Two
"Loaf-Givers"

Two "Loaf-Givers"

OR

A Tour through the Gastronomic Libraries of Katherine Golden Bitting and Elizabeth Robins Pennell

By Leonard N. Beck

Washington
Library of Congress
1984

Designed by James Wageman

Library of Congress Cataloging in Publication Data

Beck, Leonard N.
 Two loaf-givers.

 1. Gastronomy—Bibliography. 2. Cookery,
European—Bibliography. 3. Europe—Social
conditions—Bibliography. 4. Bitting, Katherine
Golden, 1869–1937—Library. 5. Pennell,
Elizabeth Robins, 1855–1936—Library. 6. Library
of Congress. Rare Book and Special Collections
Division. I. Title.
Z5776.G2B4 1984 [TX641] 016.641 82-13107
ISBN 0-8444-0404-7

Endpapers: From Jean Anthelme Brillat-Savarin,
Physiologie du gout (Paris: G. de Gonet, 1852).
Illustrations by Bertall.

Half title page: "Two women making bread."
From Olaus Magnus, *Historia delle genti et
della natura delle cose settentrionali*
(Vinegia: Appresso i Guinti, 1565).

For sale by the Superintendent of Documents,
U.S. Government Printing Office, Washington, D.C. 20402

Contents

Foreword

by Lester G. Crocker

7

Preface

by William Matheson

9

Introduction

13

Chapter One

Praise Is Due Bartolomeo Platina

19

Chapter Two

The Renaissance Discovery
of the "Inner Man"

47

Chapter Three

English Cookery Books

87

Chapter Four

La France à table

135

Chapter Five

La Cuisine moderne

165

Notes

220

Foreword

CLAUDE LÉVI-STRAUSS has told us of the importance of cooking. People make eating a social occasion, one that is tied up with the conventions of a given society and with the levels of social prestige. Cooking, he says, is a means by which nature is transformed into culture. Little wonder that men and women, quite unaware of anthropological theories, have wanted to write about the embellishment of their lives by the art of cookery. Like all art, it expresses human creativeness vis-à-vis the given.

If cookery is both a part of civilization and potentially civilizing, it takes a truly civilized man like Leonard Beck to venture as fruitfully as he has done into the hitherto unexplored bypath of books about that art. When a writer unites to stunning erudition a broad literary culture and a thorough knowledge of historical events and persons, he is bound to take us beyond the dry fact into the fertile grounds of social history. Leonard Beck has done that. The breadth of scope that embraces all of western Europe from the Renaissance on enriches our view of how people lived. We learn of the vagaries of styles of living and of manners and taste. How cookbooks came to be written and why, how they were published and received, their connection with famous men of politics, literature, and the arts are part of the culinary feast he serves up to us. How many readers know that Joseph Conrad's wife wrote a cookbook, that an imbroglio followed, and that he defended cookbooks as the only ones that are "from a moral point of view, above suspicion"? How many are aware that John Evelyn, Samuel Johnson, David Hume—among others—were readers of such books, and talked or wrote about them? Or that housewives long played the role of amateur doctors, concocting cures in the kitchen?

Devotees of French culture, scholars too, will learn of the connections between the culinary art and social and intellectual changes in that land of gastronomic worship. High-life in the seventeenth century centered on the court; in the eighteenth, on the gallant *petits soupers* in the faubourgs, soon to be aped by the aspiring upper crust of the Third Estate. There are surprises here, too. How many readers know that because a widely read cookbook increased the sugar in all its recipes, the slave trade was intensified and France's colonial ambitions affected? These are only a hint of the treats the reader will taste at Leonard Beck's board.

Admiration and the cherished memories of an ancient friendship have made it a privilege for me to write these few lines of appreciation.

Lester G. Crocker

Preface

WHEN Leonard Beck joined the staff of the Rare Book and Special Collections Division in 1973 in the newly created position Curator of Special Collections, he was already well acquainted with two of the division's collections—the Bitting and Pennell gastronomy libraries—having used them in writing biographies for *Gourmet* magazine's series "Gourmets' Lives." That assignment came to him after he sent in an unsolicited contribution, convinced that he could write a better "life" than those he had been reading in the magazine. *Gourmet* accepted his second try and following its favorable reception gave him the responsibility for the series. His schooling and years of experience at the Library of Congress had made him comfortable with the austerity of academic research but his writing for *Gourmet* presented him with the challenge of making the fruits of his research sound offhand and casual. He found the guide for his style in writing gastronomic history in Auden's

> Be subtle, various, ornamental, clever,
> And do not listen to those critics ever,
> Whose crude provincial gullets crave in books
> Plain cooking made still plainer by plain cooks.

After he stopped producing the *Gourmet* articles he kept his eye on food talk in the wide reading that is the foundation of this book. When he joined the division's staff he found himself looking at the collections with the background he had acquired since leaving *Gourmet*. A divisional report written shortly after his appointment contains the not surprising news that "as his first assignment he undertook an analysis of the Bitting Collection, a subject in which he has special expertise." In that examination he came on one of the division's great treasures, the Maestro Martino manuscript, the source of much of the information in the first printed cookbook. His account of the manuscript, the book, and its author published in the July 1975 *Quarterly Journal of the Library of Congress* was followed by articles on the Renaissance cookbooks and then on the English cookbooks in the Bitting and Pennell Collections. These articles further prepared him for his most ambitious effort, the interpretation of French gastronomic literature, printed for the first time in the concluding half of this volume.

In his foreword, Lester G. Crocker, former Kenan Professor of French Literature at the University of Virginia—a principal authority in his field and long-time friend of Mr. Beck—comments on the happy circumstance that brought a man so well qualified to write the social history of cookbooks into a position in which such writing was a natural part of his work. Though the Bitting and Pennell Collections contain American cookbooks, German and Italian cookbooks later than those discussed here, and other lesser concentrations, their greatest strengths are addressed in this book. Mr. Beck has not so much tried to provide a complete coverage of these collections as to write a history of gastronomy occasioned by a close look at these rich resources.

I share Professor Crocker's delight at the good fortune that brought Leonard Beck and the two collections together. My pleasure is even greater, for I know of the other collections—in particular the division's Houdini and McManus-Young "magic" libraries—that he has revitalized and interpreted through his writings, formal speeches, talks, and day-to-day interaction with the division's patrons. Though he marks his fortieth year of government service as I write these words, I am optimistic that the attractions of the collections will keep him with the Library for some time to come. He will be as pleased as I if this book leads the reader to the collections that have made it possible.

William Matheson
Chief, Rare Book and Special Collections Division

Two
"Loaf-Givers"

Introduction

Cookery means the knowledge of Medea, and of Circe, and of Calypso, and of Helen, and of Rebekah, and of the Queen of Sheba. It means the knowledge of all herbs, and fruits, and balms, and spices; and of all that is healing and sweet in fields and groves, and savoury in meats; it means carefulness, and inventiveness, and watchfulness, and willingness, and readi-ness of appliance; it means the economy of your great-grandmothers, and the science of modern chemists; it means much tasting, and no wasting; it means English thoroughness, and French art, and Arabian hospitality; and it means, in fine, that you are to be perfectly, and always "ladies"—"loaf-givers"....

JOHN RUSKIN

THIS paragraph from John Ruskin's *Ethics of the Dust* is used as an epigraph by Fanny Farmer for *The Boston Cooking-School Cook Book*. In the earlier *Sesame and Lilies* Ruskin had proposed his derivation of lady from "bread-giver" or "loaf-giver" and lord from "maintainer of laws." He emphasized there that these appellations of dignity have reference "not to the law which is maintained in the house, nor to the bread which is given in the household, but to law maintained for the multitude and to bread broken among the multitude." Ruskin would have thought the bookman who has performed the double service of forming a collection and then of giving it to a public institution for the pleasure of others a "loaf-giver." His term seems specially applicable to Katherine Golden Bitting and Elizabeth Robins Pennell, who have broken bread among the multitude by bequeathing their gastronomy and cookbook collections to the Library of Congress.

The task of writing on the libraries of the "loaf-givers" has been immeasurably lightened by the commentaries both ladies have published, Mrs. Bitting her *Gastronomic Bibliography* (San Francisco, 1939) and Mrs. Pennell *My Cookery Books* (New York and Boston: Houghton Mifflin, 1903). The reader is referred to these books as standards to measure what is said here and as sources to supply what is left unsaid. For the most part the talk will be of Mrs. Bitting's collection, because it is by far the more comprehensive, with 4,450 titles as against the Pennell collection total of 732. It is also because of the shockingly inegalitarian distribution of literary talent—that is, that Mrs. Pennell should have had so much more of it than anyone daring to come after her.

Mrs. Pennell was a working journalist and the author or coauthor of more than twenty-five books. She moved in literary circles with Henry James, Bernard Shaw, William Henley, William Archer, and George Moore, possibly as much in her own right as in the name of her husband, the artist Joseph Pennell. The copies of works in her library inscribed to her by these men testify to their liking and respect. *My Cookery Books* is a work rather brocaded than written; its tone is that of conversation at a tea table. Bruce Rogers's design of the book for the Riverside Press recognized and reinforced these qualities. Except for the *Gastonomic Bibliography,* Mrs. Bitting's writings seems to have been confined to about fifty notes for publication in the technical literature of food chemistry. Although the *Gastronomic Bibliography* hardly belongs in that category that Charles Lamb called "*biblia a-biblia* . . . things in books' clothing," unlike *My Cookery Books* it can probably preach only to the already converted, that is, interest only the already interested.

While the Bitting Collection happily is larger than announced by the *Gastronomic Bibliography*, the Pennell deposit is somewhat less than should be anticipated from *My Cookery Books*. A shipping agent's negligence left part of Mrs. Pennell's shipment to the Library in a warehouse to rot, the most notable victim being the first edition of Hannah Glasse once owned by George Augustus Sala, to which we shall return. The Bitting Collection has a chronology. Mrs. Bitting died in 1937. The *Gastronomic Bibliography* was published in 1939, under the supervision of her husband, Dr. A. W. Bitting, who continued his gifts to the Library until his own death in 1944. The items asterisked in the *Gastronomic Bibliography* made up the Bitting Collection in 1939; they do not completely represent it as now constituted. Mr. Bitting's noteworthy gifts included Ashmole's *Order of the Garter* (1672), Ruperto de Nola's cookbook in the Castilian version of 1525, and, the jewel of the collection, the Maestro Martino manuscript. There were other unrecorded gifts, individually less distinguished but significant in the aggregate. For example, L. and W. Glozer in their *California in the Kitchen* (Los Angeles?, 1960) comment truly enough that there are more California imprints unrecorded by the *Gastronomic Bibliography* than recorded. However, an examination of the shelves shows twenty-four California items in the Bitting Collection not reported by the Glozers, who had erroneously assumed that the Bitting Collection equated with the *Gastronomic Bibliography*.

The limitations of treatment forced by the constraints of space should be stated. While the Pennell Collection is a straightforward collection of cookbooks, the Bitting Collection is a thematic one designed to represent the very varied aspects of food and dining subsumable as gastronomy. These remarks will focus on the cookbook and touch only incidentally on topics like wine, coffee, food preservation, and domestic service, all of which have literatures too large to be explored within a parenthesis. Occasionally the sentence required to identify a minor title will be forgone so that a major work may have a paragraph to establish its importance. It is probably a reflection of this writer's personal interests that the emphasis throughout will be on the older works, that is, those of the pre-Mrs. Beeton or *Larousse gastronomique* era. This kind of self-indulgence is as much the prerogative of the librarian as of the housekeeper. The model in this connection is Jane Austen, who wrote sister Cassandra (November 17, 1798): "My mother desires me to tell you that I am a very good housekeeper, which I have no reluctance in doing because I really think it is my peculiar excellence and for this reason—I always take care to provide such things as please my own appetite, which I consider as the chief merit in housekeeping."

A brief historical sketch, a *tableau d'ensemble*, of the various national culinary literatures is an expedient mechanism for the exposition of these collections. "Another way," as the old cookbooks say, will be employed first to deal with some Renaissance and early modern publications for which the international intellectual milieu of the period seems more important than the country of origin. There should be no need to argue that the kitchen window is a good observatory from which to watch the course of history. Before Lévi-Strauss, acute social observers had known that eating is a ritual and that since man feels that what he puts in his mouth will become part of him, he will not eat everything, at any time, or at any place. "A pie for afternoon tea. The very idea," said Cousin Tabitha Twitchit in Beatrix Potter's *The Pie and the Patty Pan*. In Proust's *Remembrance of Things Past* the narrator incurs the enmity of the Princess Agrigente by getting the Guermantes to add grape juice to the orangeade served ritually at five o'clock. Doubtlessly the princess said: "The very idea." Eating and drinking are social languages compact with ideas.

Overleaf: Bartolomeo Scappi, *Opera . . . Con il discorso funerale che fu fatto nelle essequie di papa Paulo III. Con le figure che fanno bisogno nella cucina & alli reuerendissimi nel conclaue* (Venetia: M. Tramezzino, 1574?).
This illustration from the work of the Vatican cook Bartolomeo Scappi seems an appropriate accompaniment for a discussion of Bartolomeo Platina. Shown here is Scappi's dairy, one of twenty-seven plates in the book.

nenene si fa

Luochi freschi done fa lanorcri de latte

Chapter One

Praise Is Due Bartolomeo Platina

. . . merito ergo Bartolemeus
Platyna, magna sue lux et decus ille Cremone,
Sacchorum veteri ac generoso sanguine natus
munificaque manu nature ornatus et artis,
preficitur tante sub Sixto bibliothece. . . .
ROBERT FLEMMYNG

Praise is due Bartolomeo Platina,
The glory and dignity of his native Cremona,
Born of the old and generous house of Sacci,
Richly adorned both by nature and his learning,
Made prefect of the great Sistine library. . . .

IN 1475 the Italian humanist Bartolomeo Platina published the first cookbook and was appointed Vatican librarian (recent scholarship says the first).[1] These events apparently followed one another in rapid succession. On February 18, 1475, Platina became Pope Sixtus IV's librarian; the papal library was in effect institutionalized as the Biblioteca in Vaticano pubblicata by the bull *Ad decorem militantis Ecclesiae* of June 15, 1475. What is accepted as the first edition of Platina's cookbook, the *De honesta voluptate,* is ascribed to 1475. A copy is in the National Library of Medicine. A copy of the second edition, dated June 13, 1475, is in the John Boyd Thacher collection in the Library of Congress.

All members of the library community and indeed of the world of learning will join in according Platina the praise demanded by the *Lucubranciunculae Tiburtinae* (1477) of Robert Flemmyng, an English humanist attached to the papal curia. Truly and well have Platina and his successors at the Vatican realized the Sistine vision of a library "ad utilitatem omnium tam aetatis nostrae quam posteritatis literatorum hominum"—for the use of all men of letters of future ages as well as of our own.

While conceding freely that the cookbook is one of literature's minor genres, this chapter proposes to repair Robert Flemmyng's failure also to claim for Platina the praise due the author of the first cookbook. Minor literature needs no justification. As A. E. Housman, himself possibly not quite a great poet, said in his lecture *On the Name and Nature of Poetry,* "When I am drinking *Barolo stravecchio* in Turin, I am not disturbed, nor even visited, by the reflexion that there is better wine in Dijon."[2] Minor wines, minor poets, minor literary genres, like beauty, are their own excuse for being. In the *Petit Dictionnaire de cuisine* Alexandre Dumas explains that the discovery of a new dish is more important than the discovery of a new star—for whatever it is that man can do with stars he has enough already. Surely praise is due Bartolomeo Platina for the discovery of a whole new literary genre, the book about dishes!

IN the paeans for the author of the first cookbook the voice of the Library of Congress perhaps should be heard raised above all others. The recipes in his Books VI through X, in which Platina concentrates the purely culinary aspects of *De honesta voluptate,* are directly translated from a manuscript now in the

Once a fresco in the Vatican library, now preserved on canvas in the Pinacoteca, this depiction of Platina's assumption of the post of librarian by Melozzo da Forli is dated 1477. Bernard Berenson has said: "For Melozzo the figure was never impassive, never an end in itself, but always a means for embodying emotion" *(The Italian Painters of the Renaissance*, London: Phaidon Press, 1952, p. III). The pope's nephews, the figures standing in the background, seem to show the lust for power which history attributes to them. Perhaps Melozzo meant his Platina to convey the man's pride in his achievement on this day of his vindication (see detail). Photograph by the Vatican Museums.

Library's Katherine Golden Bitting Memorial Collection on Gastronomy. Like other treasures in that collection, this manuscript, the "Libro de arte coquinaria" of Maestro Martino, is not well known because it is not recorded in Mrs. Bitting's *Gastronomic Bibliography* (San Francisco, 1939). There exist today two manuscripts of Maestro Martino's work. Joseph Vehling, a collector who saw both, dated the Bitting copy as about 1450–60, making it the senior by perhaps seventy-five years.[3] It is possible that the Martino manuscript which Platina had before him is that now in the Bitting Collection. Platina did not use the "Libro de arte coquinaria" as the takeoff point for a humanistic jeu d'esprit; he translated it, and translated it very closely. The debt is honorably acknowledged, Platina saying "Ye immortal gods, what cook can surpass my Martino of Como, from whom I have taken nearly all of what I write."

All that is known about Maestro Martino is to be read in the heading of the "Libro de arte coquinaria": "formerly cook to the Most Reverend Father the Papal Camerlengo and Cardinal of Aquilea." This little implies much. Martino's employer was the papal treasurer Cardinal Ludovico Trevisan, a man of war who led military campaigns in person with the cold ferocity of a captain of condottiere. His displays of wealth, including, according to a contemporary, the maintenance

TEMPLA DOMVM EXPOSITIS VICOS FORA MOENIA PONTES
VIRGINEAM TRIVII QVOD REPARARIS AQVAM
PRISCA LICET NAVTIS STATVAS DARE COMMODA PORTVS
ET VATICANVM CINGERE SIXTE IVGVM
PLVS TAMEN VRBS DEBET NAM QVAE SQVALORE LATEBAT
CERNITVR IN CELEBRI BIBLIOTHECA LOCO

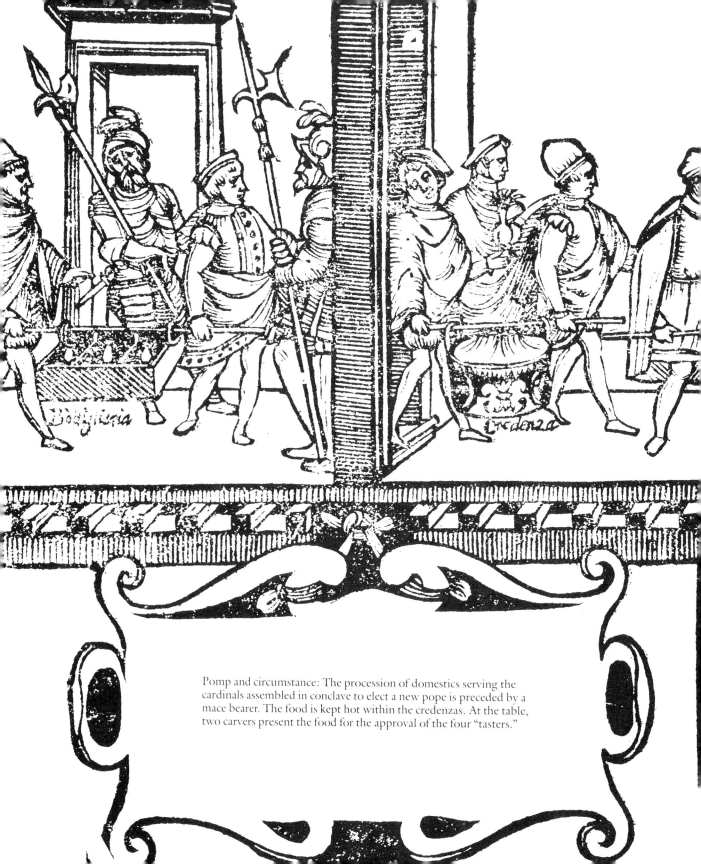

Pomp and circumstance: The procession of domestics serving the cardinals assembled in conclave to elect a new pope is preceded by a mace bearer. The food is kept hot within the credenzas. At the table, two carvers present the food for the approval of the four "tasters."

LIBRO DE ARTE COQVINARIA
COMPOSTO PER LO EGREGIO
MAESTRO
MARTINO COQVO OLIM DEL
REVERENDISS MONSIGNOR
CAMORLENGO
ET PATRIARCHA DE AQVILEIA,

Per dare ad intender qual carne merita andare arrosto, & quale allesso: Carne grossa di boue, et de vacca uole esser allessa: Carne de vitello, zio, e il perto dauanti, bono allesso, et la lonza arrosto, et le cosse in polpette: Carne de castrone tutta e bona allesso saluo la spalla, ch e bona arrosto et etiandio la cossa: Carne de porco non e sana in nullo modo, pur la schina uole esser arrosto qn, e fresco con cepolle, et il resto poi salare o come ti piace: Carne de capretto, e tutta bona allesso, et arrosto: ma la parte de drieto, e meglio arrosto: Similemente, e lagnello: Carne de capra e bona del mese de jennaro con la agliata: De la carne del ceruo la parte de nanzi, e bona in brodo lardieri. Le lonze se potono far arrosto, et le cosse son bone in pastello secco o in polpette: Similemente, e bona la carne del capriolo: Carne de porco saluatico uole esser in peperata, o in ciuero, o in brodo lardieri: Carne de lepore, e tutta

Boue.
Vacca.
Vitello.
Castrone.
Porco
capretto.
Agnello.
Capra.
ceruo
capriolo
Porco saluatico.
Lepore.

The Martino manuscript: Manuscript on paper, 21.5 cm x 13.5 cm, in contemporary binding: stamped calf on wooden boards, wormed, clasps gone. Two blank sheets, manuscript begins with the page illustrated, continues on sixty-five sheets, numbered in pencil by a modern hand. Eighteen blank sheets at end. The writing is in a fine humanistic hand. The initials, marginal titles, and chapter titles are in red. Some of the titles have not been completed by the rubricator. On verso of the second sheet, in a fifteenth-century hand, is written "Liber mej. Raphaeli Baldeli." Note by J.D. Vehling reads "Alium Martin exemplarum, scriptum ca. MDXXI, inter libros Baron Pichon videmus."

Text begins: "To know which meats are to be roasted and which boiled." The medieval cook boiled many meats before roasting and larded them to ensure tenderness. The toughness of the meat explains the prevalence of phrases like "smite hemme into gobbets" or "ramme hemme upp" in medieval English culinary literature.

of a "table for sybarites, costing more than 20 ducats daily," won for him the not entirely admiring title of "Cardinal Lucullus." It can be assumed that Maestro Martino possessed the talent for detail, the downright administrative genius, required to watch the table, the kitchen, the guests, the servants, and, above all, his terrible employer. It is to be hoped that "Cardinal Lucullus" ate with an understanding worthy of the intelligence he demanded from his cook.

Unlike the disorderly Latin culinary manuscripts associated with the name of Apicius, the work of Maestro Martino is neatly divided into chapters. In the first he talks of meat of all kinds and in the second of some rather variegated broths and stews. He goes on to condiments and sauces and then to pastries, pies, and torten. In the fifth chapter fried foods and eggs appear, and a discussion of fish concludes the manuscript. Of Martino's 250 recipes about 240 reappear in Platina, most often in the same order. Platina's own contribution includes about a dozen additional articles on fish and, most interestingly, another two dozen on cereals and vegetables. Leonardo da Vinci, who professed a vegetarianism that was more honored in the breach than in the observance, had a 1487 Italian edition of Platina in his library. Book VII of that copy answers the question as to the vegetable dishes on which this our Leonardo "doth feed, that he is grown so great." Unfortunately, Leonardo's reference to Platina's vegetable recipes in the Windsor manuscripts does not permit us to ascertain whether he meant Platina's additions or those originating with Martino.

Maestro Martino continues the classic Roman tradition of *pultes, patinae,* and *minutalia*—pottages, stews, and minced meats. The modern reader who may reproach Martino for his sweet-and-sour combinations and his meat purées possibly rejoices in today's Balkin cuisine without realizing that its techniques are those of the kitchen of imperial Rome. The besetting culinary sin of the early Renaissance was its abhorrence of the simple. Chaucer rightly complains: "These cookes, how they stampe and streyne, and grynde/And turnen substance into accident," that is, change the essential core of something into outward forms that are inherently false. But it is also true that it was not long ago that cooks like Escoffier and gourmets like Curnonsky had to fight very hard for the principle that things should have the taste of what they are. We are reading Maestro Martino's "Libro" for history, but it can also be read for pleasure, like any other good cookbook. Turning pages casually, you light on recipes for parsnip, sage, and elderflower fritters, pancakes sprinkled with honey, toasted breadcrumbs and caviar, mushrooms simmered with spices, chops baked with nuts, or poached eggs served with green sauce. This bread-and-mint-sauce combination is undoubtedly that which Ben Jonson meant in *The Staple of News* when he called for "an exquisite and poignant sauce, for which I'll say unto my cook, 'there's gold, go forth and be a knight.'"

To assay the technical stature of the "Libro de arte coquinaria," Emilio Faccioli,[4] whose *Arte della cucina* reprints the Bitting manuscript in its entirety, has confronted it with the other culinary manuscripts of the period. He thinks it more mature, that is, more coherent in methodology and more concerned with the milieux in which food is prepared and eaten, and finds in it "a sensitivity which occasionally goes beyond simple gustatory and olfactory data to touch upon the plastic values of culinary practice, on the rapport which exists between foods and the utensils used in their preparation, the preparations themselves and the effects they are intended to produce."

For a professional like Martino, Carême, or Escoffier, cooking exists as an ensemble of practical operations that must take place in precise accordance with the rhythm set by the nature of the foods themselves and the requirements of service. In a meaningful sense, therefore, Maestro Martino's manuscript is an early manifestation of the spirit of technology, the pride of *homo faber* in his competence, that is probably always present but was rarely expressed in literature before this time. Insofar as Platina repeats Maestro Martino, his is a technical book antedating those of Bernard Palissy and the others deserving the praise of Ecclesiasticus: "All these trust in their hands and each one is wise in his work."

ALTHOUGH little is known about many important areas of Platina's life, in the large it is a familiar story of the humanist enraptured by classical learning, the upward mobility possible for the talented during the Renaissance, and the centrality of the scholar's dependence on patronage. This sketch will illustrate the life by reference to the writings, on the authority of Goethe's dictum that "Leben und Werke sind eins."

He was born Bartolomeo Sacchi in 1421 of an obscure family, later taking the name Platina from his birthplace, Piadena, near Cremona in the Lombard plains. We also know that Platina served four years as a soldier in the troops of the warlords Sforza and Picconini, but how the young soldier found his way to the schools of Mantua and became tutor to the children of Marchese Ludovico Gonzaga are mysteries explicable only by his possession of extraordinary talents and motivation. When he left Mantua in 1457 to study Greek in Florence, Platina brought with him letters of recommendation from Ludovico to Cosimo de' Medici. His knowledge of Greek admitted Platina into the circle of the great and good Cardinal Johannes Bessarion, whose manuscript collection, willed to St. Mark's, is the source for many of the Aldine *editiones principes*. Later, in 1472, Platina was to deliver the funeral eulogy of Cardinal Bessarion.

franciscus Hollius

In hoc volumine hec continentur.

Platyñe de vitis mari.ponti.Historia periocunda:Diligenter re
cognita:z nunc tantum integre impressa.
Raphaellis Uolaterrani historia.De vita quattuoz Mari.ponti.
nuper edita:z in fine posita.
Platyne de falso z vero bono Dyalogus.ad Sixtū.iiij.pōti.mari.
Platyne contra amozes Dyalogus.ad Lodouicum Stellam man
tuanum.
Platyne de vera nobilitate Dyalogus.ad amplissimum Ursinum
Tranensem episcopum.
Platyne de optimo ciue Dyalogus.ad Laurētium medicē.
Platyne Panegyricus.in laudem Reuerendis.Cardinalis Uice-
ni:z patriarche Constantinopolitani.
Diuersozum academicozum panegyrici.in Platyne parentalia.

Bartolomeo Platina, *In hoc volumine hec continentur* (Venetiis: Impressum per Gulielmum de Fontaneto, 1518).

The works of Platina contained in this volume are touched on briefly in the accompanying text. The last item listed is a group of elegies read on his death.

Vatican, Biblioteca vaticana, *I due primi registri di prestito della Biblioteca apostolica vaticana... a cura di Maria Bertol*a (Citta del Vaticana: Biblioteca apostolica vatican, 1532). Facsimile in the Library of Congress. Original in the Vatican Library.

Platina's name appears twice on the first page of this register of loans. In the first paragraph he threatens to denounce to the pope those who do not return manuscripts in good time and unharmed. The third block records one of his own borrowings: "I Platina for my own use have taken from the library Piato's *Republic*. . . ." The diagonal slashes mark the transaction as completed—the manuscript has been "restitutus."

In 1462 Platina came to Rome in the entourage of Cardinal Francesco Gonzaga, son of Ludovico. Through the cardinal's influence with the newly elected pope, the humanist Pius II, he was permitted to buy a sinecure in the Collegio degli abbreviaturi, recently organized in the papal curia. The college's ostensible function was to provide a kind of editorial service; in practice it seems to have been a mechanism for subsidizing deserving humanists. When Paul II succeeded Pius and reorganized the college out of existence, the old soldier in Platina came to the fore. He demanded audiences and wrote letters threatening Paul with the wrath of all Christendom assembled in council to revenge this wrong done to scholars. As a result he spent four months in a papal prison, from which he was released only by the intervention of Cardinals Gonzaga and Bessarion.

This was the first of Platina's two prison terms. The second incarceration in Sant'Angelo (February 1468–May 1469) came about because of his association with Pomponius Leto and others belonging to a half-social, half-literary group known as the Accademia romana. Whether the impieties of these men, their jeers at priestly pomp, their Miniver Cheevy-like nostalgia for republican Rome actually constituted the conspiracy of which Paul II accused them might be questioned. Perhaps a modern sociologist would see these littérateurs and scholars as a marginal elite, at once arrogant in "in-group" consciousness and frightened by their dependence on the power center. It is clear that Pomponius Leto and Platina did not behave very well in this affair. The nineteenth-century church historian Ludwig Pastor commented on "the touching unanimity" with which they agreed on imputing all possible blame to the one member of the academy who had succeeded in fleeing the country.[5] The French say: "Les absents ont toujours tort."

Written in prison, Platina's *De vero ac falso bono* when published was dedicated to Pope Sixtus IV, but the colophon indicates that it was first offered to Paul II in propitiation. The historians of Italian literature place this work in the medieval tradition of the "consolations of philosophy" but think it relieved from mediocrity by a passage praising the mind of man, which seems unable to tolerate error but seeks it out everywhere to destroy it. Platina's *De principe*, completed in 1471 and dedicated to a Gonzaga, is sometimes mentioned in the literature about Machiavelli because of its advocacy of a standing military force. The setting for another political pamphlet, *De optimo cive,* is the Medicean court. Coming one day to visit Lorenzo, Platina finds with him Cosimo de' Medici, whom Lorenzo persuades to talk about the active public life which the good citizen chooses to lead. Moral works like *De vera nobilitate* and *Contra amores*, which today seem collections of commonplaces, probably were not so regarded in their time, the former, for example, making the revolutionary assertion that nobility is not birth, but the effulgence radiated by inner virtue.

Platina's first effort at history, *Historia Mantuae,* written for the Gonzagas about 1469, is usually summarily rejected by the historians. Cardinal Bartolomeo della Rovere, to whom Platina was to dedicate *De honesta voluptate* in 1475, praised this narrative in a latter to Ludovico Gonzaga as the equal of Caesar's *Commentaries.* To paraphrase the demolition of a similar absurdity executed by the Cambridge classicist Richard Porson: "The *Mantuan History* will be remembered when Caesar's *Commentaries* are forgotten—but not until then." Platina is taken more seriously as a historian for his biographies of the popes, the *De vitis pontificum,* translated many times into many languages. His sardonic delight in depicting the contradictions between appearance and reality is so obvious that Pastor wondered whether Sixtus had ever really read *De vitis.* While no friend of Platina, Pastor concedes "the graphic descriptions, the elegant, perspicacious, and yet concise style of the work."

If Platina's appointment to the papal librarianship was a patronage plum in return for *De vitis,* obviously his personal pride demanded that he fill his post with distinction. On February 18, 1475, the very day of his appointment, he began a register of manuscript loans in which he was careful to include his own borrowings. The bull of June 15, 1475, giving him a fixed salary and additional staff also charged him with inventorying the manuscripts and making whatever repairs were necessary. Platina must have begun the inventory well before the promulgation of the decree, because on June 18 he signed such a list to indicate his assumption of custodial responsibility. Six days after the opening of the fourth and last of the rooms in which the Vatican Library was first housed, that is, on September 20, 1481, Platina died. He would not wish his career to be summarized without noting that he gave his library a permanent physical location and increased its holdings from 2,527 manuscripts to 3,498.

THE external facts of Platina's life suggest the meanings and values in whose terms he thought it amusing, worthwhile, or necessary to write a cookbook. By making a Toynbee-like sweep of history, it would be possible to generalize that every maturing civilization—the Chinese in the fifth century, the Muslim in the eleventh and twelfth, and the Western in the Italy of the fifteenth—gives its cuisine a formal structure and decorum. But can an author and his book be considered only as a symptom of something outside them? Perhaps more can be learned about Bartolomeo Platina the cookbook author by returning to Bartolomeo Platina the soldier-student from Lombardy who had associated himself with other humanists in Rome to express his ideas of the good life.

Lombard gluttony—and both Maestro Martino and Platina were Lombards—is a stock theme of Italian regional jokes, including one still current which may please bookmen. Apparently the sixteenth-century *Compagnia della lesina* originated the witticism calling the Lombard "a wolf who begins by eating fritters in folio, goes on to eating them in quartos, and ends by eating them in reams." Since the gastronomic guides say that the cuisine of Lombardy retains the imprint of the Gonzaga court, perhaps it is still possible to taste in Mantua today the origins of Platina's interest in food.

One of the crimes the humanist from Lombardy and his friends of the Accademia romana expiated in prison was that of being "sectarians of Epicurus." Whatever its makers meant by that charge, it is a thread to guide us through a labyrinth. These friends are known because Platina occasionally connects some of them with specific recipes in the course of *De honesta voluptate*. He names others when he breaks off his discussion in Book V of the expensive fowl dishes that seem reserved for the nouveaux riches to lament his inability to play the host to his friends properly. When in the *De honesta voluptate* of 1475 Platina invokes the friendships of 1467, he seems deliberately to repeat and accept the charge of Epicureanism. This defiant acceptance is further flaunted by his choice of a title and the challenging tone of his preface.

The title *De honesta voluptate* cannot be understood without reference to the Epicurean doctrine of *voluptas*.[6] The most famous use of the Latin root in the Romance languages is in the refrain in Baudelaire's "L'Invitation au Voyage":

> Là tout n'est qu'ordre et beauté
> Luxe, calme et volupté.

In damning one attempt at translation, T. S. Eliot pointed out that the most important of the five substantives in these lines is the first.[7] Platina's *honesta* is to *voluptas* as Baudelaire's *ordre* is to *volupté*. To translate Platina's first word as *honest*, *decent*, or *legitimate* and his second as *voluptuousness*, *indulgence*, or *good living* is as far off the mark as to translate Horace's *aurea mediocritas* as *golden*

PLATYNAE DE HONESTA VOLVPTATE:
ET VALITVDINE AD AMPLISSIMVM AC
DOCTISSIMVM.D.B.ROVERELLAM.S.CLE
MENTIS PRAESBITERVM CARDINALEM
LIBER PRIMVS.

RRABVNT Et quidem ueheméter Amplif/
sime pater.B.Rouerella qui hanc nostram su/
sceptionem nequaq̄ dignam quæ tuo nomini
ascriberetur putarint:q̄ & uoluptatis & ualitu
dinis titulum præseferat . Ver̄ quū mihi atq̄ omnibus
eruditis spectata sit ingenii tui uis:& acumen mor̄ : &
honestissimæ uitæ cōstantia:doctrinæ ac eruditionis ma
gnitudo:malui te uigiliar̄ mear̄ patronum ac iudicem
siqd peruerse scriptū inest facere:q̄ alium quempiam.
Instabūt acriter maleuoli (sat scio):de uoluptate ad ui/
rum optimum & continentissimum non fuisse scriben/
dum.Sed dicant quæso ii stoicide:qui elatis superciliis
non de ui sed de nominum uocibus tantummodo diiu/
dicant:quid mali in se habeat considerata uoluptas? Est
enim huius ut ualitudinis uocabulum mediū . De uolu
ptate quam intemperantes & libidinosi ex luxu & uarie
tate ciborum:ex titillatione rer̄ uenerearū percipiunt .
Absit ut Platyna ad uir̄ sanctissimur̄ scribat.De illa uo
lupate quæ ex continentia uictus:& ear̄ rer̄ quas huma
na natura appetit loquor.Neminem enim adhuc uidi
adeo libidinosum & incontinentem:qui non aliqua tan
geretur uoluptate:si quando a rebus plusq̄ satis è cocu
pitis declinauissæ. Valet apud hos (ut uideo) Ciceronis
auctoritas:qui quidem ut Aristoteles Platonem:Pytha
goram:zenonem:Democritum:Chrysippum : Parmeni
dem:Heraclitum:sic Epicur̄ segetem & materiam eru
ditionis ac doctrinæ suæ facit:quo cū.n.tutius congre/

The argument for Epicurus: "Most Reverend Father, they will be mistaken, indeed greatly mistaken, those who think this work of mine somehow un-worthy to be dignified with your name because the words 'voluptas' and health head the title....I know full well that some unsympathetic persons will criticise me, saying that I wish to encourage a life of ease and pleasure. But I say to those persons who are so stoic and full of pride as to voice judg-ment not on the basis of the experience of 'voluptas' but on the name alone what harm can there be in well-considered 'voluptas'? I speak of the 'volup-tas' which is within the bounds of continent living and of those things which good human na-ture seeks..." (Bartolomeo Platina, *De honesta voluptate et valetudine*, Venice: Laurentius de Aquila and Sibylinus Umber, 13 June 1475).

The friends of Platina: "Those who first served peacocks and edible birds apparently were well advised because these are foods that are more delicious than any other. . . . But (as Satyrus says) common people and those not wealthy enough to support such tastes should beware of them. For they are the fare of the elegant and particularly of those men whom fortune and audacity, not virtue and labor, have . . . raised to the highest ranks of honor. . . . Pomponius eats onion and garlic with me; as do Septimius and Septumuleius Campanus, and Cosmicus does not let the night pass outside the dining room; Parthenius follows him, and Podagrosus Scaurus, nor do I pass over Fabius Narniensis or Antonius Rufus, or Moecenatis, who embrace poverty willingly. And let not Cincinnatus bear me a grudge, nor Demetrius, for calling him in for a supper of simple greens" (Platina, *De honesta voluptate . . .*).

itatibus:Iystrici haut multum diffimilia sūt.De gli/
re hoc annotatum eft:non congregari nifi plures in
eadem fylua . Et f mifceantur alienigenæ dimicando
aut uincere:aut interire.Genitores præterea fuos fe/
necta feffos infigni pietate alunt. Hyberna quiete gau
dent.Reconditi enim & hi cubant.Rurfum æftate iu/
uenefcunt,Similis & muftelis quies .

LIBER. V.
DE AVIBVS ESCVLENTIS.

VI pauones & aues efculentas ad patinas trāf
tulere:illi quidem nequaq̄ mihi diffipere uifi
funt:quum ex his obfonia fiant cæteris fua/
uiora:& regum ac principum menfis q̄ hu/
milium : & minimi cenfus hominum magis conue/
nientia.Caueant igitur plebei & populares:& quibus
(vt ait Satyrus)res legi non fufficit tale aliquid deli/
guant ne dum comedant.Lautorum hæc erunt obfo/
nia : & eorum maxime:quos non uirtus & induftria:
fed fortuna atq̄ hominum temeritas ex infima forte :
evtpote e ganeis e ftabulis e popina non ad diuitias:
qud effet ferendum:fed ad fummos dignitatis gradus
erexere.Hi funt quorum gratia pauones ac phafiani
nati aut capti uidentur.His præciofa veftis:præciofa
fuppellex:& quicquid præclarum natura extulit debet.
Cæpam & alium mecum deuor& Pomponius : Adfit
Septimius:& Septumuleius Campanus:Nec extra tri
clium pernoctet Cofmicus:Hunc fequatur Partheni/
us:& Podagrofus Scaurus:Fabium Narnienfem:An
toniū ruffū & Mœcenatē nō reiicio:q pauptatē fpōte
āplectūtur. Et ne mihi fuccenfeat Cincinnatus:hunc
quoq̄ Demetrius ad cœnam bolitoriam voc&:quan/
doquidem ita fortunæ plac&:quæ relictis induftrus

mediocrity. For want of a translation perhaps we must be content with Edith Wharton's brief paraphrase of *volupté* (and hence *voluptas*) as "the intangible charm which the imagination extracts from tangible things."[8]

The difficulty in translation is caused by the fact that the one Latin word *voluptas* is used to denote what Epicurus meant by the two Greek words for pleasure and blessedness. The popular distortion of Epicurean doctrine against which Platina argues has come about because the first of these is not properly understood as being only a means to the second. Most of what Epicurus said about the pleasures of the stomach is reducible to the rhetorical question, "If food and drink are not pleasures, what are?" Friendship is another source of the pleasure that leads to blessedness, and, indeed, the meanings of *friendship* and *voluptas* are asserted to be inextricable. Platina would have thought of the Accademia romana in reading Epicurus' admonition, "Before thinking what you have to eat and drink seek around you with whom to eat and drink."

The preface of *De honesta voluptate* is addressed to Cardinal Bartolomeo della Rovere, once in the service of Cardinal Ludovico Trevisan, at whose table Platina may have met him. The cardinal's name should have been enough in itself to ward off the charge that Platina was advocating some kind of crass and sordid sensualism. The Florentine bookseller Vespasiano da Bisticci calls della Rovere an enemy of pomp and pride who, when he invited someone to dine, would sit down with him at the same table "without genuflections and fusses."[9] The passages translated from the preface accompanying the title page illustration adequately represent Platina's advocacy of the Epicurean moderation in the satisfaction of the senses which alone leaves man free.

The title and preface place Platina's work firmly within the context of the contemporary movement of ideas. By its publication Platina announced formally that he had taken the Epicurean side in the great fifteenth-century literary controversy over whether the summum bonum is to be attained by the path of the Stoics, the Peripatetics, or the Epicureans. To attempt to summarize this debate would be to defy any reasonable meaning of the word *summarize*. Because Pope Paul II said that the Accademia romana "took Valla too seriously," we can note that Laurentius Valla began the debate by arguing in his *De voluptate* (1431) that Stoic *honestas* asks too much of man and gives him too little, fills him with pride but takes away his hope. Nature gives man both the desire for *voluptas* and the means of its satisfaction, and Valla could wish that he had fifty senses rather than only five.

Valla's rehabilitation of Epicurian voluptas was reinforced by the publication of the *editiones principes* of the *De rerum natura* of Lucretius in 1473 and the *Vitae et sententia philosophorum* of Diogenes Laertius in 1472. The first of these was to have twenty-four continental editions by 1650 and the second fourteen. Platina's preface cites both Lucretius and Diogenes Laertius as character witnesses for Epicurus. In addition to influencing Platine to write his book, Lucretius and Diogenes Laertius did the equally important job of preparing an audience to receive it. Erasmus called Epicureans the best Christians; in More's *Utopia* the adjective most frequently preceding *voluptas* is "jocund." Montaigne knew that Vergil was the greatest poet but sometimes in reading Lucretius felt he could not be sure. So he declared Epicurean *voluptas* "great and generous," thought man's condition "wonderfully corporeal," and said, "I love life and cultivate it just as God has been pleased to grant it to me. I do not go about wishing that it should lack the need to eat and drink."

With a public so thoroughly prepared, *De honesta voluptate* was ensured immediate and prolonged popularity. A contemporary joked that Platina had more buyers than Plato, a fact which has characterized cookbook sales since 1475. There were at least sixteen Latin editions by 1541, the date of the publication in Basel of the coupling of Apicius and Platina in the same covers that is the first Swiss cookbook. Two of the five Latin editions published in Italy pose minor bibliographical problems that defy resolution. Platina had worked as a corrector for the first Roman printers, Schweynheym and Pannarts, and had given the first edition of *De honesta voluptate* for publication to the great Ulrich Han of Rome. Why then was the edition of June 13, 1475, published by a Venetian printer so obscure that nothing else is known about him? In this case it is the publisher, not the place, that is surprising. Venice is where Thomas Coryat of the *Crudities* first saw the forks he took back to England, and even in Byron's time Venice was "the revel of earth and the masque of Italy." But Cividale, the place of publication of the 1480 Latin edition, has so small a part in the annals of printing that Platina's book is one of only two published there in the fifteenth century.

The first French edition of Platina, translated by Dedier Christol, prior of the Abbey of St. Maurice near Montpellier and published in Lyon in 1505, has been called the most beautiful cookbook ever published for its Gothic type and initial woodcut letters. The existence of this translation is emphasized to deflate somewhat the exaggerated accounts of the culture shock suffered by the French kitchen in 1533 when Catherine de Medici brought Florentine cooks with her to Paris on her marriage. Actually French cuisine had a cookbook author very much the peer of Maestro Martino in Guillaume Le Tirel, called Taillevent, "Maître queux" to Charles VI. In manuscript before 1392, published about 1490, Taillevent's *Viandier* was so well known that François Villon says in *Le Grand Testament* of 1461: "Si allé veoir en Taillevent/Au chapitre de fricassure." What the Italians brought new with them was the esthetics of the table called gastronomy. That is the import of the conversation Montaigne had with the steward of the kitchen of Cardinal Caraffa: "He explained to me the difference of appetites; that which a man has before he begins to eat, and those after the second and third service, how meerly to gratify it, and how to satisfy first and then to raise and sharpen it; the management of the sauces . . . the differences of sallads . . . the manner of their garnishment and decoration, to render them also pleasing to the eye. . . ."

The translators of the first two Italian editions of Platina (1487 and 1494) apparently were unaware that they were doing a back translation of a Latin translation of an Italian original. Because there is no Latin for macaroni, Platina had used the circumlocution *esicium frumentinum* for what Martino had called *maccaroni Siciliani*. The translators, although they may have dined that day on that dish, did not recognize the Latin and could think only to translate it as *exitio frumentino*. In the same way Martino's good Italian *biancomangiare*, which is *cibarium album* in Platina's Latin, becomes Greek *leucofago* in the Italian translations. This is additional proof, if proof is needed, of the truth of the Italian proverb "traduttore traditore," a translator betrays the meaning.

The same dishes can be used to illustrate the pitfalls awaiting the unwary annotator of Platina. In the fifteenth century *maccaroni Siciliani* may have meant *gnocchi*, and it certainly did not mean the pasta which in the early eighteenth century conquered Naples and then the world. In the same way *biancomangiare* must not be understood as *blancmanger* if by that word is meant today's cornstarch pudding. Platina gives two recipes for this shimmering white fish or fowl mousse with almonds, the second of which, blancmanger Catalan, poses a pretty little historical problem. The word is certainly either French or Italian, but is the dish itself Spanish, as its greatest appreciator certainly was? In the account of the adventures of that ingenious gentleman Don Quixote de la Mancha, one reads: "We have received word here, my good Sancho, that you are very fond of manjar blanco and forced-meat balls, so fond, indeed, that if there is any left over you put it away in your bosom for another day." Sancho's denial goes on to become his profession of faith as a trencherman: "No, sir, that is not so. . . . The

terasis acribus ac siccis ad .xl. misceto: inditoq̃ i pa
stillũ ad id apte ex farina subacta factum. In fur-
no aut sub textu in foco decoqui potest. Semicoctũ
ubi fuerit duo vitella ouoz disfracta: modicũ croci z acreste superfundes.

¶ In pipionem exossatum.

Ipipionem exinanitum z bene lotum: per diez
ac noctẽ in aceto acri sines: lotum deinde ac
repletum z aromatibus z herbis: elixum pro libidi-
ne: aut assum facies: Utrouis modo sine ossibus in
uenies.   ¶ Ex solo pipione duo fiunt.

Ipionem sine aqua ita apposite deplumato ne
pellem frangas. Exenterato deinde cutem in-
tegrã auertes ac diriges: directã optimo far-
cimine replebis. Integer tum omnino videbitur.
Uerum pipionem hoc modo assum: frictum: elixuz
facies. Assum semicoctum sale ac trito pane asper-
ges: inungesq̃ leiter vitello oui: ut crustam pro cu-
te faciat. Ubi incoctus omnio fuerit vehementi igne
statim torreto: quo colorazioz fiat: inde conuiuis appones.   ¶ Libaria Alba.

Ibarium album: qd aptius leucophagum di-
cetur: hoc modo pro duodecim conuiuis con-
dies. Amygdalaz libras .2. p nocte aqua ma-
ceratas: ac depilatas in mortario bene tudes: ispar-
gendo modicum aque: ne oleum faciat. Deinde capi pectus exossatum in eodem mortario conteres:
indesq̃ excauatum panem acresta prius: aut iure
macro remolitum. Singiberis preterea vnciam ac
sacchari selibrã addes: miscebisq̃ hec omnia simul:
mixtaq̃ per excretorium farinaceum in ollam mũ-
dã transmittes. Efferueat deinde in carbonub⁹ lẽto

---

igne facies: cochlearic̃ sepe agitabis: ne serie adhe-
reat. Coctum ubi fuerit aque rosacee vncias tres in-
fundes. Ad mensamq̃ aut in patinis ubi caro fuerit: aut seorsuz: sed minoribus mittes. Quod si i ca-
pos fundere institueris: quo lautius uideatur: mali
punici grana superinspargito. At vero si in duplice
conditurã diuisum voles: partem vitello oui ac cro-
co simul cum modico acreste cõfuso colorabis: quã
quidē a colore genestinam appello. Reliquam partem z alba est: ita cõuiuis ut uiri appones. Hoc ego
condimentis apitianis ante posuerim semper. Ne-
q̃ ulla ratio est cur gule maioz nostri preferãtur.
Et si.n. ab illis i omnibus fere artibus superamur:
vna tamez gula non vincimur. Nullũ.n.in orbe ter-
raz irritamentum gule est: qd nõ huc tãq̃ ad gym-
nasium popinarium translatum sit: ubi acerrime de
conditura obsoniozum omnium diseritur. Quẽ co-
quum dii immortales Martino meo comensi con-
feres: a quo hec que scribo magna ex parte sunt ha-
bita. Carneadem alterum vices: si de rebus proposi-
tis ex tempore diserentem audieris.

¶ Libarium album catellionicuz.

Arrinaz optimi risi cum duabus metretis lactis caprini in cacabo ad igne ponito ᵽcul flã-
maz: ne fumum concipiat. Pectus deinde capi eodem die mortui: ac semicocti in quadaz quasi subti-
lissima fila diuidito: in ditaq̃ in mortarium duob⁹
eo amplius tribus ictibus pistillo contundito. Ubi
lac diuidium hore efferuerit: huc idem pectus in si-
la redactuz cuz libra sacchari indes: efferuereq̃ ho-
ras quatuoz patieris agitando semper cõdituram co-
chleari: cui herebit: ut terebithia ubi decoctũ fuerit.

Platina's blancmanger: For twenty, soak 2 pounds
of almonds in water overnight, chop well, sprink-
ling them with a little water. In the same mortar
chop the breast of a capon, add the soft insides of
bread soaked in verjuice [the fermented juice of a
sour fruit or vegetable] or in the juice of lean
meat. Add an ounce of ginger, half a pound of
sugar, and mix. Strain into a clean pot; boil over a
slow fire, stirring constantly. Add three ounces
of rosewater when it is cooked.

Scappi, private cook to Pope Pius V, says that
blancmanger should be served "when it is what
the name says it ought to be, white and shining,
and the taste corresponds to the beauty" (*Opera*,
Venetia: M. Tramezzino, 1581?, p. 53).

Dequaresma.

es buena: y cozida con todo su aparejo puedes hazer plato d
lla mesma sin cortarla si no sus pieças enteras: y hazer que cu
ezga aquella salsa. y quando heruiere echarsela encima. ¶ Y
si la quieres cortada hazlo desta manera. Desque la toñina se
ra cozida cortarla: y soffreyrla vn poco con azeyte: y echale
la salsa. y dexala cozer vn buen rato: y echale vnas pocas de
yeruas deshojadas: y haz escudillas.

Arto me parece ha-
uer hablado de muchas maneras de viandas. τ delas differencias dellas. y del
seruir: τ aparejar de todas las maneras
de guisados: y viandas assi de carnal como de quaresma: τ avn que algunos di-
gan que las viandas quaresmales no so
tan prouechosas como las del carnal. A esto digo que no es
si no voluntad de personas: porque ay algunos señores que
les contentan mas vnas viandas que otras: τ diuersos ape-
titos d personas: pero como quiera que sea yo e hecho todas
mis fuerças por poner en este presente libro todo lo que yo e
sabido y alcançado: τ porque algunos ignoran algo quiero
dezir dela langosta: porque el manjar blanco no se puede hazer sin ella. o sin los pageles: τ si los pageles no fueré frescos
hazerlo dela langosta: que si no la vuiesse no se podria hazer
el manjar blanco perfecto segun dire enel siguiente capitulo.

¶ Manjar blanco.

S de tomar la langosta: τ los pageles. y avn que
son de differentes calidades de necessidad son me-
nester: pero la langosta es mucho mejor: que no el
pagel: y destos dos tomado el que mejor te pare-
cera τ cozerlo en vna olla a parte: y desq sea qua
si medio cozida sacala dela olla, o ponla en remojo en agua
(fria: τ despu

Dequaresma.   Fo.lxix.

es tomar lo blanco dela langosta que es mejor: τ a de cozer
mas rezio. τ ponerlos en vn plato: τ desbilarlo assi como he-
bras de açafran: y echar sobre este blanco desbilado agua rosada. y despues para ocho escudillas tomar quatro libras de
almendras. τ vna libra de harina. τ vna libra de agua rosada
y despues tomar dos libras de açucar fino: τ tomar las almé-
dras blancas: τ majarlas en vn mortero: de manera que no
se hagan azeyte: τ para escusar esto mojar la mano del mortero a menudo en agua rosada. τ desque sean majadas desatar
las con agua tibia que sea limpia. τ desque sean passadas tomar vn caço muy limpio que no sea estañado de nueuo / ni que
sea tampoco de cobre. τ toma lo desbilado dela langosta. τ va
le la leche que heziste. τ no toda sino aquella que conoceras
que abastara para el principio: τ antes pon la leche en dos ve
zes que en vna. τ si la echasses toda junta no lo podrias bien
conocer hasta que el manjar blanco se tornasse espesso: de ma
nera que pornas la harina poco a poco: porque no se empla-
ste. y batirlo / o traerlo siempre con vn palo hasta que sea co-
zido. τ despues hazer escudillas. τ sobre ellas echar açucar fi
no. y desta manera se haze perfecto el manjar blanco de pescado.

¶ Majar blaco de calabaças.

Tomar delas calabaças mas tiernas: y pararlas
bien raydas con vn cuchillo hasta que quedé blá
cas. τ despues cortarlas a pedaços tan grandes
como la mano: y pon agua al fuego. y quando her
uiere echarle las calabaças. τ desque sean cozidas
sacarlas. τ ponerlas détro de vn trapo limpio. τ despues haz
premirlas muy bien: de manera que salga toda la agua. y des
pues ponla en la olla. o caço donde as de hazer el manjar blá

i v

Two Spanish recipes for blancmanger for Lent:
Ruperto de Nola, *Libro de cozina* . . . (Toledo,
1525).

Manjar blanco: Boil lobster or red mullet ("but
lobster is much better than mullet"), shred it,
leaving only the white meat. Touch with saffron,
add a little rosewater. For eight, 4 pounds of
finely crushed almonds, 1 pound of flour, 1 pound
of rosewater, 2 pounds of sugar. Keep almond
milk free of taint from kitchen tools. Add flour
slowly, while beating. The second recipe is for
blancmanger of squash or other gourds.

A German recipe, ca. 1350, for blanc-manger: Take goat's milk, half a pound of crushed almonds, a quarter pound of rice ground to flour and mixed with the milk; bone a chicken breast, chop small, and add pure dripping; let it cook long enough and serve with cut violets and a quarter pound of sugar. Note that the dish is "blamensir" and that the binder is rice, both obviously non-German importations *(Das Büch von güter Spise, xiiij. Jahrhundert Witzenberg, xx. Jahrhundert Darmstadt,* Facsimile, Darmstadt: A. Kupfer, 1964).

Chaucer's blancmanger is described in *The Forme of Cury,* ed. Samuel Pegge (London: J. Nichols, 1780), written by the unnamed cook for Chaucer's royal master, Richard II. The recipe calls for ground almonds simmered in wine, beef, or chicken broth (on fast days, a fish broth), strained, mixed with chopped capon or chicken, seasoned with almond milk, strewn with fried almonds and a little sugar, with rice flour as the binder. The recipe used by his French contemporary Taillevent specifies the less effective bread-crumbs as binder.

truth of the matter is that if they happen to give me a heifer I run with the halter, by which I mean to say, I eat what is set before me and take things as they come." Another great testimony to blancmanger comes from England. When Chaucer wishes to give the ultimate praise to Roger of Ware, the cook who took the road to Canterbury with that goodly company of pilgrims, he says: "For blankmanger, that made he with the beste."

Platina's name and his title occasionally take on a life of their own. The name is used as a flag under which to sail quite a different ship in Heinrich Steiner's publication *Von allen Speysen und Gerichten* (Augsburg, 1530), the authorship of which is indicated as "durch den hochgelerten und erfarnen Platinam/Pabsts Pij des. 2 Hofmeister." Not only was the "highly learned and experienced" Platina never Pius II's chamberlain, but the text is not his, being quickly recognizable as that of the standard German Renaissance cookbook, the *Küchenmeisterei*. Steiner made amends by publishing in 1542 a genuine translation of *De honesta voluptate*, giving the author as "the highly learned philosopher and orator, the very wise and eloquent Bar. Platina of Cremona." The Lyons printer Benoist Rigaud used not Platina's name but his title. Rigaud's *Livre de honnest volupté* (1588) is a revision of his *Livre fort excellent* (1555), which has nothing to do with Platina. Rigaud published a legitimate translation of Platina in 1571. The importance of Lyons in the dissemination of Platina in France should not be surprising. Gourmets who, like the Wise Men, follow the stars of the *Guide Michelin* ratings know that Lyons has always been Paris's peer in culinary culture.

Curiously, the illustration used in Steiner's pseudo-Platina of 1530 reappears on the title page of the first Belgian cookbook, Gerardus Vorselman's *Eenen Nyeuwen Coock boeck* (Antwerp, 1560), which the author describes as having been derived from many and varied sources, including the "Ytaliaens." From Platina, Vorselman took 133 recipes, labeling 82 as "Romeyns" and leaving the others unacknowledged. The first cookbook printed in Italian, the *Eprlario*, which is attributed, oddly enough, to a Frenchman, Rosselli, is Platina with a few additions. One of the additions is a recipe for birds baked alive in a pie and so disposed that when the crust was broken the birds would fly out, certainly a dainty dish to set before a king. The "De voluptibus" of Platina which Clara in Delicado's *Lozana andalusia* boasts she far surpasses is a "bibliographic ghost" to be found only in this contemporary story of a Spanish bawd in the Rome of 1524. The first Spanish cookbook, which appeared first in Catalan in 1520 and was translated into Castilian in 1525 as *Libro de cozina*, is attributed to one Ruperto de Nola. This man

Gerardus Vorselman, *Hier begint eenen nyeuwen coock boeck* (Thantwerpen: Gheprint by dye weduwe van H. Peetersen, 1560), Lessing J. Rosenwald Collection.

This realistic illustration has its own history which partly parallels the popularization of Platina in the Germanys. The artist is Hans Weiditz, called the "Petrarca-Meister" for his work in the 1532 *Von der Arztney bayder Glück* translation of Petrarch's *De remediis*. The illustration appeared first in the Strassburg 1530 publication by Egenolphen called *Von allen Speisen...*, which uses Platina's name but not his text, and later in the same year in a reedition of that work from the press of Heinrich Steiner of Augsburg. In 1531 Egenolphen used the illustration again for a second, quite different cookbook whose title page lists Platina as one of its sources. Steiner's 1531, 1533, 1536, and 1537 reprints of the 1530 *Von allen Speisen*, wrongly attributed to Platina, carry the illustration. When in 1542 Steiner printed the true Platina, he used the same illustration. How the plate came to the Widow Hendrik Peetersen in Antwerp in 1560 for use in the Vorselman book is an unresolved problem.

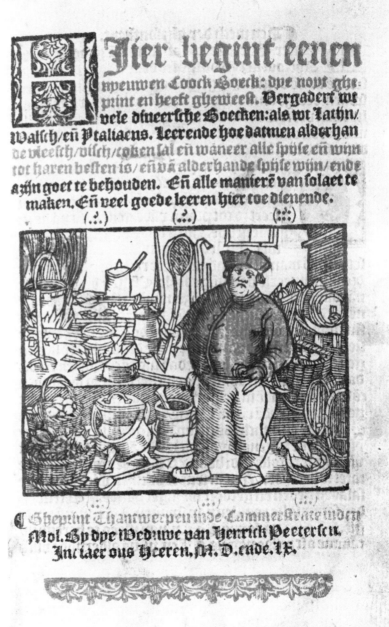

43

is described as the cook to one of the Aragonese kings of Naples, so that his work too is permeated with the Italian culinary culture represented by Platina.

The reader of *De honesta voluptate* is looking into the cocoon in which the modern cookbook is struggling to be born. The talk of medicine, gardening, and housekeeping, the vestigial elements that will be sloughed off in the evolutionary process, occurs in the first books. The second part—Maestro Martino's part—is more nearly a cookbook in the modern sense. The "modern" sense is, of course, the sense of the recipes in sequence of the Apician manuscripts of the fourth and ninth centuries and of the possibly fictitious cookbook running from onions to tunny described in a fragment of a lost Greek play, the *Phaon* of about 400 B.C.

While Martino works in the Roman or Apician tradition, it is because he is giving the same response to the same conditions, and there is no need to suppose that he read Apicius. But Platina did know Apicius and mentions him to assert that modern sauces were better than those of Rome. Professor Milham has definitely linked three of the extant Apician manuscripts with members of the Accademia romana.[10] Their interest was certainly more philological than culinary. But Platina, with his feeling for food and his knowledge and appreciation of its possibilities, would have gone on from Apicius's Latin to his recipes. Not Apicius alone, but the talk about Apician recipes with his friends at the academy dinners, held perhaps in imitation of the ritual meal of the Epicurean college to give the body its share of the pleasure enjoyed by the spirit, would have stimulated Platina to the writing of *De honesta voluptate*.

I HAVE examined *De honesta voluptate* chiefly from the outside to place it in relation to its author and to the intellectual currents of his time. In picking out this pattern I have incidentally also pulled out plums like Sancho Panza's blancmanger and Leonardo da Vinci's vegetable recipes. After a neoclassical invocation of the patron of all plum-pullers ("Forth from thy corner John Horner come!"), I have thought to conclude with plums of a different kind. There is first Platina's metaphor in comparing the ripening of the mulberry from white to dark red to the blushing of Thisbe, the Egyptian girl. The austere humanist is humanized for us by his wish that men not eat cardinals, because one summer day at the Gonzaga villa he watched these birds with pleasure and admiration.

Most pleasing are the glimpses of his friends. Caeculus makes Platina laugh when he fries eggs because he gets so absorbed in the process that he himself seems to stick to the pan. Pomponius Leto should not roast eggs on live coals: he is so absentminded that he loses two before he gets one and so poor that usually he finishes with none. Platina remembers this cinnamon sauce from the table of Filefulus; Bucinus likes this roast chicken recipe because he likes the sweet-and-sour effect; capon or pullet Catalan, according to this recipe, is as good as the best ever served by Valsichara. There can be nothing in the world more flavorful than the marzipan Platina went to eat with his friend Patritus at Senes, where it is a specialty. To use a handy phrase: Platina's medium is the recipe, and his message is Epicurus's "pleasure is not exclusive; it is not pleasure, not human pleasure, unless it is shared with a friend."

Chapter Two

The Renaissance Discovery
of the "Inner Man"

La gastronomie est la connaissance raisonnée de tout ce que a rapport à l'homme, en tant qu'il se nourrit.
BRILLAT-SAVARIN

Gastronomy is the rational knowledge of all that relates to man as one who eats.

IN *La Vie Treshorrificque du grand Gargantua* Rabelais prescribes for the education of the young Gargantua joyous table talk on "the vertue, propriety, efficacy, and nature of all that was served in at the table; of bread, of wine, of water, of salt, of fleshes, fishes, fruits, herbs, roots and of their dressing." The talkers quote the relevant passages from the classic authorities (Rabelais begins his list with Pliny and Athenaeus) and often, to make certain of a reference, the book itself is brought to the table. This chapter offers a sampling of the Renaissance and early modern books in the Bitting Collection that might have been cited in table discussion of this sort. Despite the diversity of the authorship and themes, the sampling will demonstrate that conceptually this collection is of a piece and that its parts are interlocking.

The gist of what is to be said, what Rabelais calls the "substantific marrow," is that the chief point of origin of the modern literature of gastronomy is medical humanism, that is, the humanist perception of the doctrines of Greek medicine. Man's eager but uninformed study of what can be called "the laws of inner space" had revealed only the first of these, that expressible in the terms of Aristotelian physics as "Nature abhors a vacuum." Other, more sophisticated discoveries became possible when the humanists added to Galen's concept of diet as a quasimoral judgmental act their own interest in the whole man, body as well as mind, in contrast with the medieval view of the body as dross, a mere anchor for the soul.

The three examples of medical humanism to be described here are alike in that they came in 1530 off the presses of Simon de Colines in Paris and in that they relate to two figures, Hippocrates and Galen, who are pivots on which the history of medicine turns. The first of these titles is *Hippocratis Aphorismi,* purchased by the Bittings from Jules Duhem of Montpellier, a distinguished student of the early history of aeronautical ideas. The fact of the existence of the Bitting 1530 *Hippocratis Aphorismi* contradicts the standard authority on Simon de Colines. In addition, its provenance suggests an association with Rabelais that it is not hyperbolic to call exciting.

Simon de Colines had published three little pieces from the Hippocratic canon in two editions of 1524. In one of these, the *De natura humana,* there is a kind of apology to the reader in which Colines promises soon to better this imperfectly printed translation by another edition. Philippe Renouard comments

HIPPOCRA-
TIS

Aphorismi.

De natura humana.

De flatibus.

Præsagia.

De ratione victus.

Galeni ars medicinalis.

[handwritten inscription:] ex libris Teüté ꝑ ãd
δυσκολα τὰ καλα

PARISIIS
Apud Simonem Colinæum
1 5 3 0

The annotations here further illustrate Bassaler's hand.

APHORIS-

MORVM HIPPOCRA
tis liber primus, Nicolao
Leoniceno Vicentino in
terprete.

Aphor.1.

Ita breuis, ars vero
longa, occasio autem
preceps: experimentũ
periculosum, iudiciũ
difficile. Nec solũ se
ipsum praestare opor
tet opportuna faciētem, sed & aegrũ,
& assidentes, & exteriora.

Aphor.2.

IN perturbationibus vētris, & vo
mitibus spontinis, si talia purgen
tur qualia purgari oportet, confert.
& leuiter ferunt. sin minus, contrá.
Sic & vasorum inanitio, si talis fiat
qualis fieri debet, confert, & bene
tolerant:sin minus,contrá. Inspicere
itaq3 oportet & regionem, & tem
pus, & aetatem, & morbos in qui

a.ij.

APHORIS/

MI HIPPOCRATIS, NI-COLAO LEONICENO VI CENTINO INTERPRE-TE.

EIVSDEM PRAESAGIA, GV lielmo Copo Basiliensi inter-prete.

seorsum à nobis conscriptis. Quòd vero ante hosce omnes prius exer=citari oporteat, in libris de demon=stratione. Si quis hâc artê cũ ratio-ne sit tractaturus, mõstratum est à nobis in libro qui de optima inscri-bitur hæresi. De alijs autê libris, & commêtationibus à nobis scriptis, transigere nunc minime necessariũ, cum de hisce omnibus alibi simus tractaturi in vno fortassis, aut duo=bus libris qui ita inscribentur, Gale=nus de voluminibus ab eo conscri=ptis.

FINIS.

PARISIIS
Ex officina Simonis Colinæi.
1 5 2 4.

Q .iij.

Aphorismi Hippocratis
(Parisiis: ex officina Simonis Colinaei, 1524).
Courtesy of the National Library of Medicine.

Colines promises an improved edition.
Courtesy of the National Library of Medicine.

in his *Bibliographie des oeuvres de Simon de Colines*[1] that this promise was fulfilled by the two printings of Hippocrates that Colines issued in 1539. But Renouard did not know—or, at any rate, does not list—the Colines 1530 *Hippocratis Aphorismi*. Surely it is more probable that it is this edition, rather than those of 1539, nine years later, that Colines had in mind.

Moreover, almost certainly because the 1530 printing was not recognized by Renouard, Roland Antonioli and René Sturel[2] did not consider it among the possible sources for the 1532 *Hippocratis ac Galeni libri aliquot,* prepared for publication by Gryphius in Lyon by François Rabelais. These Rabelais scholars talk only of the translations available in editions of 1524 and 1527, although the same translations, including all those used by Rabelais in 1532, are to be found in the Bitting edition.

Indeed, it might be suggested that not only the 1530 edition but the Bitting copy of that edition has some association with Rabelais. A name that can be read as Isaac Bassaler appears on the title page of the Bitting copy. What is clearly the same name in the same hand appears in the marginal annotations of the Bitting copy of Robert Grospré's *Regimen sanitatis* (Paris: Apud A. & C. Angeliers, 1540), also previously owned by Duhem. The *Gastronomic Bibliography* description of the Grospé work quotes Duhem's identification of the marginalia writer as Isaac Bassaler, a doctor friend of Rabelais. Accepting this identification, one can go on to speculate that in their talks on a topic so interesting to both of them Rabelais would have learned about the 1530 Colines imprint and even have seen the copy owned by his friend Dr. Bassaler.

The medical humanism that was clearly expressed when Henri Estienne published collections of the Greek poets, historians, and doctors as of equal value is remarkably encapsulated in this sixteenmo of 1530. The translators were preeminent among the humanists dedicated to the recovery of Greek medicine; each of the translations was in its time the standard Latin, the *edito vulgata,* of the Greek original. In a letter to Boniface Amerbach (August 31, 1518), Erasmus named Leoniceno, Thomas Linacre, and Gulielmus Cop as the great renovators of medicine. Leoniceno, here the translator of the *Aphorismi* and Galen's *Ars medicinalis,* was professor of medicine as well as of Greek and had Linacre and Vesalius as pupils. His work on the *Ars medicinalis* is noteworthy because it cleansed the Galenic doctrine of "Arabization," its adulteration by Averroes. Cop, the physician from Basel who translated *De ratione victus* and *Praesagia,* was doctor to two kings of France and to Erasmus, who dedicated to him "De

Regimēſa

hanui Oferabras

NITATIS ROBERTI

Geopretii atrebatis, non ſo-
lum medicis, verum etiam
omnibus ſtudioſis per
neceſſarium &
vtile.

Eiuſdem tractatus de Peſte.

PARISIIS.

Apud Arnoldum & Corolum Angeliers Fratres.

1 5 4 0.

Robert Grospré, *Regimen sanitatis* (Parisiis: Apud Arnoldum & Corolum Angeliers Fratres, 1540).

In recording in 1563 that he had sold this book, Isaac Bassaler wrote out his name.

cipue paleis inuoluti, bene cuſtodiũ-
tur, iuxta terram cito corrumpuntur,
Ceraſa boni ſunt ſucci, & cholerã re Ceraſa.
primunt. Vuæ paſſę ſtomachum con Vuæ paſ
fortãt, ſtomacho ieiuno ſumptæ. Ca ſæ.
ricæ, flatus ſanguinemque vitiatum Caricæ
pariunt. Pruna damaſcena ſi in pri - Pruna da
ma menſa edantur, ventrem diffici- maſcæna
lem molliunt. Amigdalę deſiccandi Amigda
extenuandique virtutem habent: ſed læ.
amaræ, vehementius efficatiúſque
thoracem & viſcera deſiccant & ex-
tenuant. Ficcus bene nutriunt, Ficus.
alui præterea vrinæque ciẽ
dæ, & renes purgãdi pro
uinciam pulcherri
me ſubeũt. Oli Oliuæ.
uæ cõditę,
appeten-
tiam
cibi reuocant, aluum
etiam difficilem leniũt.

B

senectudis incommodis," a poem on old age. Least distinguished of the group is Andreas Brentius, whose version of *De humana natura* was used by Rabelais in 1532, but not reprinted by Colines in 1539. Constantine Lascaris, the translator of *De flatibus*, is the author of the grammar that is the first printed Greek text. He can exemplify the exiles from Byzantium who brought the old manuscripts with them and taught their language to the scholars of the West.

Simon de Colines seems to have been sure that translations of Galen would interest the humanist public that was his market. Renouard lists for the period from 1520 to 1546 forty-six items by Galen from the Colines press as against two by Hippocrates and the same number by medical writers of the time. One of the Galens released by Colines in 1530 is the translation of Galen's diet book, the *De alimentibus facultatibus*, prepared by Joachim Martin, a humanist of Ghent. The Bittings' *Gastronomic Bibliography* misunderstood the title page ascription of authorship to "Ioachim Martino Gandavo" and created a ghost "Gandavo" as translator. Martin explains that he has been struck by the errors in the 1525 Aldine Galen which he as a disciple of Erasmus felt it imperative to correct. Martin's allegiance to the party of Erasmus is shown by the letter of September 15, 1528, in which the great humanist thanks Martin for sending some observations on his readings in Galen. Erasmus's own interest in Galen had been demonstrated by his translation of three little pieces from the Aldine text of 1525.

Another Colines's Galen of 1530, that annus mirabilis for the Bitting Collection, is the *De euchymia et cachochymia* translated by Guinter of Andernach, leader of the German humanists who, as if oblivious to the burgeoning vernacular, sought to make Latin the sole literary medium. Parenthetically, some three hundred years later Alexandre Martin, author of *Bréviaire de gastronome* (Paris: Audot, 1828), came across Guinter's manuscripts and called him the father of gastronomy for having invented more potages, ragouts, sauces, and *coulis* than ever Descartes discovered philosophical verities. Guinter's little half-vellum Galen also carries the *De victus ratione* of Psellus in a translation of Giorgio Valla. The English editor of Psellus, Francis Lamb, calls this author, reputedly the greatest scholar of eleventh-century Byzantium, a servile copyist of Galen like all the others after him except Averroes, who commonly differed from Galen by falling into error.

The eminent Renaissance student Professor Paul Kristeller has remarked on the surprisingly small number of humanists able to work in Greek. Another title by Valla in the Bitting Collection, his *De tuenda sanitate per victum* (Argentine: H.

Galen, *De evchymia et cacochymia* (Parisiis: Apud Simonem Colinaeum, 1530).

This title page, with its leaf in the form of a heart and its skillful use of white space, is a reminder that Colines was intimately associated with Geoffroy Tory, whose Book of Hours he published in 1525. Colines had married into the Estienne family of printer-humanists. His own humanist sympathies are shown by his publication of Erasmus's *Colloquia* in 1529, despite the censure of that work by the Paris Faculty of Theology.

CLAVDII GALENI

PERGAMENI DE EVCHYMIA ET CACOCHYMIA, SEV DE BONIS MALI'SQVE SVCCIS GENERANDIS.

Ioanne Guinterio Andernaco interprete.

Adiectus est Psellij Commentarius de victus ratione.

PARISIIS.
Apud Simonem Colinæum.
1 5 3 0

Sybold, 1528), illustrates the closeness of the connections of these men. This food-by-food discussion is extracted from Valla's encyclopedia-like *De expetendi et fugiendis rebus,* published by Aldus Manutius in 1501. Valla had learned Greek from Constantine Lascaris and his collection of Galen manuscripts was used by the Aldine press in the 1525 Galen. Bound with *De tvenda sanitate per victum* in the Bitting edition is *De ciborum facultatibus,* an excerpt translated from Paulus Aegineta's *De re medica* by Gulielmus Cop, the Basel physician and friend of Erasmus associated with the 1530 *Hippocratis Aphorismi.*

The representation accorded Galen and the other classical physicians evidences the largeness of the definition which the Bittings gave to gastronomy. In an article on "Gastronomic Philosophy," Dr. A. W. Bitting called Galen a landmark in the philosophy of food, like Moses or Buddha, for having cast the concept of the dietetic regime as the origin and center of wellbeing that dominates the history of personal hygiene.[3] The Galenic doctrine lumps food and drink together as one of the six factors external to man whose use or abuse continuously and inevitably influences health. These factors Galen called the "non-naturals," though "why," as Tristram Shandy says, "the most natural actions of a man's life should be called his nonnaturals—is another question." We leave undiscussed Galen's theory of humors and qualities, important as it is, to emphasize that the import of the doctrine of non-naturals is that man is responsible for his own health. Responsibility implies choice making, which requires knowledge and concern, and these combine to intellectualize what begins as the satisfaction of a physical need into the gastronomic approach to the table.

Galen taught that while the doctor was first a philosopher he was also a moralist because he could not intervene in the matter of health without intervening in the manner of living. The individual, who is always his own doctor, must translate his general moral and philosophical values into terms of his personal social and biological circumstances. Professor Oswei Temkin emphasizes that:

> Galen is a dietetic physician, and the moral aspect is potentially inherent in dietetic medicine, which considers most internal diseases to be caused by errors of regimen and hence avoidable. Health thus becomes a responsibility, and disease a matter for possible moral reflection.[4]

Diet conceived as a quasi-moral act of judgment has its parallel in the fastidiousness Erasmian moralists sought in the exchange of mental for sensual pleasure, of subtle for gross gratification, and, in general, of culture for nature. In Book II of his *Utopia,* Sir Thomas More explains that in Utopia where medicine is needed least Galen and Hippocrates are studied most because "medicine is the most useful of subjects." The roots of medical humanism are to be found in the humanist insistence that the individual be allowed to define himself by making choices.

The prince of humanists, Erasmus himself, is represented in the Bitting Collection by two works, to which one might perhaps wish to add a third, the manners book *De ciuilitate morum puerilium.* Erasmus's *De interdicto esv carnivum* (Basileae: J. Froben?, 1522) is in the form of a letter to the bishop of Basel concerning the scandal created by a neighbor of Erasmus who ate pork on Palm Sunday. While the point is very much the same, this is not the same work, as the *Gastronomic Bibliography* says, as the first dialogue in Book III of Erasmus's *Colloquia.* This is the dialogue called "L'Ichthyphage" in the Bitting *Colloquia* translation entitled *Les Entretiens familiers* (Genève, I. H. Widerhold, 1649). Violently allergic to fish, Erasmus had obtained ecclesiastical dispensation from his dietary obligations. This concession did not lessen his dislike, occasioned and reinforced of course by other circumstances, of church control over the daily life of men. "What porridge had John Keats?" laughed Robert Browning, jeering at those he thought inordinately occupied with the crumbs of literature. But the relationship of fish and Erasmus seems not entirely trivial when he writes (February 21, 1528) that while his heart is with the old faith his stomach is Lutheran. (As for Keats, Yeats describes him somewhere as a small boy with his nose pushed against the sweets shop window.)

B EFORE plotting other points in the early literature of gastronomy, the lines of which if drawn would converge at the Renaissance "discovery of man," this review will make the conventional tour of the collection to point out the rarities, although after a reminder that the Bittings did not intend a collection of rarities. The *Gastronomic Bibliography* describes how the Bittings, at first taken aback by the prices in the rare book market, sought counsel from the French bookseller Émile Nourry, whom they may have known from his publication of André Simon's *Bibliotheca Bacchica.* Nourry's advice was to compromise with perfection to attain the possible, that is, to collect the important titles, though not necessarily in the best editions. It is repeated here to anticipate the occasions when the reader will miss the intimacy of the first edition, the feeling

Beatus Johānes crisostomus
de reparatione lapsi.

Maistre Martin morin.

Left: Joannes Chrysostomus, *De reparatione lapsi* (Rouen: Martin Morin, June 21, 1495).

Jules Duhem's pride in this rarity is evident in his note "Un Incunable Normand rarissime," *Bulletin du bibliophile et du bibliothècaire*, n.s. II (May 20, 1932): 216-22. He wrote, "One does not know whether the perfection of the text or the purity of the print is more to be admired. The paper is excellent. The type is a beautiful German type that has already evolved toward the semi-Gothic, and apparently came from one of the most successful fonts along the Rhineland. The copy in our possession is complete and well preserved; the interior and the lateral margins have not been touched by the binder's knife."

Opposite: In the bookplate designed by Dr. A. W. Bitting, the words "Gastronomic Library" are set in the type used by Morin for the Chrysostom *De reparatione lapsi*. The signature is a facsimile of Mrs. Bitting's. The lines from the Lord's Prayer were reproduced from the Gutenberg Bible.

The book is *Les Diners de vaudeville* (Paris, 1796), one of a group of song books in the Bitting Collection. Thomas Carlyle adopted the bookplate shown only in 1853, so the book itself cannot be thought to have been in Carlyle's library at the time he wrote his "flame portrait" of the French Revolution (1835). Parenthetically, in accepting this bookplate from Henry T. Wake, Carlyle suggested the American "congress library" as a "safe and perennial place" for custody of his friend's study on the "great Franklin," a suggestion that was not acted upon (letter of November 24, 1853).

that this is the way the writer saw his work for the first time. To balance against this, attention ought also be directed to titles which at the time of purchase probably gave the Bittings the pleasure of knowing that they owned something out of the ordinary in one way or another.

A perhaps unexpected example of a gastronomic rarity is the first printed book on abstinence, the *De reparatione lapsi* of St. John Chrysostom (Rouen: Martin Morin, June 21, 1495.) This was the first incunabulum purchased by the Bittings and its typeface is used in the Bitting exlibris. Presumably then this book more than any other represented for the Bittings the pleasure of collecting—the thrill of the discovery, the excitement of the purchase, and the joy of later contemplation. This is the ninth of the thirty-nine incunabula from the press of Martin Morin, pioneer of Norman printing, perhaps best known for his *Coutumes de Bretaigne*. Chrysostom's text is that abstinence is the food of the soul, for it tames lusts, pacifies the choleric temperament, and wakes up judgment. At the moment of sale, this title was listed in Proctor's *Index,* although not in the Hain-Copinger-Reichling series of incunabula catalogs. According to Winship's *Census,* the only American copy was in the collection of John Boyd Thacher of Albany, New York. Consequently, with this purchase a pattern of events had been set up which ultimately would unite the Thacher and Bitting copies in the Library of Congress, where they had been preceded by the Yudin Collection Russian editions of the "golden-mouthed" Father of the Eastern Church.

There are other rarities in the Bitting Collection to which the collectors might have pointed with legitimate pride. At the time of their purchase of the *Martyrologium der Heiligen nach dem Kalendar* (Strassburg: Johann Pruss, 1484) there was no other copy in the United States of this source book of Alsatian social history. The *Gastronomic Bibliography* reproduces the *Martyrologium* plate of a man's figure with lines extending from the organs to the zodiacal houses at each side, in three of which the zodiacal symbols are represented as presiding over good digestion. The Bitting is still the only American copy of canon lawyer Perre Rebuffi's *Tractatus de sententiis praeivdicialibvs . . . vbi materia alimentorvm praesertim dvrante lite praestandorum, plenè explicatur,* which the publisher Joannes Gymnich of Cologne in 1595 combined with the *Tractatus de alimentis* of Johannes Baptista Pontanus, the Bohemian Jesuit Spannmüller. There is one other American copy of the 1492 edition of the *Speculum finalis retributionis*, Petrus Reginaldetus's joyful vision of the tortures of the damned on the day of the last judgment. The Bitting copy of another curious venture into eschatology, François Arnoulx's *Merveilles de l'avtre monde, contenant les horribles tourmens de l'Enfer. Les admirables joyes de Paradis* (Agen: I. Gayav, 1670), is unique in this country. Readers of the *Portrait of the Artist as a Young Man* may be interested in Arnoulx: his name and his subject matter recall the magnificent "hellfire" eloquence of Joyce's Father Arnall. The Bittings probably bought the book for the chapter entitled "Des banquets & convives qui se feront entre les bien-heureux."

Indeed, the early modern area of the Bitting Collection includes a rather substantial number of titles which, while perhaps not excessively rare, suggest that a bookman of uncommon knowledge was instrumental in their selection. It is not to denigrate the Bittings to think that the appreciation of some of these titles requires expertise of the kind one expects only of the professional bookman, in this case, presumably, the bookseller—publisher Émile Nourry. Perhaps some literate Frenchmen would recognize the *Epulum parasiticum* (Norimbergae, 1656) as a collection of contemporary satires on Pierre de Montmaur, professor of Greek at the Sorbonne and a parasite like those in Plautus who "eat and talk and talking still will eat." Bookish sophistication of a still higher order is required to know Claude Lancelot's *Dissertation svr l'hemine de vin, et svr la livre de pain de s. Benoist* . . . (A Paris: Chez Charles Savreaux, 1667) and to be aware that what seems to be a treatise on medieval weights and measures is actually a contribution to a debate on monastic diets then under way.

Neither of these works is listed in the *Gastronomic Bibliography,* but the annotation there on a comparable title, Francisco Grapaldi's *De partibus aedium* (Parma, 1516), reveals the tutelage in which the Bittings stood to Nourry. This edition, the Bittings write, is "said to be the most complete . . . and Nourry states the popularity of the work is indicated by 12 editions having been made in less than 40 years." The distinctive feature of the 1516 edition is indeed the "De verborum explicatione," which makes it twice the size of the earlier editions. Grapaldi has a sure place in architectural literature for this glossary of Latin terms, but Nourry knew and interested the Bittings in the chapters on the kitchen and the dining room, and perhaps the discussion (Book II, chapter 3) of wine, the "gratissimus liquor" whose abuse makes men lose first their legs and then their reason.

Nourry I think too much the good gastronomic bookseller himself not to know that he had a literary prototype in Cadet de Gassicourt's *Cours gastronomique* (Paris: Chapelle et Renand, 1809). In chapter 26, entitled "Gastrologie," the gastronomic bookseller (whom we shall call the gastrologist) explains that he seeks out not only those authors who treat of gastronomy *en professo* but also those who have devoted a few pretty pages to the subject. This eclecticism explains Mr. Bitting's purchase, say, of Ashmole's *Order of the Garter,* where the gastronomic interest is in the elaborate description of the feasts of that order. In addition, the titles recommended by Cadet de Gassicourt's gastrologist are so often found in the Bitting Collection as to suggest strongly something more than coincidence. This can be demonstrated by collating, so to speak, the Bitting titles against the paragraph in "Gastrologie" talking about the doctors' concern for food that is reproduced in our illustrations.

Fittingly, the first of the gastrologist's recommendations is to the father of medicine. To represent Hippocrates, the Bitting Collection adds to the 1530 Colines Raymond Restaurand's *Hippocrates De natura lactis* (Lugduni: Apud S. Vitalis, 1682) and Charles Lorry's *Essai sur les alimens, pour servir de commentaire aux livres diététiques d'Hippocrate* (Paris: Impr. de Vincent, 1757). Restaurand not only accepted Hippocrate's injunction against milk but advocated the observance of all the Hippocratic doctrines in their pristine entirety. The writings of Lorry and Restaurand illustrate the process by which Hippocrates became a kind of secular saint. Of Louis Lémery's work, which in the London edition of 1704 is called *A Treatise of Food, in General*, the Bitting Collection has a second London edition (1745) and 1705 editions from Paris and Venice. The author, one of the physicians of Louis XIV and a teacher of chemistry, obviously satisfied an international want, but his lasting distinction may be that his is the only book on digestion mentioned by Carême.

Of "the famous *Precèptes* of the School of Salerno," the Bitting Collection

---

vous remarquerez que les médecins se sont de tout temps occupés de la nourriture bonne, saine et savoureuse; aussi trouverez-vous dans cette collection le *Traité d'Hippocrate sur la manière de vivre*; les *OEuvres de Lemery*; les *Préceptes fameux de l'Ecole de Salerne*; le *Traité d'Hecquet sur les Alimens*; un *Essai sur la manière de conserver la Santé*, par Cheyne, médecin anglais; la Dissertation de Paul Eginette *de Facultatibus alimentorum*; celle de *Simeon Sethi* sur le même sujet; les Avis de *Platine* de Crémone sur le régime le plus convenable pour se bien porter (*de tuenda Valetudine*); un Traité peu commun d'un juif nommé Isaac (*de Victus salubris ratione*); les OEuvres de *Cullen*; un livre très-rare, dont l'auteur est inconnu, et qui a pour titre: *Medicus ad palatum*; et le Traité de *Cornaro* sur la Sobriété.

Ch.-L. Cadet de Gassicourt, *Cours gastronomique, ou, les diners de Manant-Ville, ouvrage anecdotique, philosophique et litteraire* (Paris: Capelle et Renand, 1809), p. 279.

The pertinent section reads: "you will note that doctors have always been concerned with good, healthful, and tasty food; and so you will find in this collection the *Treatise on the Way to Live* of Hippocrates; the *Works* of Lemery; the famous precepts of the School of Salerno; Hecquet's *Traité sur les alimens*; an *Essay on the Manner of Preserving Health* by the English doctor Cheyne; Paulus Aegineta's dissertation *De Facultatibus alimentorum*; that of Simeon Sethi on the same subject; the counsels of Platina of Cremona on the regimen most suitable for preserving health (de tuenda Valetudine); the uncommon treatise of a Jew named Isaac (de Victus salubris ratione); the works of Cullen; a very rare book of an unknown author entitled *Medicus ad palatum*; and the treatise of Cornaro on sobriety."

has a sixteenth-century Latin version—*Medicina Salernitana* (Geneva: I. Soer, 1591)—and a seventeenth-century French version—*Le Regime de santé de l'Escole de Salerne* (Paris: N. et I. de la Coste, 1649). The key precept is surely: "Se tibi deficiant medici, medici tibi siant/Haec tria: mens hilaris, requies moderata, dieta." The translation given in Sir John Harington's *The Englishmen's Docter* [sic], not in these collections, is "Use three physicians still, first doctor Quiet,/Next doctor Mery-man, and doctor Dyet." Sir John is introduced so that we may also repeat his apt characterization of the School of Salerno as "a little Academie where every man is a graduate, and can proceed doctor in the ordering of his owne bodie." Like the other works on personal hygiene in the Bitting Collection, the *Regimen sanitatis Salernitanum,* as the work is best known, was intended for the layman, not the practitioner. Its doctrine is Galen's non-naturals again: man's health is man's responsibility; man's proper concern is care, not cure. The rough verse of the *Regimen sanitatis Salernitanum* is easily committed to memory so its precepts became proverbial wisdom. Possibly no other secular text has exercised so pervasive an influence on the conduct of daily life.

The gastrologist's tongue slips in attributing to Philippe Hecquet a nonexistent *Traité sur les alimens*. What is meant is surely the *Traité des dispenses du carême* (Paris: F. Fournier, 1709), which goes beyond praising the observance of Lent to demonstrate, as the title says, "les rapports naturels des alimens maigres avec la nature de l'homme." The wits mocked Hecquet with the dry, La Rochefoucauld-like maxim that "a dietetic regime is a tedious sickness"; Le Sage satirized him savagely in the character of Dr. Sangrado in *Gil Blas.* Hecquet seems to have been the original butt of the stories about the doctor who goes to the kitchens of his patients to kiss the cooks for having made him wealthy. But the man was also doctor to Port Royal, director of La Charité, and dean of the Faculty of Medicine in Paris, to whose library he gave his great collection.

Another food reformer laughed at popularly but honored by his equals was George Cheyne, Hecquet's English contemporary. Cheyne was doctor to Hume and Richardson; Pope, the greatest poet and dyspeptic of the age, wrote Lord Lyttleton (December 12, 1736): "I love him as he loves Don Quixote, for the most moral and reasoning madman in the world." Once Falstaffian in figure, Cheyne reformed his own diet and then undertook to reform that of others in *An Essay on Health and Long Life* (London: G. Strahan, 1725). This work restates the Galenic non-naturals, somewhat modified to permit more consideration of what Cheyne called the "passions." Again the wits were merry because of Cheyne's ridiculous notion that water and milk are beverages, jeering "Suppose we e'en that milk is good, and say the same for grass, / The one for babes alone is good, the other for an ass." But there were ten editions of the *Essay* by 1740. In 1731, Sir John Arbuthnot, the most important physician of the time, who had been skeptical, published in agreement his influential *Essay Concerning the Nature of Aliments and the Choice of Them* (in the Bitting Collection only in a French translation).

The earlier of the two Byzantine physicians recommended by the gastrologist, the seventh-century eclectic Paulus Aegineta, has already been mentioned in connection with the *De ciborum facultatibus* accompanying Giorgio Valla's *De tvenda sanitate*. He appears again, this time in the company of Apicius, in the Bitting Collection in a 1541 publication from the Lyon press of Gryphius. Here a translation of that book of Aegineta's *De re medica* which deals with the maintenance of health by the dietetic regime is presented as *De facultatibus alimentorum*. The eleventh-century Simeo Sethius diligently searched the literature and queried the travelers who were so numerous in old Byzantium. His *Syntagma per literarum ordinem, de cibiariorum facultate* (Basilae: apud Mich. Isingrinium, 1538) briefly and cogently considers from the point of view of their Galenic qualities some 159 ingredients, including the musk and hashish he had learned about from the foreigners.

Of the gastrologist's last five names, the Bitting Collection can represent only the first and last, Platina and Cornaro. The absence most to be regretted is that of Ishak ibn Sulaimor al Israil (Isaac the Jew), whose *Opera omnia* of 1519 also contains the first discussion of human laughter. Here, one is told, Rabelais found that "laughter is the nature of man (rire est le propre de l'homme)," a statement with which he prefaces *Gargantua*. In chapter 1, I described the relationship of Platina, the Vatican librarian who is the author of the first cookbook, and Maestro Martino. The reader is referred to that chapter for its discussion of the fifteenth-century legitimatization of Epicureanism that is the cause, "necessary and sufficient," of Platina's pioneering venture. The Bitting Collection holds the 1503 and 1517 Latin editions of Platina published in Venice. In 1558, at the age of ninety-five, Luigi Cornaro completed the publication of the discourses that make up *Trattato della vita sobria*. Cornaro's doctrine of sobriety is perhaps best described as asking the application to the conduct of life of the principle of *misura*—harmony—that the Renaissance demanded of its art. In the Bitting Collection, Cornaro's Italian appears only in variations on the Latin version—*Hygiasticon* (London: Printed . . . and sold by C. Hitch, 1742) and *De la sobriété et de ses avantages* (Paris: L.

Coignard, 1701), by Leonardus Lessius, a theologian of Louvain admired as a moralist by St. François de Sales.

T HE gastrologist's structuring of a gastronomic library also calls for the humanist editions of the Latin and Greek classics of gastronomy. For the best known of these we leave the Bitting Collection momentarily. The Pennell Collection includes the first appearance in print of Apicius, the world's most famous cookbook author, who may have been any one of three persons and who, like Joe Miller, did not write the book for which he ever will be known. What has been handed down as *Apicius. De re coquinaria* embodies two ninth-century texts to which have been added excerpts from a Byzantine manual of the imperial period. The Pennell *Apicius* is accompanied by the Pennell *Schola apiciania* of Polynomus Syngrapheus (Francoforti: Apud Christianum Egonol-phum, 1534)—unique in this country—which also lacks an individual author in the sense that it is a collection of excerpts from writers like Paulus Aegineta, Macrobius, and J.B. Pontanus. The subject is not Apicius but food and convivial dining. The first chapter states the theme: "The table is sacred to friendship and what refers to it must not be neglected."

The editor's preface to the *Deipnosophistae* of Athenaeus in the Loeb Series argues that this book is entitled to the place given to Apicius as the great cook-book of antiquity. The Bitting Latin and Greek *Deipnosophistae* (Lugduni: Apud Viduam A. de Harsy, 1612) is the four-year labor of Isaac Casaubon, an almost legendary classics scholar. Casaubon moved from Geneva to England, there to live in the intimacy of Bishop Lancelot Andrewes, whose copy of the *Deip-nosophistae* now at Cambridge is of the same edition as the Bitting copy. The *Deipnosophistae* owned by Jefferson was the 1566 translation by Noel dei Conti from the Aldine Greek text, which, after examination, Casaubon rejected for use. Madame de Harsy's 1621 printing of *Animadversiones*, in which Casaubon justifies his text and his interpretations, is bound in with the Bitting *Deipnosophistae*.

Casaubon is reported to have regretted giving so much of his life to the editing of a work which lacked a serious moral concern. Indeed, the artists, actors, doctors, philosophers, and poets of the *Deipnosophistae* speak nothing at all of morals, although they speak a little bit of everything else. They talk of wines, of fruit, of gluttony and abstinence, of the food of the rich and of the poor, of the proper setting of a table and of the resemblances of the art of poetry and the art of

Laferatum
Oenogarum. intubera
Oxyporium
Hypotrima
Oxygarum digeſtibile
Mortaria
Ciminatum in oſtrea de conchiliis.
Apicii Celii epimeles incipit liber primus cōditum
paradoxum.

Onditi paradoxi compoſitio: mellis partes
    c   xv. in æneum uas mittunt in premiſſis inde
fextariis duobus vt in coǎturā mellis vinum
de coquas:quod igni lento;& aridis lignis calefaǎum
cōmotum ferula dū coquitur. Si efferuere cœperit vini
rore cōpeſcitur ꝑter quod fubtraǎo igni in fe redit . cū
pfrixerit rurfus accéditur.hoc fecūdo ac tertio fiet . Ac
tum demū remotum a foco poſtridie defpumatur cum
piperis vnciis quattuoriam triti maſticis fcrupulo .iiii.
folii & croci dragmę fingulę:daǎiloꝛ oſſibus torridis
qnꝗ hifdē daǎilis vino mollitis intercedente prius fuf
fufione vini de fuo modo ac numero:vt tritura lenis ha
beatur:his oibus paratis fupmittes vini lenis fextaria.
xviii.carbones perfeǎo addere duo milia .

Conditum meliromum.
Latorum conditum meliromū perpetuum:
    u   quod fubminiſtrat ꝑ viam peregrinanti:ꝓip
tritum cū melle defpumato i cupellā mittis
                                  a

Opposite: Apicius, *De re coquinaria* (Milan: Guillermus Le Signerre, 1498).

The title page of the Pennell Apicius is missing and with it the printer's designation, but this copy is established as one of the three American copies of the edition published in Milan on January 20, 1498, by Guillermus Le Signerre. The Pennell copy is still very handsome for the Roman type that William Morris used at the Kelmscott Press and for its wide margins on paper that time seems only to have mellowed. Dr. Frank Klotz and Dr. John Blackie, two great collectors, have left their names on the front endpapers. The word *paradoxi* shows the Greek origin of the first recipe; paradoxically enough, a recipe for a sugared wine that begins with honey (*mellis*) and also calls for pepper (*piperis*).

Right: Athenaeus, *Athenaei Deipnosophistarvm libri qvindecim* (Lugdvni: Apud Viduam A. de Harsy, 1612).

Mark Pattison's great biography of Casaubon puts his publishers among the "cormorants who sit hard by the tree of knowledge," but their technical achievement seems irreproachable. The last paragraph on the page shown is the first reference to the professional cook, since Simonides, the poet quoted, is thought to have lived in the seventh century B.C. The cook introduces himself here by asking "What is there that I can't do well?" The braggart cook becomes a stock character in classical comedy. Ben Jonson found here in Athenaeus the lines he used for Lickfinger in *Staple of News* (1631):

> A master cook! why, he's the man of men,
> For a professor! He designs, he draws,
> He paints, he carves, he builds, he fortifies,
> Makes citadels of curious fowl and fish,...
> He raiseth ramparts of immortal crust;
> And teacheth all the tactics, at one dinner:...
> He has nature in a pot, 'bove all the chymists...
> He is an architect, an engineer,
> A soldier, a physician, a philosopher,
> A general mathematician.

cookery. Galen appears and is introduced as the physician who has written more than all his predecessors and "is capable as any of the ancients in the exposition of his art." As the guests vie in erudite allusion and recondite quotation, one learns for example that Cadmus, who gave us our alphabetical signs, was a cook. So cookery and letters have been associated from the very first. Dr. Folliot in Peacock's *Crotchet Castle* has the *Deipnosophistae* on the tip of his tongue, and clearly Peacock's talky novels were written under the star of Athenaeus.

As was to be expected, the first "banquet" books, the *Symposium* of Plato and that of Xenophon, appear in the Bitting Collection. Perhaps unexpectedly, the profound Plato and the gay Xenophon are together under the covers of *De conviviorum veterū Graecorum, & hoc tempore Germanorum ritibus, moribus, ac sermonibus* (Basilae: ex officina Ioannis Oporoni, 1548). Cornarius, the translator, had issued a complete Latin Galen the year before; the publisher had printed Vesalius's *De humani corporis fabrica* five years earlier. The symposium is the drinking *(potos)* after the dining *(deipnon)*, so the talk in these books is not of food. This is not the case with another "banquet" book, the *Saturnalia* of Macrobius, an account of the talk at table during that holiday supposedly recorded by the author for his son's benefit. In Book VII the most prominent doctor of Macrobius's time leads a discussion on food and drink whose conclusion repeats after Galen that man must rely on his own taste and his own experience. The Bitting 1597 *Opera* of Macrobius was edited for the Plantin press by another Pontanus, this one the Dutch professor J. I. Pontanus, who is the first historian of Denmark.

An excursus is necessary here to make clear the maleficent influence of the greatest of the "banquet" books on the history of the literature of gastronomy. The villain in that history is Plato's *Symposium*, or, more correctly, what Marsilio Ficino and the Neoplatonists made of it. Ficino's commentary on the *Symposium* dismisses smell, touch, and taste as pertaining only to matter and the body and thus without significance in the appreciation of beauty. Ficino does not ask the question why, if this is so, the word "taste" should have come to be used to denote the aesthetic responses of the individual.

In the *Biographia Literaria*, Coleridge shook off the Neoplatonic inhibitions and posed and resolved this question by calling taste "the singularly happy and appropriate metaphor" borrowed from "the pregustatories of the old Roman Banquet to indicate sensitivity to the beautiful."[5] If taste was selected in preference to man's other cognitive senses, it was because of the "greater frequency, importance, and dignity of its employment and exertion in human nature." But so strong is the Neoplatonic prejudice in favor of the eye and the ear, Coleridge continues, that one refers only "sportively or by abuse of words to a beautiful flavor," although beauty is the essential concern of taste. The historian of gastronomy must wish that Coleridge had gone on to explain why the interdiction on the coupling of "beautiful" and "flavor" was first successfully violated in the France of Grimod de la Reynière and Brillat-Savarin.

The scholarly edition of the texts of Plato, Macrobius, Apicius, and the others is one part of the return *ad fontes* that the humanists pushed almost to the point of mysticism. Another aspect of this yearning to leave the vexatious present and recapture the past is the humanists' minute historical research on the mode of life of classical antiquity. This kind of learning can be instanced in Coleridge's reference to the Roman *praegustatores* quoted earlier. The breadth and depth of the humanist research effort can be gauged from the chapter "De conviviis & re cibaria" in J. A. Fabricius's *Bibliographia antiquaria*.[6] In this research the discussion of wine is particularly important. The qualities of wine are too varied and impalpable to permit description by the limited vocabulary specific to the sensations of taste. Horace and the others resorted to epithets like *generosum, dulce, molle, lene,* and *leve,* which work like metaphors. The example of the classics sanctions the free use of metaphor in gastronomic literature which will go beyond Coleridge's "beautiful taste" to the audacity of Grimod de la Reynière's "sauce with which one could eat one's grandfather."

The greatest of the Renaissance studies of the table of antiquity is acknowledged to be the *Antiquitatum convivialium* (Tigviri: C. Froschoverus, 1582) of the Swiss Johann Stuck. Cadet de Gassicourt's gastrologist and the latest English translator of Erasmus's *Colloquia*[7] join in commending this painstaking and erudite examination of 650 sources. Pierre Muret's *Dissertations sur les festins des anciens Grecs et Romains* (La Haye: C. Vanlom, 1715) pays Stuck the flattery of imitation but acknowledges its debt to its predecessor. Pedro Chacon, called the Varro of his age (the gastrologist dismisses him as "very learned for a Spaniard"), is in the Bitting Collection for his *De triclinio romano* (Rome: apud Georgivm Ferrarivm, 1588). The collector and antiquarian Fulvio Orsini added a long appendix to Chacon but there are none of the plates for which Orsini is important in the history of the Italian illustrated book. The gastrologist calls Nonnius (Luis Nunez), the pioneer student of the topographical antiquities of Spain, "modest et savant." Nonnius's *Diateticon, sive De re cibaria* (Antverpiea: ex officina P. Belleri,

a magnar
bianco

Candelier

lauorano de
pasta

passano

penelo y indora

THERMOPOLIVM
ROMANVM·

THERMOPOLIVM
CVM MILIARIIS
VASIS
CALE FACIENDI AQMAS
AD VSVM POTVVM
CVM VINO ET FRIGIDA

ANTO-

Left: Andrea Bacci, *De natvrali vinorvm historia de vinis Italiae et de conuiuijs antiquorum* (Romae: ex officinae Nicholai Mutis, 1596).

The Roman practice was to purchase from a thermopolium specially pure water which had been boiled and then cool it with snow for mixing with wine. Bacci put together this illustration of the thermopolium from the descriptions given by Seneca, Athenaeus, and others, and from remnants found in the Diocletian Baths. The first copper reservoir, the frigidarium, received the water which then passed to the tepidarium through the cylindrical tube and into the calidarium through a long series of serpentine tubes. The arrangement is so contrived that each reservoir *(miliarius)* remains equally full. The water is cooled with snow before use, for, as Athenaeus says, "no one will commend/The man who gives hot water to a friend."

Pages 72–73: Bartolomeo Scappi, *Opera . . .* (Venetia: M. Tramezzino, 1574?).

The twenty-seven plates in the book of Vatican cook Bartolomeo Scappi provide unique glimpses into the kitchens that are the backstage of the Renaissance banquets painted by Veronese. The spacious working areas and superb equipment shown are probably those of the Vatican kitchens of about 1570. The cook in the lower-left-hand corner is making what the Renaissance called blancmanger.

1645) is in effect an exposition of the references to food and drink in Horace, Juvenal, Martial, and other classic writers, though he seems always to return to the vindication of the Church's prescriptions about food. Another work on the Roman table as much Counter-Reformation as humanist in inspiration is *De victv romanorum et de sanitate tvenda* (Romae: in aedibus Populi romani, 1581). The author, Alessandro Petronio, physician to Pope Gregory XIII and Ignatius Loyola, also had some things to say about Roman public sanitation.

The Bitting Collection represents only the latter of the two great classical advocates of vegetarianism, Pythagoras and Porphyry, despite the gastrologist's express recommendation of Cocchi's *Régime de Pythagore*. Cocchi, as written by Rousseau into *La Nouvelle Héloise* and *Émile,* is an important contributor to the "back to Nature" revolution in diet still under way. Porphyry was known to the gastrologist for his doctrine that men in their perfected state would eat nothing but the fruits which plants bear in excess of their needs for reproduction. This is a great gastronomic improvement on Samuel Butler's *Erewhon,* where the righteous are limited to rotting fruit and decaying cabbage. The Bitting Collection has two eighteenth-century editions of Porphyry, one of which, the *Traité...touchant l'abstinence de la chair des animaux* (Paris: Bure l'aîné, 1747) includes the "Dissertation sur les génies" which gives Porphyry his place in demonology.

B ROACHING now the literature of wine, in obedience to that still-echoing birth cry of Rabelais's Gargantua: "À boire!" this review need not leave the area of classic studies. The authors to be cited justify George Meredith's dictum in *The Egoist* that the classicist is he "whose blood is most nuptial to the webbed bottle" because "the studious mind is . . . the obverse of mortality and throws off acids and crusty particles in the passing of the years until it is fulgent by clarity." Andrea Bacci, doctor to Pope Sixtus V and professor of botany, was honored for his learning by Cardinal Ascanio Colonna, whose arms are shown on the title page of Bacci's *De natvrali vinorvm historia de vinis Italiae et de conuiuijs antiquorum* . . . (Romae: ex officina Nicolai Mutis, 1596). This is a full and lucid scholarly account of Graeco-Roman oenology, wine and the constitution of man, the banquet practices of old, the wines of Italy, and the imported wines likely to be met in Rome. Bacci's expertise extends to knowledge of provincial variations in Italian climatic conditions and viticultural practices.

Vincentius Obsopoeus interests because this teacher of classical philology born the son of a Bavarian cook was a friend of Luther and of Pirckheimer, whom Erasmus called "the chief glory of our Germany." Brunet's *Manuel du libraire* thinks the Bitting 1648 Leiden edition of Obsopoeus's Ovid-inspired *De arte bibendi* so good in type and composition as to be attributable to an Elzevir press. Be it noted that Obsopoeus is not celebrating wine as stupifiant or anesthetic but as an alchemical agent enhancing consciousness. He would have admired the appreciation of champagne, not known to him as a sparkling wine, expressed by that unlettered sporting-man John Jorrocks: "Champagne gives one wery gentlemanly ideas." Obsopoeus's kind of lucid drunkenness is paralleled in France by Saint-Amant, Villon's successor as bard of the Pomme de Pin cabaret, whose *Oeuvres* are in our collection in the 1661 Orléans edition, that is technically as flawed as the Obsopoeus is good. A brief examination will contradict Tchemerzine's characterization of this edition as "jolie . . . bien complète et bien imprimée."[8]

The historically important, if not always intrinsically interesting, works in this category include Scacchus's early description of sparkling wine, *De salubri potu dissertatio* (Romae: apud Alexandrū Zannettum, 1622); Peccana on cold drinks, *Del bever freddo* (Verona: Stamparia di A. Tamo, 1627); and Canoniero's praise and censure of other fermented drinks as well as of wine, *Le lodi e i biasmi del vino* (Viterbo: G. Discepelo, 1608). J. B. Davini's *De potu vini calidi dissertatio* (Mutinae Typis A. Capponi, 1725) which treats of the therapeutic value of wine, is also an early treatise on hydrotherapy and is accompanied by correspondence addressed to the great historian Muratori. The first work on cider, Julien Le Paulmier de Grentemesnil's *Traité* of 1589, is in the collection only in an 1896 facsimile issued, appropriately enough, by a Norman bibliophile society. The *Vinetum brittanicum* (London: Printed by J.C. for T. Dring, 1676) of the agricultural writer John Worlidge is the first study of English cider. *The Two Discourses* (London, 1675), one of which is "Of the Mysterie of Vintners . . ." of Walter Charleton, who at twenty-two was doctor to Charles I, seem rather trivial, although prepared to be read to the Royal Society. Charleton might better have been represented in a gastronomy collection by his *Epicurus, his Morals* (London, 1656), one of the works which marks the arrival of Epicureanism in England. John French prepared himself by practice in alchemy for the writing of *The Art of Distilling*. All editions after the first (the Bitting copy belongs to the fourth edition of 1667) include a separately paginated "London-Distiller, Exactly and Truely Shewing the Way (in Words at Length and not in Mysterious Characters and Figures) to Draw all Sorts of Spirits and Strong Waters."

Scholarship and the grape itself can be represented by the *Coltivazione Toscana della viti, e d'alcuni alberi* (Firenze: Appresso i Givnti, 1622) of G. V. Soderini and Bernardo Davanzati, the first a noble Florentine who did not make his peace with the Medici and died in prison, his coauthor the editor of many texts of the classics. This work is accompanied in the Bitting volume by *La coltivazione degli vlivi*, the little study of olives of Piero Vettori, perhaps the greatest Italian classicist of his time, whose portrait Titian painted, and whose career requires five pages in Sandys's *History of Classical Scholarship*. Grapes, olives, and philosophy are combined in the rarity called *Observations upon the Growth and Culture of Vines and Olives*, written for the first earl of Shaftesbury by his grandson's tutor, John Locke. The occasion for the book was Locke's French tour of 1679, but the first printing took place in 1766. It should be remembered that Charles Lamb calls the Chinese who first discovered that it was not necessary to burn down whole houses to roast pigs, "a sage like our Locke."

THE agricultural manual that surveys the "whole house" along with the vineyard is the last of the interlocking groupings in the Bittings' conceptualization of the early modern literature of gastronomy. However, before beginning a new journey we need to finish an old one, for the recommendations of Cadet de Gassicourt's gastrologist annotated earlier hardly exhaust the medico-culinary literature in the Bitting Collection. The student of the history of science will find dispersed here the documentation of the debate on the nature of the digestive process waged after Galen called blood "food-becoming-flesh." All that can be done now is to summarize the debate by repeating that the stomach has been likened at various times to a mill, a stew pan, and a fermenting vat. For a reasonably complete cross-section of the rest of this medico-culinary literature, we return to the book-by-book enumeration inevitable in a review of this kind.

Three sixteenth-century medical imprints are reminders that astrology remained the science of sciences for the humanists as it had been for Chaucer's "Doctour of Physick." The *Artificiosa methodus comparandorum hortensium fructuum* (Coloniae Agrippinae: apud Joannem Gymnicum, 1577), a kind of astrological *materia medica,* is the work of Arnauld Mizauld, called in his time the French Aesculapius, who was adviser to Marguerite de Valois, Neoplatonist and feminist. The curiously titled *Libro llamadao El porque* (Caragoça: Impressa en casa de Iuan Millan . . ., 1567) is a Spanish translation of the *Liber de homine* of

Girolamo Manfredi, astrologer and professor of medicine at Bologna. Derived from the "Salerniternian Questions," the questions and answers concern sex, leprosy, diet, the effects of wine, the *castrati* and other oddities. *De vita libri tres* of Marsilio Ficino (Basilae: apud haeredes Andreae Cratandri, 1549) is probably in the Bitting Collection because bound with it are three little Galenic treatises on diet by Guinter of Andernach, Girolamo Ricci, and Insulanus Menapius.

However, in addition to being the prime exposition of talismanic astrology, the third of Ficino's books gives the astrologically suitable diet (white wine and very white sugar) for escape from the maleficence of Saturn. The job description of the master-cook given by Lickfinger in Ben Johnson's *Staple of News* (act 4, scene 1) requires knowledge of:

> The influence of the stars upon his meats,
> And all their seasons, tempers, qualities
> And so to fit his relishes and sauces.

The Method and Means of Enjoying Health, Vigour, and Long Life (London: Printed by J. M. for D. Newman, 1683) of Dr. Edward Maynwaring, "doctor in phisick and hermetick phylosophy" might be associated with these earlier applications to medicine of the secret knowledge of the stars in their courses. More mundane are three other seventeenth-century English imprints. Dr. Tobias Venner's *Via recta ad vitam longam* (London: Printed by R. Bishop for Henry Hood . . ., 1638) describes "the Nature, Faculties, and Effects of all such Things, as by Way of Nourishment . . . are made for the Preservation of Health." The English vegetarian book of the century is *The Way to Health, Long Life and Happiness* (London: G. Conyers, 1683) of "Philotheos Physiologus" (Thomas Tryon), "student in physics" (the man was a London hatter). Ben Franklin was one of Tryon's converts until an incident recorded in the *Autobiography* convinced him that the law of life is for big fishes to eat little fishes. It was on this occasion that Franklin formulated his instrumental definition of reason, remarking "so convenient a thing it is to be a reasonable creature, since it enables one to find or make a reason for everything one has a mind to do."

William Salmon called his publication *The Family-Dictionary; or, Household Companion* (London: H. Rhodes, 1695). Salmon was apothecary, doctor, and astrologer, like Nicholas Culpepper, whose Englishing of the Latin pharmacopeia of the College of Physicians Salmon continued to the displeasure of that body. Salmon begins by attacking quacks, since the best defense is an offense, and then

Thomas Tryon's first published work crammed all the topics announced on this title page into twenty-one pages: as Gibbon said of Tacitus, only a few pages, but the pages of Tryon. Franklin early shook off Tryon's dietetic regime, but the influence of his prose style may have been a lasting one. A mixture of visionary philosopher and dietician, Tryon was also a realist. Recognizing that men will drink, he devoted the first part of his *Way to Get Wealth* to "Directing How To Make 23 Sorts of English Wine, Equal to French."

A

TREATISE

Of CLEANNESS in

Meats and Drinks,

OF THE

PREPARATION of FOOD,

THE

Excellency of Good Airs,

AND THE

BENEFITS of Clean Sweet BEDS.

Alſo of the

Generation of Bugs,

AND THEIR CURE.

To which is added,

A SHORT DISCOURSE

OF THE

PAIN in the TEETH,

Shewing from what Cauſe it does chiefly proceed, and alſo how to prevent it.

By *THO. TRYON.*

LONDON, Printed for the Author, and ſold by *L. Curtis* near *Fleet-Bridge*. 1682.

lays down "exact rules . . . for curing the several diseases . . . incident to men, women, and children." This done, he hurries to "directions for cookery . . . the whole art of pastry, conserving, candying, confectionery . . . all sorts of English wines . . . and the mystery of pickling." Salmon's happy choice of title announces the advent of new variants in the nomenclature of the cookbook.

There are other books whose titles catch the eye. Philibert Guybert's *Toutes les oeuvres charitables* (Lyon: P. Bailly, 1640) appeared in English translation as *The Charitable Physician* and was then subtitled *"the Manner to Make and Prepare in the House with Ease and Little Expense all the Remedies Which are Proper to all Sorts of Diseases."* Guybert is a "charitable physician" because professor of pharmacy at La Charité. In Bernhard Swalve's *Querelae ventriculi renovatae* (Amstelaedami: apud Joannem Janssonium à Waesberge, 1675) the stomach has a quarrel with both doctor and patient. Swalve, a ship's doctor who lived unquietly in Hamburg, again shows his quirky humor in a work not in this collection, *Alcali et acidum, Naturae et artis instrumenta pugilica*, whose subtitle can be translated as "Nature and Art's Boxing Gloves."

The gastrologist recommends a few purely literary works to inform the gastronomer's mind and divert his spirit. One of these, the *Mensa philosophica que tractat de his quibus utimur in mensa* (Bergamo: Impressus Venetiis a Simone ex Luere, 1514), when Englished in 1649 was entitled *Philosopher's Banquet Newly Furnished with Several Dishes*. The sixteenth-century editions of the *Mensa philosophica* attribute authorship to Theobald Anguilbert; the seventeenth-century editions to Michael Scott. The first is thought to have been a German Dominican; the second is the Michael the Scot who was astrologer, doctor, and general Merlin at the Hohenstaufen court of Frederick II. He was also the "Auld Michael" of Sir Walter Scott's *Lay of the Last Minstrel*. The first of the four parts of the *Mensa philosophica* is on the gastronomical judgment of food and drink, the last on tales and pastimes with which to make merry at table. Someone has noted on the front endpaper of the Bitting copy that this work was called "libro giocondissimo e rarissimo" by G. B. Gallizioli's *Dell'origine della stampa e degli stampaturi di Bergamo* as early as 1768.[9]

Another littérateur in gastronomy recommended by the gastrologist is Erycius Puteanus (the Louvain professor Heinrich van der Put), who was thought extraordinarily prolific even in an age of great polygraphs. Sandys's *History of Classical Scholarship* dismisses his ninety-eight monographs with the comment "the topics treated in his Latin works are unimportant and he succeeded in his blameless intention of being *bonus potius quam conspicuus*."[10] His *Comus, sive Phagesiposia Cimmeria* (Louvain: Typis G. Rivi, 1611; Leiden: ex officina I. Navii, 1630) originates in that intention. In his inaugural address at Louvain University, he celebrated the high spirits of the young, then, fearful that he be accused of confusing high and alcoholic spirits, wrote a retraction. This he thought might be offensive to the high livers of Antwerp and so he wrote still another book, the very popular *Comus*, placing the characters in an imaginary land so that he might give his ideas of the good life without any possible offense to anyone.

Not recommended by the gastrologist, or, indeed, by anyone else, is the *Tractatus de butyro* of Martin Schoock, with which is bound the same author's *Diatriba de aversione casei* (Groningae: typis Johannes CöllenI, 1664). These pastiches of quotations on butter and cheese are part of a long series—other topics are herrings, truffles, and storks—written perhaps because of the "publish or perish" academic pressure existent even in the seventeenth century. This justly neglected professor of philosophy at Groningen was once important enough to be attacked by Descartes. Did the Bittings buy this book because P. Morton Shand's *A Book of Food*[11] calls this survey of cheese haters "a curious philosophical study" and associates it, curiously enough, with "the Schoolmen of the Middle Ages"?

Most interesting as a harbinger of the future of the literature is the little group of books on the dietetic regime in which the personality of the individual writer is discernible behind the screen of citations from the classics. In the twenty-two books of the Pennell copy of J. B. Bruyerin's *De re cibaria* (Lugduni: apud S. Honoratvm, 1560), each of which discusses exhaustively one type of food, the mass of classical citations is leavened by the writer's account of his own experiences and tastes. Nephew and successor to the great doctor Symphorien Champier, married into the family of the humanist Budé, Bruyerin was doctor to Henri II. Bruyerin anticipates Curnonsky and Rouff in taking the reader on a gastronomic tour of the provinces of France to demonstrate the variety of the non-Parisian cuisines. *De re cibaria* is the tool used by Şăineanu's *La Langue de Rabelais*[12] to explain the words exploded in Rabelais's pyrotechnical description of Messer Gaster and the Gastrolators' worship of their "ventripotent god."

The *Trattato della natura de' cibi, e del bere* (Romae: B. Bonfadino, et T. Diani, 1583) of Baldassare Pisanelli of Bergamo, philosopher, doctor, astrologer, and botanist, was intended to "prepare . . . the intelligence of all those who require a perfect knowledge of foods," so again the public envisaged was not an entirely professional one. Indeed, the second edition was published because of "the continued use and insistence of some princely gentlemen of this city." To facilitate consultation, the book is made up of schematic tables listing 138 foods under headings for their good and bad qualities from the point of view of Galenic humors and complections. Under the last heading, that titled "natural history," Pisanelli writes little models of conciseness, individualizing the expected classical references by comments on his own preferences. This description holds only for the Pennell first edition; the Bitting Bergamo edition of 1587 is only half the size of the first, and the Pennell Venetian edition of 1601 is even somewhat smaller.

A book annotated by Rabelais's friend Dr. Isaac Bassaler, the *Regimen sanitatis* of Robert Grospré was intended not only for doctors but for intelligent laymen who would find it "pernecessarium et utilis." This is a practical vade-mecum teaching how and what to eat, and how to distinguish the best from the better or the merely good. Grospré's prescription is always moderation. The Rosenwald copy of the first edition (Gandavi: I. Lambertus, 1538) carries a frontispiece portrait of Grospré not found in the Bitting copy of the 1540 Paris edition. The Hervé-Fierabras whose name appears on the title page of the Bitting copy was also identified by Jules Duhem as a friend of Rabelais. Hervé-Fierabras is registered as having matriculated in the Faculty of Medicine at Montpelier in November 1541, so he, like Rabelais and Bassaler, had received medical training.

The most appealing expression of the gastronomic spirit of the period may be the *Sermonivm convivialium libri x* . . . (Basilae: H. Petri, 1559) of Georg Pictorius, town physician of Ensisheim in Alsace, that well-favored land. The model for Pictorius's exposition is the *Colloquia* of Erasmus; his *personae* are stock figures in the "banquet" tradition: the roguish Critor, the laughing Gelasius, Oenophilus the wine lover, and the lucky Faustus. With the deference due to Galen the conversation begins on the manner of staying healthy but goes on to praise the wonderful things that nature has given man to eat and the exquisitely sharp sense of being alive that wine can impart. The talk is that of men who like food and seek to express their appreciation to other men who like food. The classical scholarship is there, but it is there to be shared, not shown off. Professor Leo Élaut of Ghent University finds in the *Sermonivm convivialium* charming humanist overtones and a lyric imagery like that of Ronsard and the Pleiad. Perhaps the reader is best served here by referring him to Élaut's study of the manner in which a medical humanist like Pictorius transforms the diet book into an essay on gastronomy.[13]

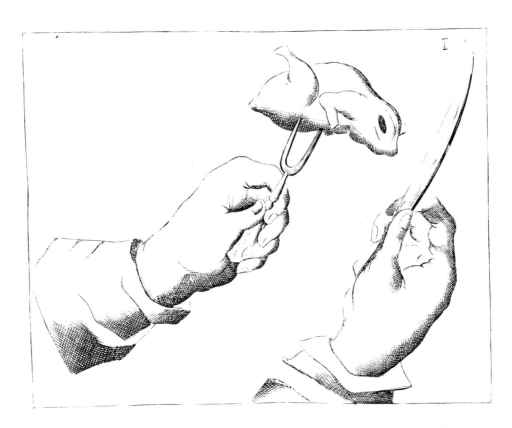

Mattia Giegher, *Li Tre trattati*
(Padova: P. Frambotto, 1639).

Giegher was in the service of the German Law School in Padua, where the practice was to carve in mid-air in the manner demonstrated. While Giegher's chapter on the folding of napkins seems to have been an innovation, his carving techniques do not go beyond those described by earlier writers like Panunto, Cervio, or Scappi. The extraordinary prices at which a Giegher book sells are attributable to the exceptional illustrations by the unnamed Italian artist.

THIS chapter will conclude with a "Renvoi" to Cadet de Gassicourt's gastrologist, whose first recommendation for a gastronomic library was the classical agricultural writers, the *Scriptores rei rustica*. The Bitting Collection has sixteenth-century examples of this literature in the original: *Libri de re rvstica* (Paris: apud Joannem Parvum, 1543), Palladius's *De re rvstica* (Lyon: apud S. Gryphium, 1549), and in French translation Columella's *Les Dovze Livres . . .* (Paris: I. Keruer, 1556) and *Geoponica* (Poictiers: I. & E. de Manef frères, 1543).

Intended for the Roman gentleman who lived on and from his estate, these manuals consider the "whole house," the *praedium* or *fundus*, as a self-contained unit providing its own food, brewing its own beverages, and spinning its own cloth. The Middle Ages wrote so little about the practices of agriculture that one wonders if the clerks were ashamed to confess knowledge or interest. The great exception is Pietro Crescenzi, who modified the classics in the light of his own experiences and those of his friends. The Bitting Crescenzi is the Italian version, *Le Cose della villa* (Venetia: Appresso F. Rampazetto, 1564), prepared by Sansovino, himself an important printer and a member of Aretino's literary circle. The gastronomic interest of this edition of Crescenzi is limited to his discussion of viniculture (Chapter 4) and of the garden (Chapter 6).

The husbandry taught by Crescenzi and the classic writers was inevitably joined by housewifery when the lady of the house worked side by side with the servants in the brewery, buttery, kitchen, and stillroom. In England Thomas Tusser appended "Five Hundred Points of Huswifery" to the second edition (1561) of his *Five Hundred Points of Husbandry* (in these collections only in editions of 1848 and 1931), saying: "Housekeeping and husbandry, if it be good / Must love one another, as cousins in blood." In 1623 Gervase Markham added *The English Huswife* to the *Countrey Contentments* he had written in 1615 to free English gentlemen farmers from reliance on non-English Romans or Greeks. Perhaps the differences between early modern and Roman manorial life were less important in France than in England. At any rate, Charles Estienne's *Praedium rusticum* (Lutetiae: apud Carolum Stephanum, 1554), after being translated and expanded by his son-in-law Jacques Liebault, had a continued popularity and usefulness in France demonstrated by the appearance of at least thirty-two editions by 1702. Works like Louis Liger's *Dictionaire (!) pratique* (Paris: Paulus-du-Mesnil, 1722), J. Demachy's *Économie rustique* (Paris: Lottin le jeune, 1769), F.J. Rey Deplanazu's *Oeuvres d'agriculture et d'économie rustique* (Paris: Meurant, 1801), and Aglae Adanson's *La Maison de campagne* (Paris: Audot, 1821), most interesting because written by a woman for women, continue Estienne into the nineteenth century.

Greatest of the modern "whole house" books is *Le Theatre d'agriculture et mesnage des champs* (Paris: A. Savgrain, 1617) of Olivier de Serres, Seigneur de Pradel, where the best chestnuts grow. Serres is thought unexcelled in the description of the real and the ideal in farm life: the rhythm of the change of seasons, the living with animals, the soil as a Demeter-like goddess to be wooed. Serres's eighth chapter is entitled "De l'usage des alimens." Perhaps something of his luminous, flavorful style is communicated in these sentences: "After the necessary foods come those that are useful and pleasant, that is to say, the preserves, so that the house does not lack food serving both to nourish the body and replenish the spirit. . . . These preserves please everyone with their exquisite preparations and rare beauties." This talk of food that replenishes the spirit seems not too far removed from Coleridge on "beautiful taste." The paragraph continues, "it will be here that the good lady of the house will find her delight in continuing to demonstrate the subtlety of her intelligence [*esprit*]." Serres's woman demonstrating her intelligence by the preparation of conserves recalls Mrs. Ramsay presiding over the *boeuf en daube* in Virginia Woolf's *To the Lighthouse* or Proust's Françoise selecting the meat for her *boeuf à la gelée* like Michelangelo his marble. In addition to making his then novel recognition of the female presence in the kitchen, Serres completes Galen and Erasmus by tacitly assuming that gastronomy, if not an art itself, is a necessary part of good living, which is an art.

Stuart Sc.

Chapter Three

English Cookery Books

All sensible and well-informed people know that cookery books are delightful reading.

GEORGE SAINTSBURY

ENGLISH culinary antiquarianism begins with Samuel Pegge's *Forme of Cury* (1780)[1] and Richard Warner's *Antiquitates culinariae* (1791) and continues immediately in the next century with Furnivall and Austin's edition of medieval texts for the Early English Text Society and William Pickering's half a dozen printings of the manuscript materials describable as "Household Ordinances." The author of the *Forme of Cury*, the earliest English cookery manuscript, who worked about 1390 as cook to Richard II, is unknown, but his French origins or tastes are clear in his work. Thereafter to live like an English milord seems always to have demanded a French cook; in Elizabeth's time William Harrison complained in his *Description of England* that noble kitchens were run by "musicall-headed Frenchmen." The English love-hate ambivalence toward French cuisine, one theme of this account, thus announces itself early.

Every book collector encounters areas where knowledge and enthusiasm are not enough to enable him to carry out his design because the pieces required never enter the marketplace. There is no example in the collections of Katherine Golden Bitting and Elizabeth Robbins Pennell of the Tudor cookbook proper, either early, like the *Booke of Cokery* printed in 1500 by Richard Pynson, or late, like the 1587 *Good Huswifes Jewell* of Thomas Dawson. Elyot's *Castel of Helth* (1541), perhaps a third of which is devoted to diet, is the closest Bitting approximation of a Tudor cookbook. Elyot is better known for his ethical treatise, *The Governour*, but he had studied medicine with Linacre. Sir Hugh Plat's *Delights for Ladies* (1644) may have been the first cookbook to give stillroom recipes. John Gerard's *Herball* (1633) mentions a parsnip bread "set forth . . . by my friend Master Plat, which I have made no tryall of, nor mean to do so." The line is quoted, not to illustrate the limits of friendship, but as a reminder that the Bitting Collection ranges beyond the cookbook to herbals like Gerard's and like John Parkinson's *Theatrum Botanicum* (1640), where the author's first concern is with the color of a flower and the flavor of a fruit or vegetable. Similarly, Fynes Morison's *Itinerary* (1617) is in the Bitting Collection because of the happy gusto with which it describes the meals and manners encountered by a gentleman on his travels in the last decade of the sixteenth century.

The Elizabethan *Health's Improvement*, written perhaps in 1594 and posthumously published in 1655 (the Bitting second edition of 1746 is important for the prefatory and biographical material) is a gossipy discourse on the "nature,

Samuel Pegge A.M. S.A.S.

A.D. MDCCLXXXV. Et. 81.

Impressit et Joh. Gustaus Brander. fini.

SIBI ET AMICIS.

On appearance, the edition of *The Forme of Cury*
by the Reverend Samuel Pegge, numismatist,
antiquarian, and writer for *Archaeologia*, was
greeted poetically in the *Gentleman's Magazine:*

> Hail once more, Sir! May health attend
> On you—and Brander, your good friend,
> Who with joint kindness have combin'd
> To teach us how our fathers din'd:
> All in "The Forme of Cury" told
> As used in Richard's days of old,
> When Cury, as it then was styl'd
> With wise Avisement was compil'd.

Gustavus Brander, the owner of the manuscript,
was a millionaire merchant of Swedish origin.
The version of *The Forme of Cury* given in
Richard Warner's *Antiquitates culinariae* (London: R. Blamire, 1791) is more easily read because
of its expansion of the abbreviations.

method and manner of preparing all the kinds of foods used in the Nation." The author, identified on the title page as "that ever famous Thomas Moffett," was a friend of Sir Francis Drake and Tycho Brahe and physician to that Mary Herbert ever famous for her epitaph as "the subject of all verse" once attributed to Ben Jonson. Moffett approves neither of "surfeiting nor self-pining," although gross eaters are warned that they stand upon the "rayser's edge." He continues in the Hippocratic prejudice against fish, for "howsoever it be sold, buter'd, fried or boiled . . . yet a stone will be a stone," but he may have been the first to recommend liver to "please the taste, clear the eyesight, agree with the stomach and encrease bloud."

The reign of that difficult man James I carries the cookbook further in the writings of Gervase Markham and John Murrell. Markham has already been mentioned as one of those who take over from the classic *Scriptores rei rustica* the occupation with the *praedium* or *fundus,* the "whole house." His *English Huswife* (1649, 1675, 1676) is a foundation stone of the culinary tradition of America as well as England, for it appears in the *Records* of the Virginia Company as early as 1620. Markham was an indefatigable hack of talent, not to say genius, whose understanding of game cookery George Saintsbury particularly commends. The second part of Markham's *Countrey Contentments,* the *English Huswife,* is self-described as "imparting the inward and outward virtues . . . which ought to reside in the compleate woman." Cookery is "the first and most principall" of the virtues of this woman, for "she that is utterly ignorant therein may not . . . challenge the freedome of Marriage, because indeed she can then but performe halfe her vow, for she may love and obey, but she cannot serve and keepe him with that true dutie which is ever expected." Markham's free use of herbs, greens, fruits, and vegetables in the "simple sallet" and the "grand sallet," which will become the salmagundi, shows that seventeenth-century England was a flowering garden.

John Murrell's *A Daily Exercise for Ladies and Gentlewomen* (1617) is singled out here as indicating the arrival in England of "conceits in sugar-workes of several kindes," "gellies," "cordiall wines," and "sucket-candies." Sugar from the West Indies, not maize or potatoes, is the great American innovation in sixteenth- and seventeenth-century cuisine. Murrell seems to have been a free-lance cook who supplemented his income by the sale at his publishers of the bread and gingerbread moulds, pots, pans, and other utensils mentioned in his books. Murrell's *A New Booke of Cookerie* (1641?), first published in 1617—that is, two years after Markham—is unmixed cookbook, with recipes "all set forth according to the now new English and French fashion."

The elegant, formal court of Charles I, which had Ben Jonson for poet and Van Dyke for painter, was the example for smaller counterparts scattered over England on the estates of the great landed gentry. Nathaniel Brooke led the publishers opening "closets" or "cabinets" to reveal the "secrets" of cookery and housewifery of the chatelaines of high degree to the discreet reader. These are the cavalier cookbooks, like the cavalier poets expressing the ideals and pretensions of a gallant, courtly aristocracy during its trial by a rude reality. They are well described by Mrs. Pennell, whose own style so often falls into what Charles Lamb called the "beautiful obliquities" of seventeenth-century prose: "Rose leaves and saffron, musk and 'amber-greece,' orange flower and angelica are scattered through them, until it seems as if the feasts could have been spread only for Phillis or Anthea. . . . The names of the dishes are a joy: the tanzies of violets or cowslips and the orangado phraises; the syllabubs and the frumenties—'all-tempting Frumenty,' the wiggs and pastries; the eggs in moonshine, the conserves of red roses, the possets without end, and almost as lyrical as the poet's, made 'with cream of lilies, not of kine, and maiden's blush for spiced wine'."

The lady of the manor practiced pharmacy in her kitchen and so quickly took over the arts of preserving, candying, and conserving as sugar became available. It is to the ladies that Sir Hugh Plat announces:

> Of sweets, the sweetest I will now commend
> To sweetest creatures that the Earth doth bear,
> These are the saints to whom I sacrifice
> Preserves and Conserves of the Plum and Pear.

Typically *The Ladies Cabinet Enlarged and Opened* (1654, 1655) begins with preserving, candying, and conserving and passes through "physick and chirurgy" to reach cookery. If the stillroom formulas in the appendix that are ascribed to Lord Ruthven are really the work of Charles I's general, no more martial pen ever wrote a cookbook.

The True Gentlewoman's Delight of that very sympathetic "Lady Bountiful," Elizabeth Talbot, dowager duchess of Kent, appears in the Bitting Collection in a 1671 edition not reported by Oxford. This work, first published as the second part of the same author's *A Choice Manual* (1659) and usually bound with it, appears separately in the Bitting Collection. The dowager duchess of Kent scandalized contemporaries almost equally by living quasi-conjugally with John Selden, a scholar of immense learning, and causing "every other day a hugh dinner to be got, and all the poor people might come that would and that which (was) spared they took home with them." The young Samuel Butler was a retainer in the duchess's household, so that her books can be read as the bill of fare of Selden and the author of *Hudibras*. One thinks in the same way of Jessie Conrad's *A Handbook of Cooking for a Small House* (1923), for which her husband, Joseph, wrote the foreword. Jessie delighted her husband's friends by preparing for them their

Printed in 1923, Jessie Conrad's *Handbook of Cookery* was probably completed by 1906, for Conrad describes it in the letter to Ford Madox Ford of January 26, 1907. Jessie was so puffed up with her achievement that Conrad said "nothing but an epidemic of indigestion setting in over all the United Kingdom after publication will subdue her." Conrad wanted to get money enough to settle all his financial difficulties. He involved Ford, who had participated in the sale of the George Meredith-Thomas Love Peacock manuscript cookbook to J. P. Morgan and was working with the publisher Byles. In sending letters of rejection to Ford and Conrad, Byles mixed the envelopes. Conrad read Byles's indignant query whether Ford thought him mad or a charitable institution to give that sum of money for a cookbook from a man whose novels never sold more than two thousand copies. Conrad threatened Byles; Byles told Ford his duty was to horsewhip Conrad. Ford tells the story of this imbroglio with great glee in *Return to Yesterday*.

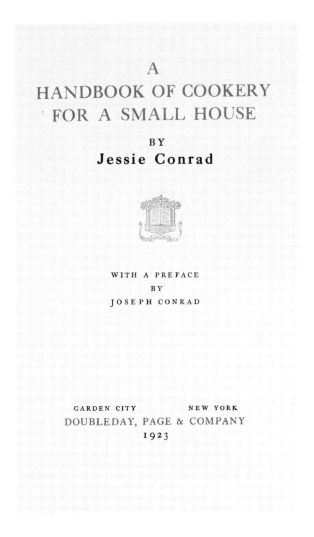

A

HANDBOOK OF COOKERY
FOR A SMALL HOUSE

BY
Jessie Conrad

WITH A PREFACE
BY
JOSEPH CONRAD

GARDEN CITY   NEW YORK
DOUBLEDAY, PAGE & COMPANY
1923

favorite dishes, the recipes for which she gives in her modest little book. Joseph Conrad has delighted all cookbook collectors since by his defense of their interest:

> Of all the books produced since the most remote ages by human talents and industry those only that treat of cooking are, from a moral point of view, above suspicion. The intention of every other piece of prose may be discussed and even mistrusted; but the purpose of a cookery book is one and unmistakable. Its object can conceivably be no other than to increase the happiness of mankind.

The appearances of *The Compleat Cook* (1656) and *A Queen's Delight* (1660, 1683) separately or accompanied by "The Pearl of Practice" in *The Queen's Cabinet Opened* (1663) and *The Queen's Closet Opened* (1656) are too complex for charting here. The queen is the unfortunate Henrietta Maria, to whom "the most experienced persons of our Time" presented "these incomparable secrets, many of which were honoured with her own practice, when she pleased to descend to these more primitive recreations." "The Pearl of Practice," which does not seem ever to have appeared separately, provides home remedies like the "Comfortable Juleb for a Feaver" or "The Water of Life," and *A Queen's Delight* the formulas for the royal perfumes used by Edward VI and Elizabeth. Our interest is in the refinement of Charles I's court as expressed in *The Compleat Cook, Expressly Prescribing the Most Ready Ways Whether Italian, Spanish, or French for Dressing of Flesh and Fish, Ordering of Sauces, or Making of Pastry*. Note that there is no English ready way.

A "woman's liberationist" *avant la lettre*, Hannah Woolley is being discovered today for the trenchant, truculent eloquence of her attacks on male chauvinism. Our concern is limited, however, to the author of *The Ladies Directory* (1662), who observed "methinks I hear some of you say *I wish Mrs. Woolley would set forth some New Experiments*" and in response published her *Queen-like Closet* (1674, 1684?). *A Supplement to the Queen-like Closet* (1674) is bound in with the Pennell copy. In this closet are to be found kickshaws, ragoos, fricassées, syllabubs, and other dishes sure "to gratify Noble Persons in their Gusto's." Her cookery is medieval in the recipes for veal to be prepared to "eat like" sturgeon, pig like lamb, and beef or mutton like venison. Her household management section gives the medical receipts for the "Griping of the Guts" and other digestive disorders doubtlessly occasioned by her recipes. Her poetry plummets to depths not attained again until Julia Moore, the "Sweet Singer of Michigan," took up her lyre, proving that there is always room at the bottom.

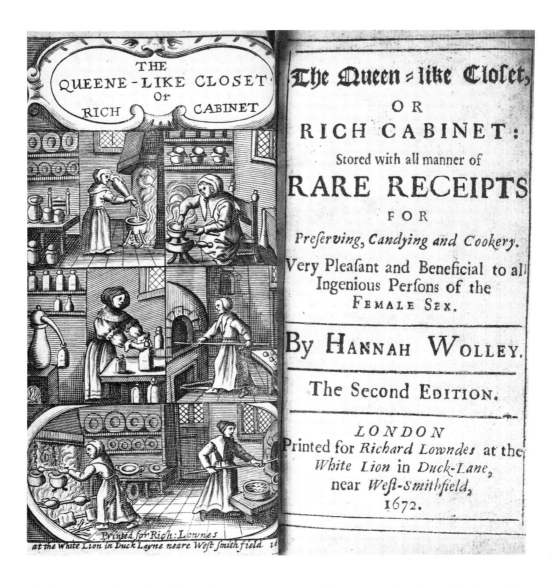

In a letter to another print collector (August 12, 1769), Horace Walpole lamented, "Mrs. Wolley I could not get high nor low." It was once thought that hers is the portrait in *The Accomplisht-Lady's Delight* and John Shirley's *Accomplished Ladies Rich Closet of Rarities,* but these attributions have been disproved. Hannah Wolley's admirers must be content with the energetic little figures de-

picted here as portraits of her spirit, if not of her person. This is the spirit the anonymous bard celebrated when he wrote:

In her very way of looking
There was cognizance of cooking.
Underneath her skirt were peeping
Indications of housekeeping.

Mary Halfpeny
her Booke
1678
ye orange puding
take ye outward rines of 4
oranges boyle ym very tend
der in severall waters
yn beat them in a ston mo
rter very fine with half
a pownd of suger & half
a pownd of butter yn put
to it 2 hand fulls of bread
crumes wth: 10 eggs having
but: 2 whits & ye Juce of 3
orangs mix all these toge
ther bake it wth a sheet of
past under it: half an
howr bakes it

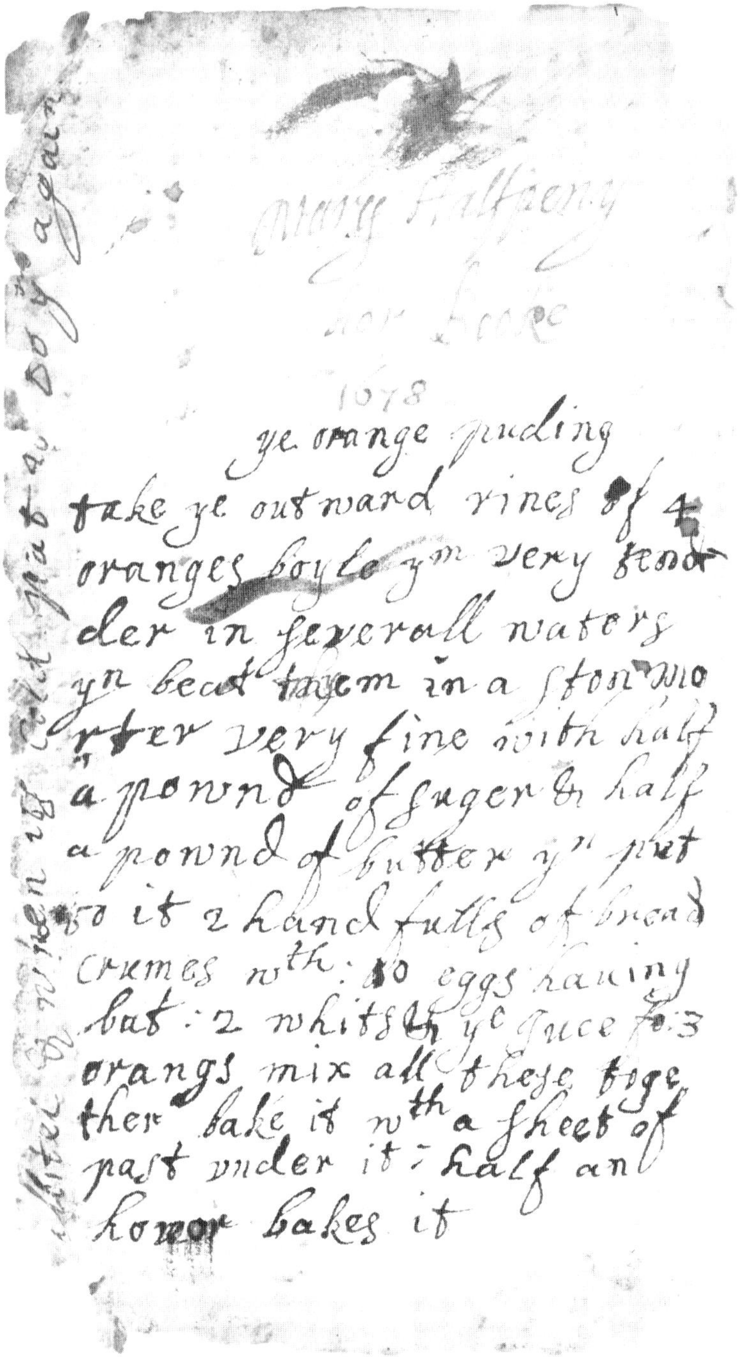

The cookbook sometimes also served as a family record, as shown here. "Brother John Halfpenny when he was at Trinity Colidge" presented this copy of Hannah Wolley's *The Queen-like Closet* to Mary Halfpenny. She wrote her own recipes for syllabubs and gooseberry wine, orange pudding and "plane" cake, on the flyleaves. The book became the property of Anna Warden at an unrecorded date. However, James and Rebecca Keeling, sometime in the middle of the seventeenth century, do tell us the hours when Thomas and Rebecca were born unto them.

The Pennell copy of *The Accomplisht Lady's Delight in Preserving, Physick, Beautifying* and *Cookery* (1675), sometimes attributed to Hannah Wooley, carries A. W. Oxford's bookplate, although Oxford's bibliography refers only to a second edition of 1677. This copy is imperfect; regrettably, there is a gap where the index promises the "art of angling" and one is left wondering if Dame Julia Berners has been remembered. The Bitting copy (1706) belongs to the "ninth edition, enlarged," is very much smaller, and was without the "art of angling" from the beginning. Of the two the first is the more attractive edition, with larger type, better paper, and plates that are not worn. It seems possible to generalize for these books that a progressive deterioration in book production occurs in each edition after the first. The section interesting us is "The Compleat Cook's Guide, or, Directions for the Dressing of all Sorts of Fl Fowl, and Fish the English and the French Way." There are three plates in the Pennell edition, one of which shows the appropriate shape for humble pie.

John Shirley's *Accomplished Ladies Rich Closet of Rarities* (1696) is one of those hack-written "how-to" books produced in large numbers for a mass audience that are thumbed out of existence, so today the booksellers call any copy they sell "excessively rare." Shirley wrote "not only for the delight but for the Accomplishment of the Female Sex," so he begins with distilling, preserving, carving, cosmetics, stain removal, cooking, baking, and bills of fare before laying down the rules of deportment for the young gentlewoman. Shirley wrote "almost a hundred hardbound books," according to his publisher, the very eccentric Anglo-American John Dunton, who was himself the author of *The Ladies Dictionary* (1694), a fat little book designed to interest the female sex "from the lady at the court to the cook-maid in the country" that is in the Library's Oliver Wendell Holmes Collection. The last of the genre that will be mentioned here, *The True Way of Preserving and Candying* (1681, 1695) was specially intended by its author "for my scholars," a reminder that there was a cooking school in London.

The Restoration, that "very merry, dancing, drinking, laughing, quaffing and unthinking time," returned the cookbook from the lady of the manor to the professional cook and reinforced the French influence. Murrell excepted, Robert May was the first professional to publish a cookbook after *The Forme of Cury* of 1390. That statement should not be thought to imply any continuity between the two cooks. May's vocational schooling indicates the absence of a tradition: the son of a London cook, he was sent off to Paris at the age of ten to be trained in his father's craft. Curiously for a time when gentry were gentry and every one else

What wouldst thou view but in one face
all hospitalitie the race
of those that for the Gusto stand
whose tables a whole Ark comand
of Natures plentie wouldst thou see
this sight, peruse Mais booke 'tis hee

THE
Accomplisht Cook,
OR THE
ART and MYSTERY
OF
COOKERY.

Wherein the whole A R T is revealed in a
more easie and perfect Method, than hath
been publisht in any language.

Expert and ready Ways for the Dressing of all Sorts of
FLESH, FOWL, and FISH, with variety of SAUCES
proper for each of them; and how to raise all manner
of *Pastes*; the best Directions for all sorts of *Kickshaws*,
also the *Terms* of CARVING and SEWING.

An exact account of all *Dishes* for all *Seasons* of the
Year, with other *A la-mode Curiosities*.

The Fourth Edition, with large Additions throughout
the whole work: besides two hundred Figures of several Forms for all manner of bak'd Meats, (either
Flesh, or Fish) as Pyes, Tarts, Custards, Cheesecakes,
and Florentines, placed in Tables, and directed to the
Pages they appertain to.

Approved by the fifty five Years Experience and Industry of *ROBERT MAY*, in his Attendance on
several Persons of great Honour.

London, Printed for *Obadiah Blagrave* at the *Bear* in St.
Pauls Church Yard, near the Little North-Door. 1678

According to the preface of *The Accomplisht Cook,* May was born in 1588 and, therefore, would have been seventy-two years old in 1660, the date of this portrait. One of May's "Triumphs and Tragedies in cookery" is unquestionably the masterpiece of the kind. It calls for a pastry ship with guns made of marzipan, a wounded stag of pastry filled with claret to simulate blood, and pastry cattle. Among these are distributed two pies, one filled with frogs and the other with birds. The cattle and the ship were blown up with powder trains, the stag would bleed when the arrow was removed, and the birds and frogs would come out of their pies. May promises that "the flying birds and skipping frogs, the one above, the other beneath, will provide much delight and pleasure to the whole company."

merely people, May recognizes the existence of a middle class, saying that for those who "cannot reach to the cost of rich dishes, I have descended to their meaner Expenses." May's *Accomplisht Cook* (1660, 1678, 1685) opens with a three-page recipe for an olio, presumably in deference to Catherine of Braganza, but constantly looks back to the puddings, pies, and roasts of Charles I's England, "those golden days wherein was practised the Triumphs and Tragedies of cookery." The Frenchness is there—May gives nine recipes for snails—despite his sneers at the "epigram dishes" with which the French "have bewitched some of the gallants of our nation."

Will Rabisha's *Whole Body of Cookery* (1673) announces recipes "according to the best tradition of the English, French, Italian, Dutch," but this kind of multinationalism was a temporary phenomenon. Charles II and his brother preferred French cuisine and "Dutch Billy" the cooking of his home country, so that English cuisine again did not have the support of the example of the court. While May writes for master cooks and young practitioners, Rabisha addresses himself to a wide audience, although knowing that the "Fraternity of Cooks" will berate him for revealing its mysteries to every kitchen maid. Giles Rose is one of Mrs. Pennell's enthusiasms for his dramatic diagrams of trussed birds and skewered joints, "the like never before extant in any language." The title of his *A Perfect School of Instruction for Officers of the Mouth* (1676, 1682) gives away its origin in *L'Escole parfaite des officiers de bouche,* from which most of the illustrations are taken. Among the officer of the mouth's concerns are carving and table service, so Rose gives directions for laying long and round tables, for folding napkins into beasts and birds, for "carve-peeling" apples and pears in twelve ways and oranges in eighteen.

THE pace of this enumeration must be slowed now. Towering personalities like Sir Kenelm Digby and John Evelyn cannot be fitted tidily into a rapid review. Poet, courtier, duellist, diplomat, swashbuckling naval commander, dabbler in science and the occult, Digby was judged a "noble and absolutely compleat Gentleman" by Henry Peacham in his *Complete Gentleman* and "an arrant mountebank" by John Evelyn. Mrs. Pennell said once that Digby and the openers of cabinets and closets wrote the best bedside books, although later naming Markham as the prettiest of them all. I will not comment on *The Closet of the Eminently Learned Sir Kenelme Digby* (1671), which in the

Pennell copy is bound with *Choice and Experimented Receipts in Physick and Chirurgy* (1668). As the preface says, Sir Kenelm's name "does sufficiently auspicate the work" so that "it needs no Rhetoricating Floscules to set it off."

The first of the *Two Treatises, By . . . the Honourable and Truly Learned Sir Kenelm Digby, Knight* (1669), the one on home remedies and cosmetics, does not give the secret of the "Viper Wine for the Complection," to which was attributed both the beauty and the death of Venetia Stanley (Lady Digby), whose portrait Van Dyke painted and whose death Ben Johnson commemorated in the *Eupheme* poem series. The separate title page of the second of the *Two Treatises* reads: "the other, of cookery, with several ways, for making metheglin, sider, cherry-wine, &c. together with excellent directions for preserving, conserving, candying, &c." The modern writer Elizabeth David, to whose opinions other students of cookbooks defer, suggests that the first large group of recipes for metheglin (the drink from fermented honey) be read aloud for the sound, like litanies and magic rituals, and that the reader then go on to enjoy this beautiful example of English baroque literature in the usual way.

Digby introduces his friends to you with their recipes, e.g., "The White Metheglin of My Lady Hungerford," "The Queen Mother's Hotchpotch of Mutton," or "My Lord d'Aubigny eats Red Herrings thus boyl'd." It is a special pleasure to meet the "crème fouetée of My Lord of St. Albans," that is, Francis Bacon. Digby gives his own recipes for "Hydromel as I Made It Weak for the Queen Mother and Was Exceedingly Liked by Everybody," "A Good Quaking Bag-Pudding," and "To Make Ale Drink Quick" and tells the reader that a dish must be left to thicken "until you see your shadow in it" or "till it begins to blink." The example of his style most frequently cited occurs in his account of the instructions for the brewing of tea given by a Jesuit newly returned from China: "The water is to remain on it no longer than whiles you can say the *Miserere* Psalm very leisurely . . . thus you have only the spiritual part of the tea, which is much more active, penetrative, and friendly to nature." The recital of a set piece like the *Credo* to time a cooking operation can be found as early as 1475 in the first cookbook, Platina's *De honesta voluptate*.

At the Royal Society on March 1, 1665, Samuel Pepys heard a "very particular account of the making of the several sorts of bread in France, which is accounted the best place for bread in the world." The speaker was John Evelyn, the other of England's two great diarists. Thirty-four years later John Evelyn turned to gastronomy again to write *Acetaria. A Discourse of Sallets* (1699). Evelyn sees the

The truly Learned and Hono.^ble
Sr Kenelme Digby K.^t Chancellor
to the Q.: Mother
Aged 62.

Gross sculpsit

Kenelm Digby was succinctly characterized as "one of the few soules that understand themselves" by his contemporary David Lloyd (*Memoirs of the Lives...of Those that Suffered,* London, 1688). Lloyd continued: "The rest learn from this epitaph:"

Under this tombe the Matchless DIGBY lyes,
DIGBY the Great, the Valiant and the Wise
This Age's Wonder for his Noble Parts
Skilled in six Tongues, and learned in all the Arts.

composition of a salad as an exercise in harmony: "Every plant . . . should fall into their places like the Notes in Music, in which there should be nothing harsh or grating: And tho admitting some Discords (to distinguish and illustrate the rest) striking in the more sprightly, and sometimes gentler Notes, reconcile all Dissonances, and melt them into an agreeable Composition." He counsels the housewife to model after Milton's representation of Eve "dressing of a sallet for her Angelical Guest," but also gives practical advice on the avoidance of metal knives.

Evelyn lists seventy-three herbs and plants as salad ingredients but says of garlic "tis not fit for Ladies Palats, nor those who court them, farther than to permit a light touch on the Dish, with a Clove thereof." These ingredients are to be sprinkled "discreetly" with spring water and swung together in a clean coarse napkin. Evelyn insists on sweet wine vinegar and requires that the oil not be "high coloured nor yellow but with an eye rather of a pallid olive green without smell or the least touch of rancid." He accepts pepper and rejects saffron ("we little encourage its admittance into a sallet"). A steel knife must not be used, and the salad dish must be of porcelain or of Holland delft. His injunction that the stirring continue "until all the furniture be equally moistened" comes to mind today when one is served a quartered iceberg lettuce head on whose edge a dab of salad dressing has been deposited. The seasonal table of salad plants ending the book satisfies a request made by the then obscure Robert Boyle some years before.

In the century which we now leave, English cookery had ceased being more than half medieval and become more than half modern. Most obvious is the solo appearance of meat, that is, the disappearance of the medieval meat stews, the mawmenees and mortrells. This is evidenced in the cookbooks by May's 112 recipes for beef, in high society by the formation of the Sublime Society of Beefsteaks, and in literature by the verse "The Roast Beef of Old England." Along with beef come the dairy products, butter for vegetables, pastry, sauces—indeed, melted butter is *the* English sauce—and cream and milk for custards, puddings, and caramels. English puddings make Misson, a French traveler, break out into capital letters: "BLESSED BE HE THAT INVENTED PUDDING for now it is a manna that hits the appetite of all sorts of people." English cookbooks now talk about the *bouquet garni,* cream soups, heavy stocks, and *pate feuilletée* which can be associated with the Frenchman La Varenne. Even the style has changed. The trailing anacolouthas and tangled parentheses of Sir Kenelm Digby give way to the Addisonian well-made sentence. At the end of the coming century, Mrs. Raffald will write with most un-Cavalier matter of factness a sentence like: "Stick your pig

At the end of this copy of John Evelyn's *Acetaria* are thirteen lines in Evelyn's hand on the cooking of carrots and cucumbers. Mrs. Pennell made this purchase at the 1913 sale of the library of the great Shakespearean scholar Edward Dowden of Trinity College, Dublin. It had once been part of the extraordinary collection of Richard Heber. Godfather to Sir Christopher Wren's son, Evelyn worked with Wren on founding the Greenwich Hospital and rebuilding London. After having had dinner with Sir Christopher and Samuel Pepys, Evelyn called them in his diary "two extraordinarily ingenious and knowing persons." Evelyn's initials are intertwined underneath the inscription to Sir Christopher.

Pages 104-5: "Mr. Burchell's First Visit." From Oliver Goldsmith, *The Vicar of Wakefield* (London: R. Ackermann, 1823). Illustrated by Thomas Rowlandson.

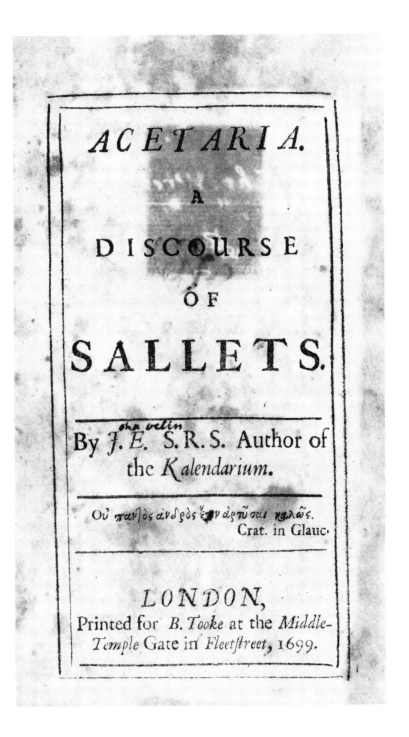

ACETARIA.

A

DISCOURSE

OF

SALLETS.

By *J. E.* S.R.S. Author of the *Kalendarium.*

Οὐ παντὸς ανδρὸς ἐςιν ἀρτῦσαι καλῶς.
Crat. in Glauc.

LONDON,
Printed for *B. Tooke* at the *Middle-Temple* Gate in *Fleetstreet,* 1699.

just above the breast bone, run your knife to the heart, when it is dead, put it into cold water."

THE cookbooks for the transition from the seventeenth to the eighteenth century, from Stuart to Hanoverian England, were written by Henry Howard and Patrick Lamb, the former, cook for the duke of Ormond and the earl of Winchester, the latter, cook in the kitchen of all the rulers of England from Charles II to Queen Anne. Howard's *England's Newest Way in All Sorts of Cookery* (1708, 1747) is the first to give diagrams for the setting of the table which show that the large medieval dish had given way to numerous smaller dishes in geometric array over the whole table. He also gives recipes for cakes, marmalades, and sweets, though this area is more fully represented for the time by Mary Eales' *Receipts* (1718). Patrick Lamb's *Royal Cookery* (1710) introduces the recipes used at St. James, Kensington, Hampton Court, and Windsor with the wit and elegance befitting his intention to represent the "grandeur of the English court and nation." Lamb's specialty is the ragoût, for which he gives twenty-three recipes, and one's eyes will linger on his recipe for "dressed Salmon in Champaign Wine." There are also "Near Forty Figures (Curiously Engraved on Copper) of the Magnificent Entertainments at Coronations, Installations, Balls, Weddings, &c, at Court" that show the permutations and combinations possible then in stocking a table. The *Royal Cookery* was the one cookbook in the library of Sir Robert Walpole, "The Great Man" satirized as a sybarite by Pope, Gay, and Swift.

The shift from men writing for men cooks to women writing for women housekeepers is prefigured by Richard Allestree's *The Ladies Calling* (1673) and the anonymous *The Whole Duty of Woman* (1734), which make cookery, along with the church and children, the business of the sex that has been admonished to be good, letting who will be clever. The change does not take place all at once and neither form ever completely dominates. Mary Kettilby's 1714 *A Collection of Above Three Hundred Receipts in Cookery, Physick, and Surgery; for the Use of All Good Wives, Tender Mothers, and Careful Nurses* (1734) is followed by Robert Smith's 1723 *Court Cookery* (1725) and John Nott's 1723 666-page *Cooks and Confectioners Dictionary* (1724, 1726, 1727.) Nott gives almost two thousand recipes, findable by what he calls "a copious alphabetical index," originating with "the nicest and most curious Dames and Housewives" of England and "the best Masters" of France, Spain, Italy, Germany, and other countries. However, after Smith and Nott in

THE
WHOLE DUTY
OF A
WOMAN:
OR, A
Guide to the FEMALE SEX.

From the A G E of *Sixteen*, to *Sixty*, &c

Being Directions, How Women of all Qualities and
Conditions, ought to Behave themselves in the
various Circumstances of this L I F E, for their
obtaining not only Present, but Future Happiness.

I   Directions how to obtain the Divine and Moral
VERTUES of *Piety, Meekness, Modesty, Chastity,
Humilty, Compassion, Temperance, and Affability*, with
their Advantages; and how to avoid the opposite
VICES.

II. The Duty of *VIRGINS*, directing them what
they ought to do, and what to avoid, for gaining
all the Accomplishments required in that State.
With the whole ART of L O V E.

III. The Whole Duty of a WIFE.

IV. The Whole Duty of a W I D O W, &c.

Also Choice Receipts in Physick and Chirurgery:
With the whole A R T of Cookery, Preserving,
Candying, Beautifying, &c.

Written by a L A D Y.

THE EIGHTH EDITION.

LONDON: Printed for *A. Bettesworth* and *C. Hitch*,
at the *Red-Lyon* in *Pater-Noster-Row*; *R. Ware*, at
the *Sun* and *Bible*, in *Amen Corner*; and *James
Hodges*, at the *Looking-Glass* on *London Bridge*. 1735.

The physical conditions of housekeeping explain the significance of the guides to morality for women outlined on this title page. In an essay entitled "The Woman's Burden," J. H. Plumb says, "kitchens were active all the year around to a degree which would daunt and depress even the most dedicated housewife today. Wives and daughters made everything, the processes were slow, the labour, even with the help of servants, backbreaking. . . . Except in the highest ranks of the aristrocracy, the women worked, perhaps slaved would be a better word, in their houses. This, as much as childbirth, led to the subjection of women."

chronological line is the *Compleat Housewife* (1730) of E. Smith—even the British Museum *Catalogue* does not know the Christian name—which is the harbinger of the series of best-sellers written by women from their own experiences in "fashionable and notable homes."

The line of demarcation in the employment of men and women in the kitchen is made clear by Swift's 1734 *Instructions for Servants:* "Although I am not ignorant that it has been a long time since the Custom among People of Quality to keep Men Cooks, and generally of the French Nation, yet because my Treatise is chiefly calculated for the general Run of Knights, Squires, and Gentlemen both in Town and Country, I shall therefore apply to you Mrs. Cook as a Woman." Swift's "Mrs. Cook as a Woman" seems a pallid abstraction that should be personalized by recalling Pepys's Susan, "a pretty willing wench, but no good cook." William Verral in the 1759 *Art of Cookery* makes it clear that even the woman cook regularly employed in an establishment could expect to be displaced on gala occasions. The higher cookery has been reserved for men only until very nearly our own times. In *His Gift* Kipling uses only the masculine gender: "A good cook is a King of men. . . . Beside being thunderin' well off if 'e don't drink. It is the only sure business in the whole round world."

Unlike most Renaissance and early modern cookbook authors, E. Smith writes for the beginner, and she is among the first to give menus for every month of the year. Recipes are grouped according to subject although not arranged alphabetically; the progression of the meal is that which we expect: soup, fish, meat, and sweet. The large sections on pudding and pastry indicate the sharp decline in the price of sugar. There is a section on the purchase of meat and much discussion of the problem of preservation. The French influence is muted but present. While deploring popular admiration of "the French tongue and French messes," she expresses the intention "to present you now and then with such receipts as I think may not be too disagreeable for the English taste."

Between E. Smith and Hannah Glasse, the next landmark on this cook's tour, there are other writers who merit comment in passing. First perhaps is Edward Kidder, whose octavo *Receipts of Pastry and Cookery* (1740?) is curious because the man ran two cooking schools ("ladies may be taught at their own houses") and because the title page, the forty-two pages of text printed on one side only, and the eight plates are all engraved on copper. Nathaniel Bailey, author of the *Dictionarium domesticum* (1736), is also a translator of Erasmus and the author of the *Dictionarium Brittanicum*, which lies at the base of Dr. Johnson's great lexico-

THE
Country Housewife
AND
LADY's DIRECTOR,
IN THE
Management of a HOUSE, and the Delights and Profits of a FARM.

CONTAINING

INSTRUCTIONS for managing the Brew-House, and Malt Liquors in the Cellar; the making of Wines of all sorts.

DIRECTIONS for the DAIRY, in the Improvement of Butter and Cheese upon the worst of Soils; the feeding and making of Brawn; the ordering of Fish, Fowl, Herbs, Roots, and all other useful Branches belonging to a Country-Seat, in the most elegant manner for the Table.

Practical OBSERVATIONS concerning DISTILLING; with the best Method of making Ketchup, and many other curious and durable Sauces.

The whole distributed in their proper MONTHS, from the Beginning to the End of the Year.

With particular REMARKS relating to the Drying or Kilning of SAFFRON.

By R. BRADLEY,
Professor of Botany in the University of Cambridge, and F. R. S.

The Sixth Edition.
With ADDITIONS.

LONDON:

Printed for D. BROWNE, at the *Black-Swan* without *Temple-Bar.*

MDCCXXXVI. 1736

[Price 2 s. 6 d.]

Richard Bradley's *Country Housewife and Lady's Director* (1736) is an excellent example of the English country housewife book, a split-off from the Latin "whole house" book described in chapter 2. Other works of this genre whose intention is "to teach the farmer's wife / With satisfaction how to live / The happy country life" include *The Farmer's Wife or the Complete Country Housewife* (1780). Bradley was the first professor of botany at Cambridge and very probably the first academic luminary to prepare a cookbook. His may also be the first English recipes for pineapples and turtle soup.

graphical venture. Cookbooks and dictionaries are alike parts of the eighteenth-century urge to order and methodize. Unlike Dr. Johnson, Vincent La Chapelle dedicated his work, *Modern Cookery* (1733, 1744, 1751), to his employer, Lord Chesterfield. Carême thought La Chapelle's book the only work of his predecessors worthy of the profession. The phrase reminds one of Charles Carter, who in his *Compleet City and Country Cook* (1732, 1736) boasts that he comes of "a long line of predecessors." Others, in roughly chronological order of first publication, are *The Young Lady's Companion in Cookery and Pastry* (1734), John Middleton's *Five Hundred New Receipts* (1734), Sarah Harrison's *Housekeeper's Pocket Book* (1748, 1755), *The Lady's Companion* (1740), Eliza Haywood's *A Present for a Serving Maid, or, The Sure Means of Gaining Love and Esteem* (1743, 1771), calculated to make both mistress and maid happy, and the even more prettily named *Adam's Luxury and Eve's Cookery* (1744), which is devoted to the kitchen garden and "the cheap, healthy, and palatable dishes it can yield."

E. Smith and the others are only J. Alfred Prufrocks, attendant lords meant to "start a scene or two," immediately to be overshadowed by the classic eighteenth-century English cookbook, Hannah Glasse's *Art of Cookery*. For Hannah Glasse we can do no better than to quote Mrs. Pennell's pithy summation: "Her fame is due not to her genius, for she really had none, but to the fact that her own generation believed that there was 'no sich a person,' and after generations believed in her as the author of a phrase she never wrote." It is curious that "first catch your hare" should still be credited to Hannah Glasse. Readers of Boswell know the dinner table conversation about the authorship of the *Art of Cookery* that occasioned one of Dr. Johnson's all too quotable pronouncements: "Women can spin very well, but they cannot make a good book of cookery." Johnson's attribution of authorship to the physician Sir John Hill has proved as poorly founded as Johnson's observation on women cookbook authors. To be consistent, he should also have denied to Hannah Glasse the authorship of her *Compleat Confectioner* (1770, 1772, 1800) and *The Servants Directory* (1760).

But this conversation would never have taken place if *The Art of Cookery* by "A Lady" had not already caught public attention. Was it because the book had appeared in a thin folio, instead of the customary quarto, so that the wits could talk of a "pot folio"? Was it because, as Hannah Glasse says, it was "not wrote in the high polite style"? Or because of the author's designation on the title page as "A Lady" and the English love of a peer? Anne Cook, whose "Essay on the Lady's Art of Cookery," included in her *Professed Cookery* (1755), is an explosion of invective, thought so: "Look at the Lady on the Title Page/How fast it sells the book and gulls the age."

Mrs. Glasse said that she wrote the *Art of Cookery* to warn that "if gentlemen will have *French* cooks, they must pay for *French* tricks." She breaks off a recipe for the French way of dressing partridges to interject: "I think it all an odd jumble of trash." However, she does give some of her recipes "French names to distinguish them, because they are known by these names." This true-born Englishwoman's aversion to all things Gallic in the kitchen might be explained by the competition given her book by La Chapelle's *Modern Cookery*. Her particular grievance is *coulis,* the basic stock of eighteenth-century French cuisine—Patrick Lamb has fifteen recipes for *coulis*—in whose making she would replace the whole veal and whole ham by a pound of veal and half a pound of bacon. Voltaire's jibe that the English have sixty religions and only one sauce is only too familiar. It ought to be pointed out therefore that Hannah Glasse gives more than thirty recipes for sauces and mentions a sauce boat as well.

The Bitting Collection has Hannah Glasse's second edition (1747), the third edition (1748), the London editions of 1771, 1778, 1843, and the Alexandria, Virginia, editions of 1805 and 1812. The Pennell Collection holds the London editions of 1751, 1763, 1765, 1774, and 1786, the last being the product of a combine of twenty-six publishers. Glasse's popularity is difficult to explain because her book is precisely like so many other books that came before or would come after. Her debts are quickly detected; for example, the chapter on creams comes out of the first edition of Smith's *Complete Housewife*. Like Smith, she writes for beginners; like Smith again, Glasse accepts vegetables and warns against overcooking. Her book is medieval in its recipes for larks and a series of dishes in which one meat is made to look like another; it is modern in its recipes for rice pudding and ice cream.

Calling it ugly for one Englishwoman's table to look exactly like every other Englishwoman's table, she gives no diagrams of table settings. She does provide the innovations of a chapter listing in the first part of the book, an index at the end, and a chapter written for ships' captains. Richard Briggs, cook at the White Hart Inn, was also interested in seafaring men and in the *English Art of Cookery* (1794, 1798) gives recipes like Glasse's "fish sauce to last a year" and "catsup to last twenty years." Glasse and Briggs are writing for the Englishmen who went down to the sea in ships to build an empire and then to beat off Napoleon.

We have noted—in order to dismiss—Dr. Johnson's opinion that Sir John Hill wrote *The Art of Cookery*. A presentation inscription in the Bitting copy of the

British Jewel (1769), a copy that is unique in this country, further confounds the confusion by charging that the *Art of Cookery* was copied from this little book and that the copier was Sir John Hill. Mrs. Bitting points out that this duodecimo and the folio and quartos in which Hannah Glasse appears have only three recipes in common. David Garrick's verse: "For Physics and Farces his equal there scarce is; His Farces are Physic, his Physic a Farce is," as unjust as it is witty, calumniates the Sir John Hill who prepared the twenty-six folio volumes of *The Vegetable System* and introduced the Linnean classification into England in his *British Herbal*.

What Macaulay said about Boswell as biographer holds true for Hannah Glasse as cookbook author of the eighteenth century: She is first and the rest are nowhere. But the rest are a very respectable and numerous lot indeed. A new reading public that had been created by the expansion of literacy bought cookbooks because of the increase in leisure, which eighteenth-century moralists called "idleness." Equally important was the call for "self-help," for while that phrase appears only in the next century, surely the doctrine is implicit in the social teachings of contemporaries like John Wesley. Other factors were the stability of food prices almost until the end of the century and the freeing of book publishing from the licensing acts. As the literature of the kitchen expands into and over the horizon, our task will become limited to pointing out the best-sellers found in the Bitting Collection. It is still possible at this point to trace further some of the routes of development that we have only reconnoitered. Before reverting to the chronological line, these remarks will attempt photos of a relatively high degree of resolution of the cook/home doctor book, the confectionery book, the housekeeper book, and the Scottish cookbook.

The lady of the house as doctor, or woman as ministering angel, is a persona to be found in the literature until well into the nineteenth century. E. Smith dedicates her 200 medical recipes ("never before been printed") to the generous, charitable ladies who wish to help their poor neighbors, and Mary Kettilby apostrophizes: "O Heavenly Charity, how often have I seen thee employ the Rich in Waiting upon the Poor!" Mary Kettilby also feels it necessary to assure the professionals that they are not hurt by the housekeeper-medicos, because the patients treated are neither in the range of the doctors' visits "nor in a capacity of gratifying their trouble." The author of the *Family Magazine* (1750) thinks her cures unimpeachable because copied from the commonplace book of a doctor.

Hannah Glasse said, "I shall not take it upon me to meddle in the physical way further than two receipts," the two being the classics of the genre: Dr.

Meade's cure for the bite of a mad dog and the "four thieves" plague preventer. Mrs. Pennell's favorite in this literature was Elizabeth Price's *New Book of Cookery* (1782) for its cure for a malady too familiar to us all: "For the lethargy," says Mrs. Price, "you may sniff strong vinegar up the nose." The cook/home doctor books continue on even after the appearance of the very popular medical guides like Dr. William Buchan's *Domestic Medicine* in the next century. The poet Felicia Hemans in her *Female Instructor* (1835) offered "moral and religious essays, interesting tales, and memorials of illustrious women." But feeling all this not enough for the instruction of females, she hastens to conclude: "to which are subjoined, medical receipts." The great Victorian household book, Mrs. Beeton's, contains sections on home medicine and common diseases written by "an experienced surgeon" whose style happens to coincide exactly with the style of that extraordinary layperson Mrs. Beeton.

In France, the special nature of pastry and confectionery making had been recognized when La Varenne followed his *Cuisinier françois* with the *Pâtissier françois*. The secession of English confectionery from cookery and its demand for its own literature are manifest in the *Receipts* (1718) of Mrs. Mary Eales, "Confectioner to her Late Majesty Queen Anne," a copy of which in the 1742 edition was included in Thomas Jefferson's 1815 library. Eales makes extensive use of imported ingredients, including "Seville" and "China" oranges. The recipe in Hannah Glasse's *Compleat Confectioner* (1772, 1800) calling for milking the cow directly into the "everlasting syllabub" reveals the unchanging way of life of the English countryside. After Glasse come *The Court and Country Confectioner* (1770) of Borella, confectioner to the Spanish ambassador, Robert Abbot's *Housekeeper's Valuable Present* (179?), and Frederick Nutt's *Compleat Confectioner* (1790, 1807, 1815). In the next century two great generalist cooks, Francatelli and Mrs. A. B. Marshall, like La Varenne, also successfully tapped the confectionery book market. The specialists include William Jarrin, to whose *Italian Confectioner* (1820, 1827, 1844) William Kitchiner referred his readers, William Jeanes (*Gunter's Modern Confectioner*, 1875), and Edward Mackenzie (1833) and W. Stavly (1829), who use the same title: *The New Whole Art of Confectionery*.

The title pages of the housekeeping books often accompany the author's name with a statement of her years of experience and sometimes even with the names of her employers. So we learn that the author of *Family Friend* (1802), Priscilla Haslehurst, was "for twelve years housekeeper in the families of W. Bethel and others of the greatest respectability." She is topped by Charlotte

Mason of the *Lady's Assistant* (177?), "a professional housekeeper, with upwards of thirty years experience in families of the first order." Mary Smith of *The Complete Housekeeper, and Professed Cook* (1786), "late" housekeeper to Sir Walter Blackett, Lord Anson, and Sir Thomas Sebright, seems to have had no feeling for orthography. One identifies easily enough her "soup a la rain," and "roe boat sauce," but only after noting that the recipe begins "take eight eggs" will her "hamlet" be understood. The families cited seem not to have been displeased by the appearance of their names on the title pages. Mrs. Pennell owned a copy of *The New Experienced English Housekeeper* of Sarah Martin, "many years housekeeper to Freeman Bower Esq. of Bawtrey," which belonged to Bower and had been annotated by him. The Bitting copy of this work (1795) has been rebound by some diligent housekeeper to incorporate about three hundred pages of manuscript recipes and household notes. If this is included, the Bitting Collection totals twenty-nine manuscript cookbooks, which belong to the English eighteenth and nineteenth centuries, as do five of the six in the Pennell Collection. The exception there is in German and is dated 1716.

Whom were the books written for? Apparently for the lady of the house first and then for her servant. When Hannah Glasse explains that her book is "not wrote in the high polite style" for her "intention is to instruct the lower sort" and Mrs. Raffald says that her book is "wrote in my own plain language . . . so as to be understood by the weakest capacity," they are talking to the lady or the housekeeper about the ultimate user, the servant. The situation is clear from Cre-Fydd's *Family Fare* (1866), which poses the rhetorical question: "Ask any young housewife in moderate circumstances whether, when she has put the newly-purchased cookery book into the hands of her cook, she has not been ultimately disappointed." It is a tenable generalization that no middle-class English lady regularly did the cooking. Dora receives David Copperfield's suggestion that she study housekeeping "with something that was half a sob and half a sigh" and ended in what was wholly hysterics. Mrs. Bennet in *Pride and Prejudice* wanted her daughters married, but not domestic in any housekeeping sense. Let Charlotte Lucas make mince pies, but "for my part, Mr. Bennet," said his good lady, "I always keep servants that can do their own work."

To find an ethnic cuisine in the "right little, tight little island," like Dr. Johnson and Smollet we take the road north out of London. The cuisine of Edinburgh, rooted historically in the Auld Alliance with France, was at its apogee in the "Scottish Enlightenment" of David Hume, Adam Smith, Dugald Stewart, and Sir Walter Scott. Hume in retirement boasted of his talent for cooking, "the science to which I intend to devote the rest of my life." In his *Philosophical Essays* Dugald Stewart, friend and correspondent of Jefferson, draws an analogy between cookery, poetry, and the fine arts, for they all concern what is understood by "sweet" and "bitter," effects that are essential to the composite beauty which is the final artistic creation. The recipes with which the philosophers stuffed their escritoires would have come from Scottish cookbooks like Elizabeth Cleland's *A New Easy Method of Cookery* (1770), Hannah Robertson's *The Young Ladies School of Arts* (1767), Susannah Maciver's *Cookery, and Pastry* (1784, 1805), Mrs. Frazer's *The Practice of Cookery, Pastry, Pickling, and Preserving* (1800, 1804), and John Ciard's *The Complete Confectioner and Family Cook* (1809). These books are the necessary gloss for *Noctes Ambrosianae*, the memorial to Scottish conviviality and talk of "Christopher North" (John Wilson of *Blackwood's*).

The greatest of Scottish cookbooks was published when Sir Walter Scott ruled the literary world and indeed is so closely associated with him that he is rumored to have had a hand in its writing. The book is the *Cook and Housewife's Manual* (1837). The title page gives the author as "Meg Dods," whom novel readers will recognize as the landlady of St. Cleikum's Inn in Scott's novel *St. Roman's Well*. Isobel Johnstone ("Meg Dods") was editor and publisher of the *Edinburgh Weekly Chronicle* and a woman admired by De Quincey. "Meg Dods" is still to be consulted for the traditional Scottish dishes: haggis (Burn's "great chieftain o' the pudding race"), cockaleekie, oatcakes, and particularly the dried and salted fish of the breakfast table, for, as Dr. Folliott says in Peacock's *Crotchet Castle*, Scotland is "preeminent in the glory of fish for breakfast." The cookbook proper is preceded by the "Annals of the Cleikum Club," which narrates how Peregrine Touchwood, Esq., sought to avoid ennui by studying the culinary mysteries. Included is the syllabus of a course of lectures on cookery whose theme is announced as "Man is a cooking animal."

Of the men professionals of the post-Glasse period, John Farley, "principal cook of the London Tavern," is selected for mention because Elizabeth David particularly commends his *London Art of Cookery* (1804) for its potted meats, John Mollard of the same tavern because his *Art of Cookery* (1808) makes the art "easy and refined," and Collingwood and Woolams, "principal cooks at the Crown and Anchor Tavern," because their *Universal Cook* (1801) is one of the few English cookbooks ever translated into French (1810). Not a cookbook but a guide to dining room etiquette is *The Honours of the Table* (1791) of John Trusler, priest

a Spare-rib of Pork

turned doctor, noteworthy for instructions like "As eating a great deal is deemed indelicate for a lady (for her character should be divine rather than sensual) it will be ill mannered to help her to a large slice of meat at once, or fill her plate too full."

William Verrall of the White Hart in Sussex interests as an English tavern-keeper who had been apprenticed to a French cook. Verrall's master was Monsieur St. Cloud, cook for the duke of Newcastle and later for "Marshal Richlieu." Verrall gives as "the chief end and design" of one part of his *A Complete System of Cookery* (1759) "the whole and simple art of the most modern and best French cookery." Elsewhere he lays down the maxim: "Point de légumes, point de cuisinier." (No good garden things, no French cook.) One wonders what had happened to the English garden since Markham. A copy of Verrall annotated by Thomas Gray is preserved in the Egerton Mss. of the British Library. Gray filled up the front and back pages with additional recipes, some of them taken from Isaac Walton. In the *Compleat Angler* Walton introduced a recipe in this way: "This dish of meat is too good for any but anglers, or very honest men, and I trust you will prove both, and therefore I have trusted you with this secret." Walton, we can be sure, would have granted Gray his choice of recipes.

While the men cookbook authors competed fairly equally, Elizabeth Raffald far outpaced in sales and editions the other women writers like Elizabeth Moxon (1775, 1776, 177?, 1789), Ann Shackleford (176?), or Elizabeth Price (176?). Elizabeth Raffald dedicated her *The Experienced English Housekeeper, for the Use and Ease of Ladies, Cooks &c* (1771, 1775) to Lady Elizabeth Warburton of Arley Hall, Cheshire, whose employ she had left for marriage and Manchester. In the following eighteen years, Mrs. Raffald had sixteen daughters. In addition to this active maternity business, Mrs. Raffald ran a confectionery shop, managed several inns, conducted a school of cookery for young ladies and a registry office for servants, compiled several Manchester city directories, and wrote for the newspapers. *The Experienced English Housekeeper* is intended for gentry like Lady Warburton. Mrs. Raffald's aims are to "please both the eye and the palate" and to join "economy with neatness and elegance"; her recipes are "wrote purely from practice." She gives no medical recipes, no instruction for servants, and very little on laying the table, while emphasizing confectionery, candied fruits, and jellies. One notes in turning pages an illustration of a "New Closed Stove with Fire Ports Burning Coal" instead of charcoal or wood. There were thirteen genuine editions of *The Experienced English Housekeeper* from 1769 to 1806 and almost twice that number of spurious and pirated editions in the same period.

This review of the eighteenth century in the Bitting and Pennell Collections will close with a look at the century's little literature of gastronomy, that which treats not so much the art or science of cookery as the art of dining. The best representative of English neoclassical culinary aesthetics—that is, of the table qua table and not as an extension of the kitchen stove—is William King. Students of the main-traveled road of English literature encounter him as one of the subjects of Dr. Johnson's *Lives of the Poets*. His *Art of Cookery, In Imitation of Horace's Art of Poetry, With Some Letters to Dr. Lister . . .* (1709) was on publication ascribed to the author of *A Tale of a Tub*. The object of King's satire, Apicius Coelius's *De opsoniis et condimentis; Libri decem* (1709) of Martin Lister, doctor to good but gouty Queen Anne, seems now a conventional enough piece of scholarship which should be remembered by Americans as one of the two cookbooks in the library of Thomas Jefferson purchased in 1815 by the Congress. Jefferson's copy also belonged to the 1709 edition; this and the 1705 edition were published in only 100 copies. The association with Swift is not entirely absurd. King's derision of Lister's scholarship as misplaced originates in the same fear of the extravagances of intellect in which Swift jeers at the makers of sunbeams in *Gulliver's Travels*.

King's *Art of Cookery* lives on, while his *Art of Love* is no longer read. But his *Art of Making Puddings* is also forgotten, so that it is not possible to generalize on the relative interest of his subjects. Another writer of the time on puddings was Henry Carey, the musician, the author of the beloved "Sally in our Ally." In the Bitting copy his *A Learned Dissertation on Dumpling . . . With a Word Upon Pudding* (1726) is accompanied by his *Namby Pamby, a Panegyric on the New Versification,* which gave Ambrose Phillips the name "Namby Pamby" by which Pope dissected him in the *Dunciad.* Another Phillips in the period is John Phillips, too often designated only as the nephew of Milton, though his *Cider* (1717) is one of the best of the series of eighteenth-century didactic poems. The last of the poets of the time in the Bitting Collection is probably the least. Dr. John Armstrong in his *Art of Preserving Health* (1744), important perhaps as an experiment in blank verse, is capable of describing egg haters as those "who the generous nutriment detest/Which in the shell the sleeping Embryo rears."

IT is necessary now to recognize chronology and confront the nineteenth century. Throughout the English war against revolutionary France and Napoleon, the hegemony of French cuisine in the English kitchen had never been questioned. The Royal Court was more interested in drink than food: Beau Brummel, the tone giver, recalled "once having eaten a pea." As for the country gentry, Janeites know that after Mrs. Bennet's great dinner she boasted: "Even Mr. Darcy acknowledges that the partridges were well done, and I suppose that he has two or three French cooks at least." The important infusions of French cuisine in this period came from Clermont and Ude. Clermont described his *Professed Cook* (1812) as based on Menon's French cookbook but modified by what he had learned from English food tradesmen. The Bitting copy belongs to the tenth edition. Louis Ude, once chef to Napoleon's mother and to his uncle, left France because of differences of opinion on the arithmetic of his bills. His English fame was made at Crockford's gambling house, where he served supper from midnight to five in the morning during parliamentary sessions while the members thronged the hazard tables. Lord Bossnawl in Peacock's *Crotchet Castle* would have his cook read only Ude. Ude's kind of cuisine is revealed in his characterization of a recipe as being "so simple a woman could do it." The Bitting Collection has the first edition of Ude's *French Cook* (1813); the Bitting 1841 copy belongs to the fourteenth edition.

One of the financial cornerstones of the great publishing house of John

Murray was Maria Eliza Rundell's *A New System of Domestic Cookery,* the first fully developed household encyclopedia and cookbook. Lord Byron wrote John Murray: "Along thy sprucest bookshelves shine / The works thou deemest most divine / The Art of Cookery and mine, My Murray." Most editions after the first seem to have been printed simultaneously in the United States and England. The seventieth edition was reached in 1846. The collections include editions of London (1810, 1822, 1838), New York (1814, 1815), Philadelphia (1810), and Boston (1807), as well as the Baltimore edition (1819) where the name has "suffered a sea change" into *American Domestic Cookery.* The distinctive note is struck by the very first section: "Miscellaneous Observations for the Use of the Mistress of a Family." Clearly Mrs. Rundell sees her reader as a young woman who has recently taken on the duties of domesticity and must be taught the routines of management. Mrs. Rundell is traditional in her remarks on carving and on cooking for the sick but modern in grouping together each kind of dish. Part 5, that on sauces, is larger than similar sections in her predecessors. Hannah Glasse has a section on foods to take on the journey to India, Mrs. Rundell a section on mulligatawny, curries, etc., that is, the foods that the "nabobs" brought back. There are twelve recipes for potatoes; writing eighty years earlier, E. Smith had ignored the potato.

William Kitchiner lists the 250 cookbooks he had plowed through before he began to write his own and dismisses them all as olla podridas of confused, indigestible scraps. His own *Cook's Oracle* (1818, 1822, 1823, 1829, 1830, 1833) might be added to the list as the 251st for its bombast and self-importance. In his long introduction, Kitchiner declares that his recipes were "accumulated by a perseverance, not to be subdued or evaporated by the igniferous Terrors of a Roasting Fire in the Dog-days—in defiance of the odoriferous and calefaceous repellents of Roasting, Boiling, Frying, and Broiling." As W. Carew Hazlitt remarked, two editions of Kitchiner sold out before the critics had recovered breath enough to voice their indignation. Kitchiner presents 574 recipes, "all eaten with unanimous applause by a committee of taste, composed of some of the most illustrious gastrophilists of this luxurious metropolis." (All? Even recipes like number 547, "Toothache and Anti-Rheumatic Embrocation?") The name given this committee of taste was Eta Bita Pi; tardy members were refused admission and admonished: "Better never than late."

Kitchiner urges economy by purchasing seasonally and gives marketing tables at the end of the book. As a doctor his real interest is not so much in recipes as the maintenance of health in general. His is the reigning English Regency

Bubble and Squeak, or fried Beef and Cabbage.—(No. 505.)

MADE DISHES, &c.

This page from William Kitchiner's *The Cook's Oracle* (London, Edinburgh, etc.: Printed for A. Constable, …1823) offers a recipe for "Bubble and Squeak or fried Beef and Cabbage." Kitchiner's depiction of the duet of beef and cabbage on the range inspired Tom Hood to rime:

> Teach my burning soul to speak
> With a bubble and a squeak.
> Of Dr. Kitchiner I fain would sing
> Till pots and pans and mighty
>   kettles ring.
> O culinary sage (I do not mean the
>   herb in use
> That always goes along with goose)
> How have I feasted on thy page!

cookbook (there were eleven editions by 1840) and a *Shilling Kitchiner,* not in the Library's collections, appeared as late as 1861. He did require precise measurements of ingredients before Fanny Farmer and used some turns of phrase that Brillat-Savarin deigned to borrow. William Jeanes's judgment in his *Gunter's Modern* (187?) can be accepted: "In Kitchiner there is a great deal to amuse, if not much to learn; a trifle can be gained, and nothing lost."

Elizabeth David describes Eliza Acton's *Modern Cookery* (1845, 1859) as "the final expression, the crystallization, of preindustrial England's taste in food and attitude to cookery. The dishes she described and the ingredients which went into them would have been familiar to Jane Austen and Lord Byron, to Fanny Burney and Tobias Smollet." Miss Acton was forty-six when Longmans told her that there was no market for poetry by maiden ladies and that she should write a good sensible cookery book. Compelled to renounce bad verse for good cookery, she revenged herself by contrasting "poor author's pudding" and "publisher's pudding," which, she says, "can scarcely be made *too rich.*" The book was an instant success: there were three editions in the first year, two more in the second, and Longmans let the copyright lapse only in 1918. The Bitting 1845 edition, an American version based on the second London edition, was prepared by Sarah J. Hale of *Godey's Lady's Book*.

The reader for whom Miss Acton writes is not the professional cook but the lady concerned with keeping the men around her—the Victorian "lords of creation"—in good humor. She prescribes a good table, so lavish indeed that one forgets that she is writing in the period that the economic historians call the "Hungry Forties." A poignant reminder of those "old, unhappy, far-off things" is the Pennell *Cheap Receipts and Hints on Cookery; Collected for Distribution Amongst the Irish Peasantry in 1847* (1847). Miss Acton seems to have been the first to separate the ingredients from the recipe and to have thought to include a small group of recipes headed "Foreign and Jewish." The first book on this kind of ethnic cookery in the Library's collections is *The Jewish Manual* (1846). Miss Acton's 1855 and subsequent editions show her awareness of the new understanding of nutrition associated with Liebig.

Miss Acton's *English Bread-Book for Domestic Use* (1857) is more than an expansion of the chapter on bread making in her *Modern Cookery*. One of the idylls in William Cobbett's *Cottage Economy* (1833) depicts the woman of the house kneading bread dough and calls upon the onlooker to kiss the beads of perspiration away. Miss Acton, who had actually inspected the establishments of the baking industry, so far from kissing the bakers, rushed into print to urge each family to do its own baking. The tocsin for the war against adulterants had earlier been sounded by Frederick Accum in *A Treatise on Adulterations of Food, and Culinary Poisons* (1820) and *A Treatise on the Art of Making Good and Wholesome Bread* (1821). The blue-grey cover of the former carries the design of a spider in its web about to devour a fly, surrounded by a pattern of intertwined serpents with a skull and crossbones at top. Underneath is the biblical quotation (2 Kings 4:40): "There is death in the pot." Eighteenth-century precursors in this war that seems never completely won include Jasper Arnaud's *An Alarm to all Persons Touching Their Health and Lives* (1740) and *Poisons Detected, or, Frightful Truths. By my Friend, a Physician* (1757).

Miss Acton's success was achieved despite the competition offered by two great cooks, Soyer and Francatelli. The latter was for a time manager of Crockford's, Ude's old post. He moved on to the Royal Household as maître d'hôtel and cook-in-ordinary to Queen Victoria, and then to the Reform Club, once Soyer's domain. His *Modern Cook* (1846, 1895) was published in 1846 by Richard Bentley, publisher-in-ordinary to the queen, and went through twenty-nine editions before 1896. Francatelli's *Cook's Guide and Butler's Assistant* and *Plain Cookery Book for the Working Classes,* not in these collections, both appeared in 1861 and his *Royal English and Foreign Confectioner* a year later (1862, 1891).

Francatelli seems to have wished to compete with Ude and Soyer for popular acclaim, but it was a competition for which his lack of the common touch disqualified him. A reviewer in the *Athenaeum* put it cogently: "M. Francatelli is throughout much astonished at his own humility in addressing people who have to dangle their meat on a string when it is to be roasted for want of a meat-jack. He is also profoundly ignorant of the manners, customs, and prejudices of the class he addresses." Francatelli continued Carême's use of the dining table to display architectural constructions in sugar and paste which it would have been vandalism to cut. However, he did advocate the service *à la russe* as simpler than the prevailing service *à la française* and preached against the waste of food. His speciality was desserts: it is said that he taught Queen Victoria to appreciate the flavor of pistachio.

Mirobolant, the French cook in *Pendennis* who makes a dinner all in white to express his loved one's virginal soul, is not Alexis Soyer, or at most is only one aspect of him. Thackeray admired Soyer the professional—he was known to break other engagements in order to eat one of Soyer's Reform Club specialities—and his liking for the man is shown in the references to him in *Punch* and the *Book of Snobs.* Mrs. Beeton probably had Soyer in mind in her reference to "brilliant foreign writers, half philosophers, half chefs." Soyer's first major work is the *Gastronomic Regenerator* (1847), which, although priced at a guinea, sold two thousand copies within two months of its appearance and reached a fourth edition in a year. After fifty pages of general considerations, there are two sections: "Kitchen of the Wealthy" and "Kitchen at Home," with 274 recipes and an elaborate diagram of Soyer's kitchen. Soyer emphasizes substance over presentation, saying: "Although the eye must be pleased to a certain extent, my principal business is with the palate."

For the historian of British food ways, the *Modern Housewife or Menagère* (1852), which translates the brilliance of the *Gastronomic Regenerator* into the world of the English housewife, is more interesting than its predecessor. The *Modern Housewife* takes the form of a series of letters from a Mrs. Baker instructing a friend in every department of cookery, including the nursery dinner, comforts for invalids, and the feeding and management of servants, guests, children, and husbands. The sequence gives a complete picture of the food habits of a middle-class English family of the time from the beginnings in a small shop to the achievement of the prosperity of the well-established merchant. The *London Times* review of the *Modern Housewife* pronounced it as "at once a grave essay in prose and a most felicitious poem; it deals with that undoubted reality, the human stomach, yet with a pen essentially romantic and imaginative. It is at once didactic and dietetic, dramatic and culinary." By 1853 *The Modern Housewife or Ménagère* had sold thirty thousand copies. The edition of 1853 shows us the Bakers fallen into poverty though "quite as happy and more settled in mind than when they were better off."

A Frenchman of the generation of 1830, Soyer was spiritual brother to Delacroix and Berlioz and, like them, driven by torrential gusts of energy. When the potato famine ravaged Ireland, he set up soup kitchens in Dublin and returned to London to do the same in Spitalfields. He was an ingenious tinkerer, with more than two dozen patented gadgets for the chef and the housewife; he marketed sauces and relishes which would have made the fortune of a more commercially minded man. Thackeray laughed that the best-loved man in England was a Frenchman, for whose name and good things were in as many people's mouths as Soyer's? When the management of the Crystal Palace exhibition of 1851 gave Schweppes the inside food concession, Soyer took over Gore House on the outside where Albert Hall now stands. Rebuilding it as the "Gastronomic Symposium of all Nations," a complex of restaurants, he expressed uninhibitedly the execrable taste he had everywhere outside the kitchen. *Punch* wrote:

> *But now Gore House hath been by thee*
> *So glaringly defaced,*
> *However good thy palate be,*
> *We must dispute thy taste.*

For the *Pantropheon, a History of Food and its Preparation* (1853) Soyer wrote 450 pages of text supported by over 30 pages of references in small print. This scholarly work by the formally uneducated Soyer "surprizes by himself," as Dickens' Count Smalltork puts it so well, the history of everything in cookery. In the next year Soyer brought the *Gastronomic Regenerator* down to the lower middle-class. His *A Shilling Cookery for the People* (1855) sold 10,000 copies on the day of issue and reached 60,000 by the sixth week and 260,000 copies by 1857. In 1855 Soyer found the cause to which he could give himself and went off to the Crimean War to do for the food of the armies there what Florence Nightingale did for their

A

SHILLING COOKERY

FOR

THE PEOPLE:

EMBRACING

AN ENTIRELY NEW SYSTEM OF PLAIN COOKERY
AND DOMESTIC ECONOMY.

BY ALEXIS SOYER,

AUTHOR OF "THE MODERN HOUSEWIFE,"
ETC. ETC.

"Religion feeds the soul, Education the mind, Food the body."
SOYER's *History of Food.*

One Hundred and Tenth Thousand.

LONDON:
GEO. ROUTLEDGE & CO., FARRINGDON STREET.
NEW YORK: 18, BEEKMAN STREET.
1855.
[*The Author of this Work reserves the right of translating it.*]

The frontispiece to *A Shilling Cookery* shows the Alexis Soyer of 1855, the Soyer who designed his own waistcoats, cravats, and hats (always worn in the manner he called "le zoug-zoug") and dazzled Victorian England with the rings on his fingers, the chains on his waistcoats, and the stick pins in his cravats. The portrait of Soyer that is the frontispiece to his *Culinary Campaign* (1857), published only two years later, shows a man very much sobered by the experience of war.

nursing. His account of the war is the *Culinary Campaign* (1857). The time remaining before his death Soyer devoted to the problems of military feeding, leaving unfinished a projected *Culinary Wonders of all Nations*. For the English nineteenth century, Soyer was *the* cook, a distinction attested by his admission to that national Valhalla, the *Dictionary of National Biography*.

Mrs. Beeton's *Book of Household Management*! This good book, with its Miltonic epigraph, "Nothing lovelier can be found in woman than to study household good," is as integral a part of the Victorian era as Prince Albert, crinolines, or piano legs in bloomers. Its history can be summarized briefly. In editing her husband's journal, *The Englishwoman's Domestic Magazine,* Isabella Beeton called on her readers to supply recipes for inclusion in a new book. From November 1859 to October 1861 *The Book of Household Management* appeared in monthly parts in this magazine. The Bitting copy of the first edition (1861) is made up of 1,172 pages of small and closely spaced print, 500 wood engravings, and 50 colored plates which may be the first of their kind in a cookbook. The middle-class woman working her way up the Victorian social ladder had found her mentor, for unlike Soyer and Acton, Mrs. Beeton dealt with household management and the personal life of the lady. In 1863 the recipes and other parts relating to the kitchen were published separately, with some alterations and additions, as the *English-woman's Cookbook*. After Isabella's death, the financially inept Sam Beeton transferred the copyright to Ward, Lock, and Tyler. Their editions retained Mrs. Beeton's name but were edited by the German-Swiss C. Herman Senn, who added Edwardian richness and lost Mrs. Beeton's English housewife's touch.

It is characteristic of Mrs. Beeton that while she emphasizes that Victorian status symbol the joint, she also provides ninety-five recipes in the section called "Cold Meat Cookery" for having the joint reappear in forms not too much resembling the original. One of her tricks here is to work with two joints, say lamb and pork, at the same time. Mrs. Beeton is the first to give the months when the dish is seasonal, the cooking time, the number of people served, and the average cost per person, so that the Victorian housewife might know, for example, that her "Useful Soup for Benevolent Purposes" would require six and a half hours and cost one and a half pence per cup. Mrs. Beeton did not say "take a dozen eggs," but she did say "clean as you go, for muddle makes more muddle" and "a place for everything and everything in its place." She also said "dine we must, and we may as well dine elegantly as well as wholesomely," and for this much can be forgiven her. *The Book of Household Management* is, as it sets out to be, "practical, reliable, and economical," the values of the middle-class ladies for whom it was written. Mrs. Beeton in the kitchen expresses Victorian England, the society of appearance and convention but also of vitality and enterprise, as eloquently as the middle-class woman on the throne.

Although no English cookbook has ever exercised a comparable influence, there were numerous other such works in the halcyon days of Queen Victoria. The later Victorian manuals on how to be middle class occasionally show an uneasy awareness of cracks in the seemingly monolithic social structure. May Hooper's preface to her *Little Dinners* (1894) warns: "It cannot be too strongly urged upon the ladies of the middle classes, that there never was a time when it was so necessary for girls to be instructed in every branch of domestic economy. We cannot misread the signs of the times, or doubt that, unless the men of the next generation can find useful wives, matrimony will become a greater difficulty for them than it is now." One of the signs of the times was a new restraint in the display of conspicuous consumption, for Samuel Hobbs's *Kitchen Oracle* (1887) marvels: "Such a wonderful change has taken place that half the dishes described by Soyer, Ude, and Francatelli are now scarcely heard of or seen."

While Mrs. Beeton remained a fixed star, the cookbooks first of the publishing house of Cassell, then of C. Herman Senn (editor, *Food and Cookery*, and chef, National Training School), and somewhat later of the cooking school teachers like the Mesdames Fairclough, Marshall, and Whitling waxed and waned in popularity. In the flash Edwardian epilogue to Victorianism, traditional England so changed that the period must be called a transitional one (though recognizing that the historians will demur that every period is transitional). Its study would take us beyond the range of these collections. There was, for one example, a change in the locales of hospitality. Mrs. Beeton took it for granted that people invited each other to their houses for dinner. The man-in-the-city dined at a chophouse, the man-about-town at his club, and ladies were never seen eating in public. But after 1870 a wave of immigrants from the Continent served haute cuisine in restaurants like Gatti's and Romano's, where Frank Harris ruled the walk. Col. Newnham-Davis ("The Dwarf of Blood"), writing for the *Pall Mall Gazette,* Mrs. Pennell's employer, begins a new branch of the little literature of gastronomy. He is the first man-about-restaurants reporting to the people who regularly dine out. For those who felt restaurants still not quite the thing, there were the hotels—not so much Rosa Lewis at the Cavendish remembered in Evelyn Waugh's *Vile Bodies,* as Escoffier at the Carlton and the Savoy. The great Escoffier is an international figure, but his work was done in London.

This is possibly the first appearance of chromolithograph work in England and certainly its first appearance in a cookbook. The title page design shows fruit, corn, and livestock surrounding a plaque bearing the hand-lettered title in green and red. Another twelve plates, amusing and sometimes elegant, scattered throughout the recipes, show a silver tureen of scalloped oysters, a crenelated Christmas pudding, a ring of apples in custard, and a game pie with the feet protruding through the crust. The colors are still bright and clear in the Bitting copy. Every ingredient and much of the equipment are illustrated, so that a wood or steel engraving will be found on almost every page.

Another fundamental change has taken place in gastronomy as a result of a wholesale recasting of class relationships. In "Mr. Bennet and Mrs. Brown," Virginia Woolf dates this shift in social values as happening in or about December 1910. She thinks it demonstrated in literature by Samuel Butler and George Bernard Shaw; in life, "in the character of one's cook. The Victorian cook lived like a leviathan in the lower depths, formidable, silent, obscure, inscrutable; the Georgian cook is a creature of sunshine and fresh air; in and out of the drawing-room, now to borrow the *Daily Herald,* now to ask advice about a hat." Two world wars have continued this transformation. When servants were the merit badges of the Victorian middle class, domestic service was, after agriculture, the largest area of employment. Now the English cook has gone—not out to buy a hat but away. In *Mrs. Dalloway* Virginia Woolf points to the social fiction that the luncheon served that hot day in June 1923 had not been paid for, needed not be paid for. A like fiction today is that the hands that prepared the food and set the table are those of someone other than the lady of the house.

THE little literature of gastronomy of the early English nineteenth century can be given the same kind of summary review as that for the eighteenth-century product, with which it suffers in comparison. Without Grimod de la Reynière and Brillat-Savarin this literature might have been written but certainly not in the same way. The century begins well with the *Culina famulatrix medicinae* (1805) of "Ignotus." The *Tabella cibaria* (1820) of the emigré Abbé Denis Macquin is a remarkable jeu d'esprit in a Latin verse possible only for someone scholarly enough to have been a professor of classics and witty enough to be an intimate of William Beckford, author of *Vathek.* Launcelot Sturgeon's *Essays Moral, Philosophical and Stomachical* (1822) is memorable for what may be the first appearance of "Turkey boil'd is turkey spoil'd / And turkey roast is turkey lost, / But for turkey braised / The Lord be praised." But then come the epigoni of the French Masters, for example, William Green's *Art of Living in London* (182?), Sydney Whiting's *Memoirs of a Stomach* (1855), and the anonymous *Gastronomy, or, The School for Good Living* (1822), which in the 1814 edition had dispensed with the first two words of the title. The kind of humor endemic in this period is demonstrated by the full title of *The Apician Morsels* (1829, 1834) of Dick Hummelbergius Secundus (Hummelbergius was a Renaissance editor of Apicius), i.e., *Apician Morsels . . . Containing a New and Approved*

CULINA

FAMULATRIX MEDICINÆ:

OR,

RECEIPTS IN MODERN COOKERY;

WITH

A MEDICAL COMMENTARY,

WRITTEN BY

IGNOTUS,

AND REVISED BY

A. HUNTER, M.D. F.R.S. L.&E.

Qui Stomachum regem totius corporis esse contendunt, vera niti ratione videntur. .... SERENUS SAMMONICUS.

1st. ed. 1804.

THE SECOND EDITION.

YORK:

Printed by T. Wilson and R. Spence, High-Ousegate:

For J. MAWMAN, in the Poultry, London, and for WILSON and SPENCE, York;

Sold also by J. WHITE, Fleet-street, and J. HARDING, St. James's Street, London; A. CONSTABLE and Co. Edinburgh; and by J. TODD, SOTHERAN and Son, and J. WOLSTENHOLME, York.

1805.

In the editions after the first of *Culina famulatrix medicinae,* "Ignotus" is revealed as Dr. Alexander Hunter, founder of the York Dispensary and the York Mental Hospital. The book's dedication is "To those Gentlemen who freely give two Guineas for a Turtle Dinner at the Tavern, when they might have a more wholesome one at Home for ten Shillings." However, the preface says that Hunter's intention is to inform the doctors as to what it is that their rich patients have been overeating so that they can better cope with the "occupational disease" of the wealthy. Dr. Franklin's dialogue with the gout is reprinted in the text.

Code of Eatics: Illustrating the Veritable Science of the Mouth, Which Includes the Art of Never Breakfasting at Home and Always Dining Abroad.

Despite its obvious debt to Brillat-Savarin, *The Art of Dining* (1853, 1874) of Abraham Hayward is conceded to be the best English writing of the period. Hayward had won some modest fame with his translation of *Faust* in 1833; two years later he published in the *Quarterly Review* his "Gastronomers and Gastronomy" and found himself a celebrity. He followed with an article in the same journal on Thomas Walker's *Aristology* and in 1851 combined the two articles as *The Art of Dining*. Walker had founded the appropriately named journal *The Original*, for which he wrote "Aristology: or The Art of Dining," still pleasant for its insistence that food be served punctually, simply, and in an atmosphere

"Transmigration." Frontispiece from *Culina famulatrix medicinae.*

free of annoyances. Walker's definition of the ideal meal was much quoted: "turtle, followed by no other fish but whitebait, which is to be followed by no other meat but grouse, which is to be succeeded by apple fritters and jelly." Hayward took obvious pleasure in pointing out that the seasons in which whitebait and grouse are at their best do not coincide. Carlyle called Hayward "the best of our second-rate men"; the *Art of Dining* may be the best of the second-rate books in the little literature of gastronomy.

The epigraph for this chapter on English cookery literature comes from George Saintsbury's preface to the first publication of Ann Blencowe's 1694 *Receipt Book* (1925). Saintsbury, professor of English at Edinburgh, is reported to have read everything in English and French literature and to have remembered everything he read. He expanded the Baconian precept that reading makes a full man to prescribe reading—and writing—about food and drink for the fuller man. His *Notes on a Cellar-Book* (1921, 1923; both copies signed), part memoir, part cookbook, is also a kind of laughing dissertation for the highest degree in oenology. For the ideal dinner Saintsbury prescribes the sonnet form: fourteen guests: male and female rhymed *abab;* the menu something simple like soup, fish (trout), fillets of beef, roast duckling, apricots, and sardines *Dieu sait comment* ("a prescription of my wife's named by me"), accompanied by sherry, champagne, and chartreuse over the coffee.

André Simon was honorary cellarer of the Saintsbury Club, which met to dine twice yearly on the birthdays of Shakespeare and Saintsbury. Bred to the wine trade, Simon did much in his authoritative writings, a half dozen of which the Bittings acquired, to assure the English that wine was not invented by the French nor meant to be consumed only by them. He was instrumental in forming the International Wine and Food Society, to which he gave the collection described in his *Bibliotheca Bacchica* (1927). Francis Meynell of the Nonesuch Press wrote the preface for the 1951 edition of Simon's *Art of Good Living* (1929). Meynell's *All My Lives* gives glimpses of the Saintsbury Club dinners, though he errs in ascribing to Simon Theodore Hook's classic observation that when one dines alone the bottle comes around so much more often.

The unfinished business on our agenda is the fate of George Augustus Sala's copy of the first edition of Hannah Glasse. Sala was honored by Thackeray and Dickens as the outstanding journalist of his time, although Matthew Arnold pointed out the touch of the second-rate about this man in *Friendship's Garland*. As Sala tells the Glasse story, he got married one day, walked back to

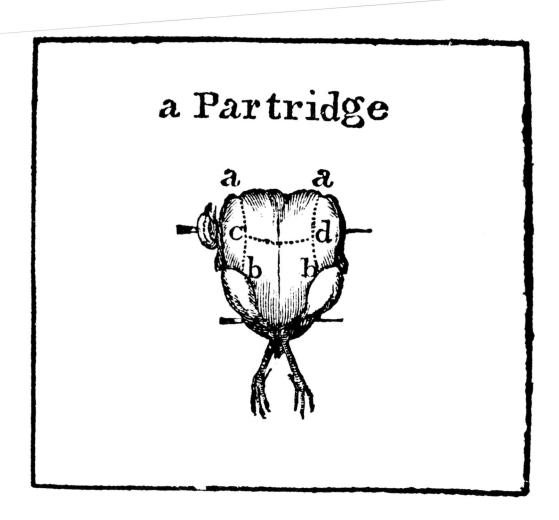

work, and "on the way I bought for sixpence a copy of the first edition of Hannah Glasse, of which scarcely half-a-dozen copies are known to be in existence. So you see I secured two treasures in one afternoon." According to the correspondence in the *Daily Telegraph* (May 8, 1876), there were then actually only three known copies. In an act of raw vandalism Sala had this rarity disassembled so that he might elaborately interleaf it with his own notes. When the Sala copy came upon the market, Mrs. Pennell was able to secure it for only ten pounds. Habent sua fata libelli.

The banality of Sala's *Thorough Good Cook* (1895) should not be unexpected. When Sala visited America, he grew enthusiastic about Delmonico's, that is, the international cuisine he would have been served in London, Paris, or Berlin, while Thackeray remembered New Orleans cookery and Boston oysters big as babies from his American journey. Possibly in the ultimate history of the literature of gastronomy, Sala will be remembered largely for his association with a book far better than anything of his own. Auguste Kettner in Soho's Church Street was the first restaurateur to open his kitchen to all comers at a time when kitchens were probably even worse than George Orwell describes them in *Down and Out in Paris and London.* An anonymous letter to the *London Times* (the author was E. S. Dallas, one of the *Times*'s principal reviewers) in 1869 publicized this phenomenon. Sala became Kettner's patron and when in 1877 *Kettner's Book of the Table* appeared anonymously, it was dedicated to Sala.

It has been established that the author of *Kettner's Book of the Table* was E. S. Dallas, by 1877 very much crushed by time and circumstance. His book's value transcends the revelations of contemporary kitchen and marketing practices, interesting though they are. The pen is that of a writer distinguished enough to have been a friend of the Rossettis and a member of the Garrick Club. Dallas's *Poetics* was reprinted in 1972; he himself thought his chief work the *Gay Science,* a title he took from the troubadors' characterization of their art of poetry as "gai saber." Dallas's thesis here is that the science of criticism is the science of the laws of pleasure. He had read in Coleridge that the immediate effect of science is truth, while that of poetry is pleasure. Perhaps it is this approach, combined as it is with great erudition lightly worn, that makes *Kettner's Book of the Table* one of the classics of gastronomical literature.

Chapter Four

La France à Table

Tout Français, à ce que j'imagine
Peut faire, tout au moins, un peu de cuisine.
ANONYMOUS

Every Frenchman, from what I have seen,
Can do at least a little cuisine.

THESE remarks on the French gastronomic literature of the Bitting and Pennell Collections will be a sketch of what should be an extended study. A full and properly structured account of the French gastronomic attitude would trace its relationships to French history, art, thought, and the great consolidator of all these, the literary tradition. Such an account could be begun in the Rare Book and Special Collections Division by the consultation of a third group of books there, that assembled by Raymond Toinet for his study of the *écrivains moralistes.* The term denotes the seventeenth-century commentators on *esprit et moeurs,* that is, attitudes and manners, particularly the worldly intelligence of how to please others and ourselves. This brief excursus will describe summarily the new collective sensibility documented by the Toinet Collection that displaced the old tragic view of life in the seventeenth century.[1]

If until our own day France has set the standards in cuisine, it is because a privileged elite has acted out the *moraliste* precept that the purpose of intelligence is not to understand the world but to enjoy it. The other French minor arts that adorn the conduct of daily life—those exemplified by the pottery of Rouen, the porcelain of Limoges, the furniture of the *ébénistes* of the faubourg Saint-Antoine—also originate in this teaching. Indeed the arts of agreement are so closely allied that the highest French gastronomic ideal is their integration in the dining room in a small *Gesamtkunstwerk* of the kind Wagner thought to make of opera. La Varenne's pioneering *Le Cuisinier françois* (first edition, 1651) is a landmark in the sudden emergence of a uniquely French culinary art; another, as significant for gastronomy writ large, is Colbert's takeover of Les Gobelins in 1662. These events occur as part of the brilliant ordering given by the French seventeenth century to the torrential creativity of the Italian Renaissance.

While the explanations for French gastronomy are largely social, some intellectual innovations discernible in the Toinet Collection are clearly relevant—among them, the *honnête homme* social code and Epicureanism. On assuming the Brillat-Savarin chair of the *Académie des gastronomes,* Curnonsky called his predecessor an *honnête homme* of the seventeenth century. If we sought to demonstrate the acuity of Curnonsky's perception, we would find *honnêteté* and the other new intellectual stances conveniently exemplified for us in the Toinet Collection by one person, Saint-Evremond. In the *Lettre sur les plaisirs* this symptomatic figure in a changing world said: "The principal end for which wisdom was given us, was to direct us in the enjoyment of our pleasures." Saint-Evremond picked up the *voluptas* theory of pleasure, but went beyond earlier Epicureans in calling for the active search of pleasure, not merely the avoidance of pain. As an *honnête homme* with realistic expectations of himself, others, and the world, he knew that life can be good because it offers simple and natural pleasures: "what can be better than a peach?" The continuing French reputation for frivolity originates in the seriousness with which the seventeenth-century *moraliste* took the pleasures of food, clothing, and love.

To make the world an object of pleasure, the seventeenth century sought also to make it social and communicable. Representative of the extensive commentary on conversation in the Toinet Collection is the chevalier de Méré, whose *De la conversation* says that the purpose of conversation is to give others a good opinion of themselves and of us. This chef d'oeuvre of the intelligence is achieved by "knowing and judging." Other seventeenth-century *moralistes* expanded on Méré by introducing the concept of taste as the faculty of the spirit which transcends knowledge in making judgment, distinguishing and preferring the beautiful without the use of fixed, precise criteria. Seventeenth-century conversation invented first the salons, occupied with manners, taste, and the appreciation of women, and then a little later the cafés, informal salons and places of rendezvous.

The significance for French gastronomy of Saint-Evremond on pleasure and of Méré on conversation can be made clear by contrast with the English experience. Perhaps Froissart was the first to jibe that the English take their pleasures sadly; it was A. P. Herbert who said that the English accept pleasure only in a noble cause. As for conversation, a French restaurateur in England, the very anglophile X.–M. Boulestin, lamented the English failure to talk of food, which he knew is all the better for being talked about. An English observer of the French, Arnold Bennett, overheard an animated dinner table conversation he thought typical because "I felt all the diners knew profoundly and passionately what they were talking about." The diners finally agreed that women can't cook an omelette because they worry it so much that it cooks unevenly; however, they do better than men with bouillon because they will skim it more constantly. The talk then turned to wine and here Bennett breaks off, saying only "when these people begin to talk of wine they never stop." French gastronomy thrives because gastronomy is a spoken language and in France there are many like Bennett's diners who speak gastronomy, as Molière's *bourgeois gentilhomme* spoke prose, naturally and without knowing it.[2]

NO French cookbook appeared in the first half of the seventeenth century, the time of the organized ill-will and violence of the religious struggles. In 1651 Pierre David of Paris published the great pathbreaker, La Varenne's *Cuisinier françois,* the most important work after Platina's *De honesta voluptate* with which the historian of gastronomy has to do. La Varenne's success alerted publishers to the commercial possibilities of the cookbook. A French student puts the total of cookbook editions (not titles) from 1651 to 1789 at 230; that is, 75 in the second half of the seventeenth century and 155 in the nine decades preceding the outburst of the French Revolution. The average number of copies per edition in the period is thought to be 1,200, so that the total number of cookbook copies published between 1651 and 1699 can be calculated as 90,000 and from 1700 to 1789 as 273,600. The count is a conservative one, excluding the "whole house" and medical books which often gave much space to food and drink. What these figures say about cookbook popularity is brought out by another datum: French book production reached five hundred titles annually only shortly after the middle of the eighteenth century.[3]

Working in the spirit of the time La Varenne and his successors made cookery into an art of generally applicable techniques and basic units. The first recipe in the first edition of La Varenne is for bouillon, the stock which Marin's *Dons de Comus* of 1739 called "the jewel of the kitchen," and without which, Escoffier said in the *Guide culinaire* of 1903, nothing can be done. Signalling the end of medieval anarchy and renaissance fantasy, the book is organized methodically in accordance with the unfolding of the meal itself. Louis XIV's cookbooks regulated cuisine by the same assumption as that by which the contemporary state-organized institutes regulated architecture, music, the beaux-arts, and even the language and literature: beauty lies in the whole, but the proper subordination of the parts to the whole is achieved through the use of reason.

The point of this tour is that the cookbook is not a personal expression. It is cut out for a specific audience and therefore can be understood only by reference to the social context of which it is an epiphenomenon. The writer must give the public what it wants, although often it does not know what it wants until it reads the writer. The period of the advent of the French cookbook was characterized by a sense of present material and cultural wellbeing and by rising expectations for the future. The art historians say that the portraits by Le Brun and Philippe de Champaigne of the owners of the new hôtels in the faubourgs breathe the same richness and self-satisfaction as the hôtels themselves. Madame de Maintenon wrote the archbishop of Paris (October 22, 1698): "There are new ragoûts every day, and *gourmandise* is *à la mode*." Contemporary observers parodied the gastronomic excesses that obviously were there to be parodied: Boileau, pretentious bad taste in "Le Repas ridicule," La Bruyère, the pedant gourmet Cliton with his "sure palate" in *Les Caractères*.

No American library reports possession of a copy of the first edition of La Varenne's *Cuisinier françois* (Paris: Pierre David, 1651). Thirty editions of this work appeared before 1727 under such names as *Cuisinier françois, enseignant la manière . . .; Cuisinier françois, ou, l'école des ragoûts; Cusinier méthodique; École des ragoûts ou le chef-d'oeuvre du cuisinier; Nouveau cuisinier français ou l'école des ragoûts; Nouveau et parfait cuisinier françois;* and *Vray cuisinier français*. Of these thirty, the Bitting and Pennell Collection each hold the 1656 edition printed by Adrian Vlacq of The Hague, and the Bitting Collection has in addition the 1682 Paris release of Jean Ribou, Pierre David's associate and cellmate in the Bastille, and a 1688 printing by J. Canier of Lyon. It should not be assumed that all editions of a seventeenth-century book carry the same material. The stock recipe appears in first place in the 1656 and 1682 editions; it does not appear at all in the 1688 edition. The 1682 title page states that the edition "is augmented by a new *Confiturier*"; the 1688 title page promises a *Traité de confitures* (which is not the same as the 1682 inclusion) but leaves unannounced the *Pâtissier françois* that ends the book.

The publisher's preface to the first edition does not reappear in the editions available to us. Because in gastronomy (as in religion) the earliest works are the most important, we shall quote Pierre David's claims to distinction for his publishing venture from a secondary source, Bertrand Guégan's fine *Fleur de la cuisine française*. David points first to the novelty of his book, "whose matter and title seem new in Paris, there being nothing like it in print," and then to the breadth of its interest, its utility in houses "where money is not a consideration, as well as those of more modest expenditures." The historian thinks David restrained in his congratulations to his author. In this book La Varenne had dealt the medieval cuisine of spiced stews and exotic birds a mortal blow and crowned the stuttering culinary art of the Renaissance.[5]

Talking of editions not present in these collections is a breach of decorum in which we shall continue because of the interest of two *rarissime* La Varenne items, dissimilar in the printing skills they represent, but equally curious historically. The nineteenth-century bibliophile's craze for Elzevir imprints made the first edition of La Varenne's *Pâtissier françois* the sensation of the auction halls. The historian of gastronomy values this edition for a preface which says: "Having learned that foreigners greet very favorably certain new books that carry the word French in their titles . . . I present boldly *Pâtissier françois* . . . since there has been until now no other author who has given instruction in this art." The other extraordinary La Varenne item is the version of *Cuisinier françois* prepared for the series called "Bibliothèque bleue" or "Bibliothèque de Troyes," cheaply made books peddled, along with needles and ribbons, in the farming villages, so alien to and sometimes alienated from Paris and Versailles. Phrases like "now you will hear" show that these books were meant to be read aloud to illiterates. Did the peasants hear La Varenne's recipes as another version of the Land of Cocaigne stories?

The Library's collections do show the evidence that the cultural tide that once went from Italy to France had been reversed in the Italian translation of La Varenne, *Il Cuoco francese,* in six editions as early as 1703 and as late as 1815. Cuisine was an important weapon in the cultural imperialism that in the beginning of the eighteenth century would have one Frenchman, Leblond, plan the city of St. Petersburg and at the end would have another Frenchman, L'Enfant, plan the city of Washington. The appearance of Pierre de Lune's great *boeuf à la mode* in Pepys's *Diary* illustrates the manner of French cuisine's peaceful invasions. On May 12, 1667, on their way homeward, Pepys reports that he and his wife "bethought ourselves of going alone, she and I, to a French house for dinner . . . and in a moment almost have the table covered, and clean glasses, and all in the French manner, and a mess of potage first, and then a couple of pigeons *à l'estuvé,* and then a piece of *boeuf-à-la-mode,* all exceedingly well seasoned and to our great liking . . . but to see the pleasant and ready attendance that we had, and all things so desirous to please and ingenious in the people, did take me mightily." Forty years after the first La Varenne, Massialot could preface his cookbook with the boast: "We pride ourselves in France on being superior to other nations in cuisine as we are in a thousand other excellences."

The place directly after La Varenne must be given to Nicolas de Bonnefons, whose 1654 *Délices de la campagne* is in the Bitting Collection in the 1662 and 1715 editions. The title indicates its descendance from the old "whole house" book, but the dedication is *"aux dames mesnagères,"* the housewives, not to the princeling or noble expected. The preface continues the break with tradition by talking of expense, concluding "you will do as much as your position permits, leaving to the great the expenditures that must be made for the glory of their houses." The first of the three books, that on bread and baked goods, is dedicated to the ladies who

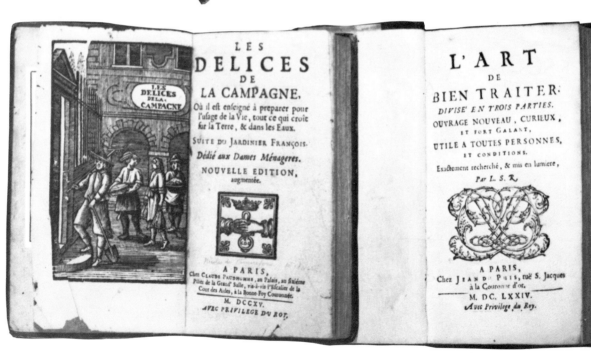

142

The starting point in the movement of gastronomy from Versailles to Paris, from the court to the middle classes, is La Varenne's *Cuisinier françois* (La Haye: Adrian Vlacq, 1656). Following it are Bonnefons's *Délices de la campagne* (Paris: A. Cellier, 1662), remarkable for its insistence on simplicity, and the *Art de bien traiter,* (Paris: J. du Puis, 1676) "new, curious, and very gallant." Perhaps *L'Escole parfaite* (Paris: J. Ribou, 1676) should have been placed somewhat out of line to indicate that it makes a step backward to medieval cookery. It is followed by the work whose title *La Cuisinière bourgeoise* (Paris: Chez Guillyn, 1746) proclaims the completion of the transition and recognizes a new social datum: women, middle class women, are concerned with the kitchen.

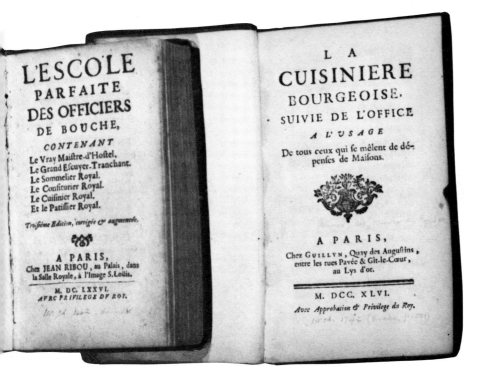

prepare their own bread, because bread is the French standard for excellence in food. The second book is on *racines,* that is, roots or vegetables, and is dedicated to the Capuchins, best gardeners of the religious orders. The vibrations of the word *racines* in the seventeenth-century ear may be communicable to Americans who remember Edward Markham's "Man with the Hoe," who has "the emptiness of ages on his face." La Bruyère's *Caractères* depicts the *animaux féroces* bent over working in the fields, who on standing are revealed to be human. These "ferocious animals" return at night to their lairs where they live on "black bread, water, and *'racines.'*"

In the third book, that on meat and fish dedicated to the *maîtres d'hôtel,* Bonnefons takes his place among the great purifiers of taste, with Escoffier, who said "make it simple," and Curnonsky, who decreed that things should have the taste of what they are. "This book," he writes, "has for subject the true taste which ought to be given each kind of fish and meat, which most cooks do not care about, since . . . they think they need only to disguise and garnish their dishes in confusion." Bonnefons demands that a cabbage potage taste only of cabbage and a leak potage only of leeks, and not of minces, mushrooms, or spices. While he has specified the potages, "what I say about potages I mean for everything and it should serve as a law for everything that is eaten." It has been said that the whole of Western philosophy is a commentary on Plato. In a sense the development of French gastronomy is a realization of Bonnefons. If, in fact, his performance sometimes limps behind his principles, as Bertrand Guégan charges, his prophetic stature is not thereby diminished.

Bonnefons presented *Délices de la campagne* as a supplement to his 1651 *Jardinier françois,* which the Bitting Collection holds in the second edition of Raphael Smith (Amsterdam, 1655). Both works are included in the Bitting 1684 volume entitled *Traitez de jardinage.* The subtitle of *Jardinier françois* reads: "How to cultivate trees and the kitchen garden, and the manner of preserving fruits and making all kinds of preserves, conserves, and marzipan." In describing the pleasures offered the five senses by the garden, the preface singles out the fruits, which, "while seasoned only by nature, are so excellent, each in its kind, that fruit by itself best satisfies the palate." This purity of taste was recognized by John Evelyn, whose first work on horticulture is a translation of the *Jardinier françois.* The plates made for Bonnefons by François Chauveau were copied for use in Evelyn's *Kitchen Gardener.* They are missing from the Bitting copy. Evelyn also translated some of the extremely influential work of La Quintanie, genius of the *jardins-potagers* provided him at Versailles itself so that he might demonstrate with peas in May and asparagus in December the ability of the French king to force even nature to serve him. Another worker in the King's gardens, Ballon, wrote a well-received *Nouveau Traité des oranges et citronniers* (Paris: C. de Sercy, 1692) to convince the French that the best way of getting gold out of the ground is to plant orange trees.

La Varenne had worked for the marquis d'Uxelles, a marshall of France; Bonnefons had been valet de chambre to the king. L.S.R., the author of *L'Art de bien traiter, ouvrage nouveau, curieux, et fort utile* (Paris, 1674), may have been Rolland, *officier de bouche* to the princesse de Carignan, or, more probably, a Robert otherwise unidentified. Obviously he had witnessed the *ambigus, collations,* and *soupers* at Fontainebleau, Saint-Cloud, and Vaux-le-Vicomte that he describes in pages that sometimes seem to prefigure Watteau's "Embarquement pour Cythère." While Robert attacks La Varenne, his accusation is in effect a testimonial to the latter's importance: "I know that until the present moment his book has carried off the glory of having laid down the rules and the methods. I know that the plebes and even some rather enlightened people read it as if it were something sublime, agreed upon, and perfect." In the essentials Robert's cuisine seems not to differ from that of La Varenne, although he grows indignant about *tripes de morue fricassées* and the idea of feeding Frenchmen jerusalem artichokes as if they were Arabs. He deplores yesterday's cuisine for its prodigious excesses and praises today's cuisine for its exquisite choice of dishes, the finesse of their seasoning, and a table where mouth and eye are equally charmed. Bertrand Guégan thinks Robert a gastronomer as distinguished as Grimond de la Reynière, a cook unexcelled in his own day, and a prose stylist as skilled as many who appear in the manuals of literary history. Robert's contemporaries were of a different opinion; there was only one edition of *L'Art de bien traîter* after the first.

The Widow David continued her husband's business, printing with Jean Ribou *L'École parfaite des officiers de bouche,* although her name had disappeared from the title pages by the time of the Bitting 1676 edition. This book, or rather group of booklets, is made up of the "Vray Maître-d'hostel," "Grand Écuyer-tranchant," "Sommelier royal," "Cuisinier royal," and "Pâtissier royal." The publisher's warning against confusing the first booklet with *Le Maistre-d'hostel royal* and so mistaking substance for shadow was advertising effrontery unequalled until the advent of Chilean wines labelled "Beware of French Imitations." *Le Maistre-d'hostel royal* is the title of the work that Pierre de Lune gave Loyson to publish in 1662, although Pierre David had printed his first work, the 1656 *Le Cuisinier.* (These two de Lune titles are not in our collections and exist in this country only in single copies.) Ribou and the Widow David added injury to their insult to de Lune by taking over the section on eggs and *pâtisserie* in de Lune's *Le Cuisinier* for their "Cuisinier royal." Ribou had similarly pirated one of Molière's plays, coming out of the ensuing court action with a small fine and the right to publish the first edition of *Tartuffe.* Except for the material stolen, *L'École parfaite* is a medieval cookbook, a fact which did not prevent it from reaching fifteen editions as against de Lune's two.

The seventeenth-century code of *honnêteté* had evaluated man in relation to an ideal of social life conceived in terms of the royal court. The first title in the literature of *honnêteté,* Faret's 1649 *Honnête homme ou l'art de plaire à la cour,* and the word *royal* suffixing the components of the 1680 *École parfaite des officiers de bouche* explicitly make this relation. The radiation of court style outward and downward had been begun by the salons and the *honnête homme* during the reign of Louis XIV. After his death, social life and high style were taken over by Paris, which earlier had been, in La Bruyère's phrase, only "the ape of the court." The elegantly artificial Paris of the Regency and Louis XV expressed itself in small parties and gallant *soupers* of the kind painted by Moreau le Jeune. The books that follow are transcripts of the new society of the eighteenth century, a century of beautiful surfaces, when art was woven into the fabric of social life perhaps more than at any other time.

THE author making the transition into the next century and new culinary era is Massialot, at various times in the service of the king's brother, the duc de Chartres, and the marquis d'Arcis. His 1691 *Cuisinier royal et bourgeois,* which in the Bitting English version of 1702 is the *Court and Country Cook,* is royal because used in royal kitchens, bourgeois because useful for those who ordinarily make do with just enough but are often obliged to make a show. The Bitting copy of the third French edition of 1689 carries the inscription of a Grandbois who identifies himself as cook to the marquis de Montcalm. Voltaire's self-portrait in verse, "Le Mondain" (1736), in which he describes his love of modern pleasures and of the luxury that is a necessity ("le superflu, chose si nécessaire"), asks how good the "good old days" could have been without Massialot. In a letter written forty years later recalling Massialot (April 7, 1777),

Voltaire lamented that he himself belonged to "the good old days" so that the newest "new cuisine" was not for him.

Massialot followed his first work with the 1692 *Nouvelles Instructions pour les confitures, les liqueurs, et les fruits,* of which the Library holds the 1716, 1733, 1734, and 1740 editions. An earlier example of this specialty literature is the *Traité de confiture,* a rough reworking of La Varenne published by Thomas Guillain of Paris in 1689. For his sugared entremets, marmalades, compotes, and preserves Massialot prescribes a high new sugar: fruit ratio of 1:1, thereby speeding sugar on its triumphal march. After Massialot, the Regency put sugar into everything, even champagne. So the French maritime fleet scurried to bring slaves to Guadeloupe and Martinique and in the negotiations of the Treaty of Paris (1763) France rejected "the few hectares of snow" of Canada in favor of the sugar islands.

Beginning with the Pennell 1714 edition, when the word *nouveau* appeared in the title, Massialot's cookbook was progressively enlarged, reaching its final form in the two-volume edition of 1724-30. Perhaps at the publisher's initiative, a third volume appeared in 1739 carrying the name Vincent La Chapelle on its title page and concluding with fifteen pages of La Chapelle's recipes. The story is an odd one only recently disentangled.[6] The recipes of La Chapelle's *Modern Cook,* published in 1733, when he cooked for Lord Chesterfield, and translated into French in 1735, when he was in the household of the prince of Orange, are word for word repetitions from Massialott, sometimes in the same sequence. The Bitting Collection lacks the first four volumes of La Chapelle's 1742 French second edition. The interest of this edition, however, is the fifth volume's promise of new menus, new table arrangements, and new preparations "far above the capability of the *Cuisinier royal et bourgeois.*" La Chapelle then lifts these promised novelties from the work that he has just denigrated.

In 1739 Prault in Paris published *Les Dons de Comus* by Marin, then cook to Madame de Gesvres, wife of the king's first gentleman of the chamber, and later in the employ of the maréchale de Soubise. Marin's title page describes this work as intended even more for those who wish to give dinners "in the newest taste" than for the professionals. This awareness that a change in taste was taking place had been expressed first by Massialot in titling his *Nouveau Cuisinier* (1714) and again by La Chapelle in his *Modern Cook* (1733). When in 1742 Menon added a third volume to his 1739 *Traité de la cuisine,* he called this supplement boldly *Nouvelle Cuisine.* The principles of this "new cuisine" are nowhere actually spelled out. Perhaps they can be extrapolated from Marin's comment prefacing his *fricassée de poulet* recipes: "In general, *fricasseé* is good only in so far as it is simple," or his obiter dictum in the bouillon recipe: "I prefer the simplest way, which I think best for the palate and for health."

This acceptance of the new as necessarily better than the old suggested by Marin's title page was made explicit in the preface to *Les Dons de Comus,* so explicit that it provoked a skirmish in the literary "Quarrel of the Ancients and the Moderns," then being waged on both sides of the English Channel. The authors of this preface were, rather surprisingly, the two Jesuits Brunoy and Bougeant. The Jesuit fathers distinguished between an old and a new cuisine, the latter, they say, being more varied, simpler, cleaner, and even more "savant." The "quintessences" of the dishes are obtained in "a kind of chemistry" so calculated that "nothing dominates but everything is felt, to give the dishes that unison that painters give colors and to render them so homogeneous that only one fine and piquant taste results from their different savours." Marin's kind of chemistry originates in his extensive use of the concentrated stock or *fonds: fonds clair,* from veal and fowl, *fonds brun,* from beef. It is this chemistry that explains the story of the cook who boasted he could put fifty hams into one small vial.

A defender of the old order of things, Desalleurs l'aîné, answered in *Lettre d'un pâtissier anglois, au nouveau cuisinier françois* (n.p., 1739?), of which the Bitting Collection has one of the two American copies. Desalleurs' immediate target was Marin, the cook who thought to perfect cuisine by submitting it to the rules of geometry; his ultimate argument was with all those he saw as seeking to Newtonize human affairs. Desalleurs caricatures Marin's preface in words like "A ragoût for a delicately voluptuous people is a geometrically chemical dish that is composed entirely of intellectualized quintessences and is utterly free of any mondanity!" When Meusnier de Querlon, novelist and periodical editor, took on the writing of an apology for Marin, he did not confront Desalleurs directly but instead eulogized the philosophic spirit in general and a cuisine structured by geometry in particular. Desalleurs reads like the Swift of the *Battle of the Books;* Meusnier like the d'Alembert of the introduction to the *Encyclopédie,* calmly confident that the Newtonian jinii can never be wrested back into the bottle.

Traditional cuisine is brought to completion and its successor announced by one man, Menon, perhaps unequalled in publication activity until Gouffé and Dubois in the nineteenth century. Menon's *opera* in the aristocratic tradition are listed here in the order of the edition in our collections. The earliest is the 1750 *Science du maître d'hôtel, confiseur,* which is the supplement to *Science du maître d'hôtel, cuisinier,* which the Library has only in the Pennell 1789 edition. The three volumes of the Bitting *Nouvelle Cuisine* (1751) first appeared in 1742 as a continuation of Menon's 1739 two-volume *Traité de la cuisine,* which the Library does not have. The Bitting *Traité historique et pratique de la cuisine . . . pour . . . tous ceux qui veulent donner à manger honnêtement* (1758) is a first edition, as is the Library's *Manuel des officiers de bouche* (1759). The most ostentatiously aristocratic of all Menon's works is appropriately the *Soupers de la cour,* a work which was rare in 1828 when Grimod de la Reynière vainly called for a reprinting. The Library has the first edition of 1755 but only two volumes of the 1778 edition, a deficiency somewhat compensated for by the presence of the rare English 1767 translation entitled *Art of Modern Cookery Displayed.*

Janus-like at the crossroads, Menon then looks toward the future and a public which will forgo truffles and *coulis* to achieve simplicity and economy. The dedication of his *Cuisinière bourgeoise* of 1746 is to "all those who are concerned with household expenses." Other works had described themselves as designed for the bourgeoisie, but only as an afterthought. The *Cuisinière bourgeoise* is the first to be given over entirely to the female cook in the bourgeois kitchen. The Bitting Collection has the first edition, published by Guillyn in Paris, and the 1771 Brussels edition by Foppens, Guillyn's rival in cookbook publication throughout the period. Mrs. Pennell owned the Paris editions of 1777 and 1798. At least thirty-two editions had appeared by 1789. The Russian translation of 1791 elsewhere in the Library's collection is the second Russian edition. The phrase "cuisine bourgeoise" was destined, in the French phrase, *à faire sa fortune,* and is still occasionally to be seen on the windows of the restaurants of Paris.

Menon's preface gives the reasons for this success: "I have used simple, good, and new dishes, of which I have made intelligible explanations understandable to all." Unmistakably recognizing food as a symbol of the social hierarchy, Menon says, "It is not for the nobles that the author writes but for the bourgeois, but it can be said that he ennobles bourgeois dishes by the treatment he gives them." What goes beyond the capacity of the bourgeois kitchen, he declares, should be reserved to the great and "those whom great opulence puts in a position to imitate them." Baron Grimm thought it worthwhile to call the *Cuisinière bourgeoise* to the attention of the highly select subscribers to his *Correspondence littéraire* (letter of February 1, 1757) as "a book which will hold its place in a French library." Grimm commented further: "The cooks of this country have acquired a great reputation all through Europe. In our day they have carried their art to its highest perfection."

Baron Grimm's admiration of the achievements of the cuisine of his age is typical of the eighteenth-century Enlightenment's self-congratulation on modern superiority over the past in all things. La Chapelle, who in 1733 and 1735 ostentatiously flaunted the word *modern* in the title of his books, dated the culinary past as recently as twenty years earlier, a date probably picked with Massialot in mind. Certainly the decisive change had occurred before the advent of the French Revolution. Louis-Sebastien Mercier, writing in the *Tableau de Paris* of 1783, stated flatly: "We have known how to eat for only half a century. The delicate cuisine of Louis XV was unknown to Louis XIV. . . . Who can enumerate the dishes of the new cuisine? It is an absolutely new idiom."[7] After Carême's adaptation of the eighteenth-century culinary idiom, changes occurred, but always within the known matrix. Only now, with the advent of *cuisine minceur,* have the principles inherited from the eighteenth century been questioned.

THIS laying out of books in the order of their appearance may give the impression that one book supplanted another and was in turn supplanted. That is not factually the case. In the extraordinary twenty-year period 1739-59, when more than half of the 1700-89 cookbooks were published, all authors and all specialties seem to have coexisted in prosperity. The preface to the 1758 *Dons de Comus* announces the publisher-bookseller's ability to supply readers with a full assortment of books on cookery, confectionery, and pastry. The anonymous author of the *Manuel des officiers de bouche* (Paris, 1759) used his preface to apologize for adding another to the books with which the public was already deluged. However, Menon is the one author who more than any other can be said to represent the culinary art as it was when Carême began his career. A typical example of Menon's influence is given by the little *Étrennes aux vivants* (Paris: Chez Leclerc, 1785), which lists nine titles for further reading. Except for the specialist books, Massialot's *Confiturier royal* and Sieur d'Emy's *Art de bien faire les glaces d'office* (Paris: Le Clerc, 1768), these are all the work of Menon.

In the last half of the century the old dietetic regime approach to the kitchen is revived in a rather new format, the dictionary. The *Dictionnaire des alimens, vins et liqueurs* (Paris, 1750), attributed to Briand, its publisher, accepts Menon's separation of haute cuisine and cuisine bourgeoise and adds a third variety "cuisine sensuelle," simpler than the others. Briand promises instruction in all culinary levels and medical information on all his recipes. This work apparently makes the first French reference to pâté de foie gras, mentioned earlier in a sixteenth-century

German text. The *Dictionnaire portatif de cuisine, d'office, et de distillation* (Paris: Chez Vincent, 1767) adds to the recipes in the areas announced in the title "medical observations on the properties of food and the dishes most suitable for each temperament." The title page makes the distinction in the kitchen employment of men and women by addressing itself to the "chefs d'office and most skillful cooks" in the masculine gender and to the "cooks who are employed only at bourgeois tables" in the feminine. The most extensive of the dietetic regime books is not a dictionary but Jourdan Le Cointe's three-volume *Cuisine de santé*, published by Briand again in 1789-90. Not surprisingly, his ideas on diet and nutrition are those of Galen; surprisingly, he thinks the cuisine of Italy superior in delicacy to that of France.

Of the three cookbooks to appear during the French Revolution, the Library holds only the *Manuel de la friandise* (Paris: Janot, 1797), which the booksellers' catalogs today call *introuvable*. In the rhymed prolog the author describes himself as a man of wit who loves nature, simplicity, *gigot* without sauce, and his cook Isabeau. He had earlier written a little economical cookbook (the *Petit cuisinier économe*), but he intends this book for those who wish and can afford the very best. In fact, however, his recipes for the very best are renamed versions of what he found in the *Cuisinière bourgeoise*. The temporary disappearance of the cookbook should not be unexpected. The Revolution had promised the French people liberty, equality, and fraternity; it had said nothing of food and drink. The return to order under Napoleon meant a return to satisfied appetites, but after ten years of privations a people eager to eat had to be reminded of the pleasure of eating well. The next period will be one of crisis and renewal for gastronomy.

THE mechanism of exposition thus far in this tour of the Bitting and Pennell collections has been the stringing of one book after another as links in a chronological chain. However, the role of tour guide imparts the liberty to comment freely on whatever presents itself without restriction by any governing pattern. Surely a tour guide should hail the gastronomic brilliance of the little court maintained at Luneville by Stanislaw Leszczynski, made duc de Lorraine after the Russians forced him from the throne of Poland. His *officier de bouche*, the Alsatian Gilliers, wrote the *Cannameliste français* (Nancy: Lescure, 1768) from his experience in satisfying Stanislaw's extraordinary sweet tooth. The gold- and silversmiths value Gilliers for the plates designed by Dupuis and engraved by Lotha representing the elegant *surtouts, pièces montées, goblets*, and

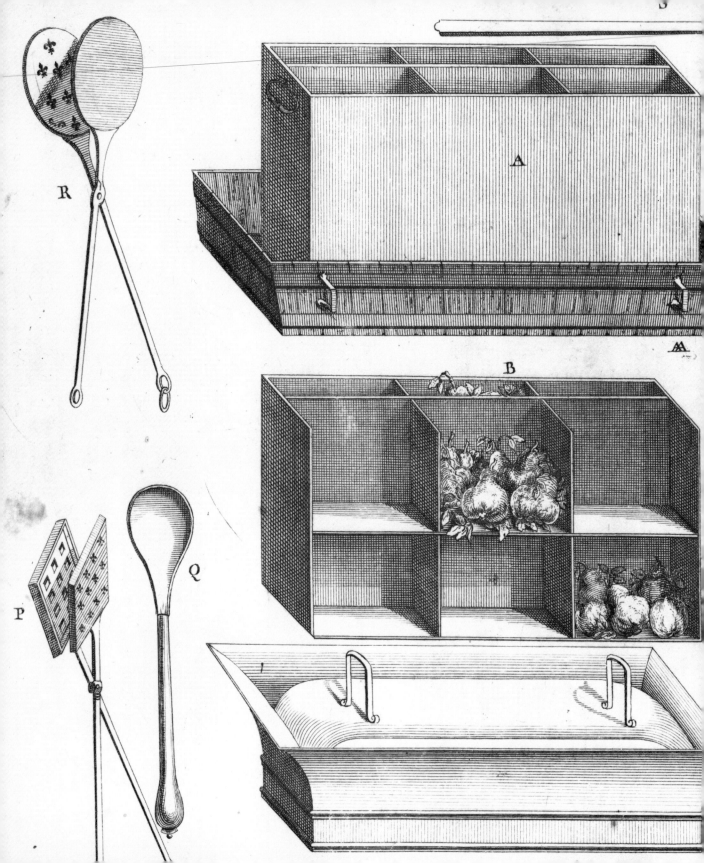

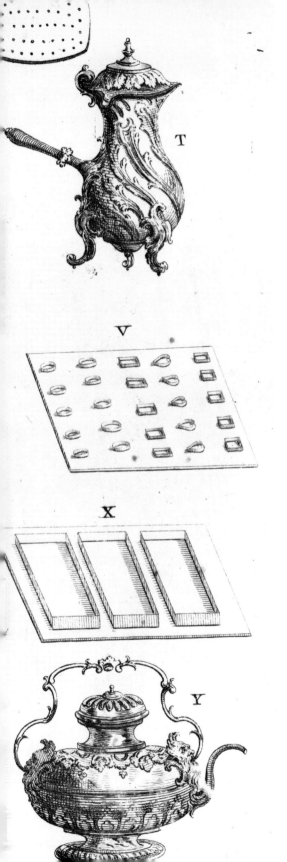

Gilliers, *Le Cannameliste français . . .*
(Nancy: J.B.H. Leclerc, 1768).

   Gilliers' plate displays the utensils of the *officier de bouche*, particularly the copper *cave*, where ice cream or ices were kept in wooden ice buckets while waiting service. Figure A is the top of the *cave*, figure B the *cave* itself, with some ice cream moulds inside it and the *cave* case beneath it. The book's next plate shows some of the moulds Gilliers used in making what he called *fromage glaceés* or *neiges*, that is, ice cream. A frequently repeated story is that Jefferson brought the recipe for ice cream home from France. Actually Mary Eales tells how "to ice cream" in her 1714 *Recipts*, a book which Jefferson owned in the 1748 edition.

cafetières of Stanislaw's table. Edmond de Goncourt praised the recipes, particularly the candied violets, roses, and jonquils, which he called entremets of odor and perfume fit for a banquet of the Thousand and One Nights.[8]

The biologist Pierre Buc'hoz was also attached to the Luneville court, though the personal service a popularizer of science with a bibliography including almost two hundred monographs could have rendered the duke seems minimal. The Buc'hoz works in the Library's collection, the dissertations on tea, coffee, and chocolate, all of 1787, the *Traité usuel du chocolat* of 1812, and the *Art alimentaire ou méthode pour préparer les aliments les plus sains pour l'homme* of 1783 constitute only a small fraction of his effort at popularizing the knowledge of "household economy." As prolific as Sir John Hill, Buc'hoz equally merits Dr. Johnson's characterization of Hill as "an ingenious man, but of no great veracity." The great non-literary contribution to gastronomy of the Luneville court was the *baba-au-rhum,* which was sometimes served to Stanislaw almost meter-high. Less well known is the role of his daughter, Maria Leszczynska, in popularizing *bouchées de la Reine* and *fricassée de poulet.*

The architects had thought to keep the servants out of the new social life by introducing the special dining area separated from the kitchen. The nobles then went into the kitchen to play at inventing new dishes, so that some pages of a nineteenth-century cookbook read like an armorial of the old nobility of France. Two books mark the advent in the kitchen of the gifted amateur who has taste by virtue of his patent of nobility. Very early is *Plaisirs de la vie* (Aix: Iean Roize, 1655), whose title page gives César Pellenc as author and whose preface dedicates the book to Pellenc's employer, the baron de Villeneufve, Cereste, etc., etc. A previous owner has recorded in spidery handwriting on the endpapers that the marquis de Logey said that the author was the nobleman and not the cook. The coyness of some passages in the preface seems to confirm this. Almost all the execrable eight-syllable ten-line stanzas are recipes, although some pages at the end are devoted to the pleasures of hunting, gambling, music, and love, against which the serious eater is warned. Vicaire could find only one copy of Pellenc in France; the Bitting copy is unique in this country.[9]

The *Cuisinier gascon* (the Bitting copy is the first edition of 1740) is dedicated to the prince de Dombes, "one of the best cooks in France," by the author—the prince de Dombes. A grandson of Louis XIV and Madame de Montespan, the prince was a frequent guest of Louis XV in the *petites appartements* of Versailles, in whose kitchens he prepared, sometimes with the assistance of the king, the dishes his book describes. His preface disclaims any pretensions to the knowledge of

Menon or the intelligence of the *Pâtissier anglais;* no, all that the author prides himself on is taste ("je ne me pique que de goût"), clearly in the two meanings of that word. We are to understand that the gifted amateur, particularly the gifted noble amateur, can have taste although lacking in both knowledge and intelligence. The gifted amateur pose breaks down when the *Cuisinier gascon* must deal with the great sauces: he does not attempt their preparation, instead referring the reader to the dullard professionals. The 217 recipes bear names like potage à la wooden leg, caramel without malice, green monkey sauce, and nasty chicken. The recipe for stuffed calves's eyeballs au gratin, in which the eyeball is replaced by a whole truffle, is as surrealist as anything in Marinetti's *La Cucina futurista.*

The most amusing book of these collections is either *Roti-Cochon* or the *Festin jozeuse.* The Bitting copy of the *Roti-Cochon* vocabulary is a facsimile, now a rarity itself, edited in 1890 by the bibliographer Georges Vicaire, with the patronage of Baron Jerome Pichon. The greatest gastronomic bibliophile of his time, Pichon was also responsible for the 1892 reprinting of the 1490 Taillevent, the first French cookbook. Our illustration of this ingenious vocabulary for young gourmets can show only one type of the cuts used, while the printer seems to have drawn upon everything in his stock. Lebas prepared his *Festin joyeuse* (Paris: Lesclapart père, 1738) out of "the wish to give ladies the means of teaching their subordinates by song how to make sauces and ragoûts." His last twenty-four pages provide the music of the airs indicated with each recipe, e.g., the recipe for *dindon à la saingaras* is to be sung to the air "L'amour plaît malgré les peines." Watteau painted marquesses down into shepherdesses; Lebas elevates his *oie au vin blanc* recipe into a villanelle and his *dindon en daube* into a rondeau. While Lebas may be the first in music for the kitchen, Christophe Ballard, music master of the King's Chapel, worked in an old, indeed classic, genre, the drinking song. In his two-volume *Nouvelles parodies bacchiques* (new because the 1673 first edition was *Parodies bacchiques*) the words are accompanied by the music. The curious frontispieces that enhance the interest of this work are intact in both volumes of the Bitting 1714 edition.

These two groups of three titles, the first giving a still timely solution for the servant problem, the other embodying the polemic on a drinking custom associated with a religious festival, belong among the great oddities of the literature. The Bitting copy of the 1713 *Maltote des cuisiniers* is an 1833 reprint issued by the great bibliographer Joseph Techener and is apparently unique in this country. Bound with it are the undated *La Conferance des servantes* and *La Responce des servantes.* The common subject is the *"anse du panier,"* the commission which the

96 *Poſt Pira ſume potum.*
Aprés la Poire, faut boire.

LES POMMES
& les Poires font
bonnesàl'Eaurofe
avec force Sucre.

Les POIRES de bon Chretien font meilleures que les POMMES de Turc.

Roti-Cochon
(Paris: "Pour la Société des bibliophiles françois," 1890).

This facsimile of a seventeenth-century approach to teaching children both Latin and French (now itself a rarity) was issued by Georges Vicaire, the bibliographer of French gastronomy. Vicaire attributed this educational oddity to the enterprise of Claude Michard of Dijon, the Burgundian printer, since Burgundians proverbially have "guts of silk," but subsequent research has demonstrated the existence of a non-Burgundian original. The figures here, so expressive in their naiveté, probably were not specially made but came out of the printer's stock on hand. Like every work intended to teach children to read, the original *Roti-Cochon* was quickly thumbed out of existence.

servant extorts from the tradesman for giving him her master's trade. The old servant's advice to the young is, succinctly expressed, "steal"; the corresponding advice to the employer is a resigned "let them steal." The custom of selecting a king to preside over the table on the eve of Epiphany and of having those in attendance say: "Le roi boit!" each time the king drank, was so prevalent that the festival itself was called "Roi-Boit." Jean Deslyons, dean of the cathedral at Senlis, attacked the licentiousness of "Roi-Boit" in his address to the theologians of France, the *Discours ecclesiastique contre le paganisme des roys de la feve et du Roi-Boit* (Paris: Despres, 1664). He was answered in the same year by Nicolas Barthélemy, a lawyer in Senlis, in the *Apologie dv banquet sanctifié*. J. B. Bullet wrote the last of these books, *Du festin de Roi-Boit* (Besancon, 1762), as a historian rather than a moralist.

THIS next group of books has been put aside so that we may gloss the sentence earlier in this chapter beginning "No French cookbook appeared in the first half of the seventeenth century . . .," and at the same time examine the notion that the arrival of Catherine de Medici at the court of France in 1533 brought about a culinary revolution. To do so we shall have to call upon a witness not in our collections, the *Grand Cuisinier de toute cuisine,* also titled *Fleur de toute cuisine,* a fourteenth-century manuscript revised by Pierre Pidoux and published in 1540. The only French cookbook to appear after 1533 and before 1651, it has gone through four editions by 1575, all now so rare that in preparing his *Bibliographie gastronomique* in 1890 Vicaire could not find a copy anywhere. The popularity of Pidoux's medieval text argues forcibly that the hypothesis of a Medicean culinary revolution should be dismissed as unproved and unprovable.

The Bitting Collection has both the books following Pidoux, the *Thrésor de santé* (Lyon: I.A. Huguetan, 1607) by "one of the most famous and celebrated doctors of the century" (probably the publisher himself) and the *Pourtraict de la santé (Paris: C. Morel, 1606),* which is really by a great physician, Joseph Du Chesne, Paracelsian chemist, and doctor to Henri IV. These are, as the titles indicate, health regime books first and cookbooks second. While the first work is somewhat more moderate in the uses of spices than the second, neither can be thought of as embodying a culinary revolution. The fact remains that no specialized cookbook appeared until La Varenne's *Le Cuisinier françois* in 1651.

Moreover, if the health regime and "whole house" books are excluded, *Le Cuisinier françois* is not only the first cookbook to appear in the seventeenth century but the first in the more than a hundred years by which it is separated from Pierre Pidoux.

The Bitting books do demonstrate an unquestionable Italian influence on French Renaissance cookery, but one which cannot be linked with Catherine de Medici's marriage in 1533. The *Epulario* of Rosselli, in the Bitting Collection in an eighteenth-century Venetian edition, was early translated in both France and England, where it was styled *The Italian Banquet*. However, Rosselli's recipes were taken entirely from Platina, who was first translated into French in 1505, more than a quarter of a century before Catherine came to Paris. The *Bastiment de receptes* (Lyon: A Lescu de Coloigne, 1541) is a translation of the work in which the Italians opened up a new area—jams, jellies, candied fruits, and sweets of all kinds—into which the French eagerly rushed. In its other pages the *Bastiment de receptes* is medieval, a "book of secrets" giving perfume recipes and home sick-room remedies. The Bitting copy of the first edition is unique in this country and, Mrs. Bitting thought, in the world. Certainly this edition is not reported in the catalogs of the British Library or the Bibliothèque nationale.

L ASTLY, there is a rather large grouping of books concerned with the refreshments that ease and grace social life by lubricating conversation and stimulating individual wit without the possible consequences of the hard liquors. This literature explains the equation café = coffee, "divine coffee unknown to Virgil but adored by Voltaire," which the abbé Delille sang because "it gladdens the heart without altering the head (sans alterer la tête, il épanouit la coeur.)" Like the café, the salon was a social invention, a direct working of the seventeenth-century wish to humanize the world by social intercourse. The artists still congregate in the cafés, because the spectator attitude into which the café habitué falls is the same as the analytical observation of the painter and writer. To represent the café, the Bittings chose Maximilian Rude's *Tout-Paris au café* (Paris: M. Dreyfous, 1875) and Alfred Delvau's *Histoire anecdotique* (Paris: E. Dentu, 1862.) While both works will always be marginally interesting—Rude was a friend of Baudelaire and Delvau's work is illustrated by Courbet and Rops—perhaps neither is more than minimally informative.

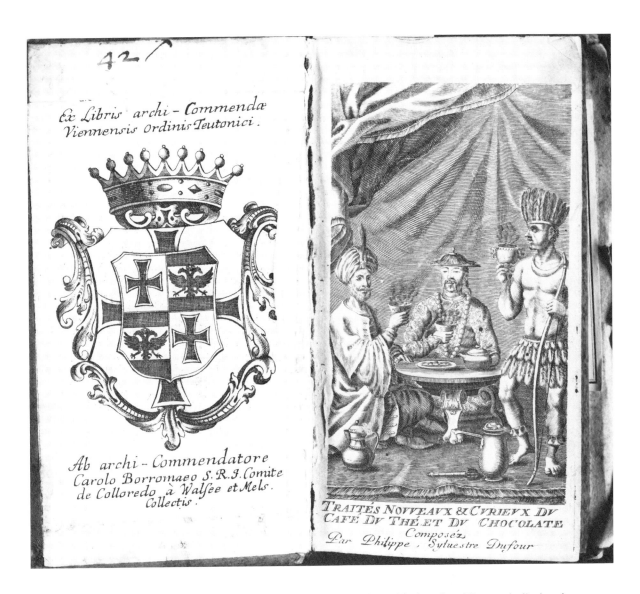

TRAITÉS NOVVEAVX & CVRIEVX DV CAFE DV THÉ ET DV CHOCOLATE Composéz Par Philippe, Sylvestre Dufour

Philippe Dufour, *Traitez nouveaux & curieux du café, du thé et du chocolate* (La Haye: A. Moetjens, 1865).

Dufour's frontispiece shows the three new drinks in the hands of men of their country of origin. First is the Turk or Arab with coffee, which then, like tea, was drunk out of a handle-less cup; in the middle, a Chinese with tea; next, an Indian with chocolate. The vessels displayed before the figures have retained their form until the present day: the pear-shaped coffee mug, the wide-bellied teapot, and the thin, ovaloid chocolate pot with the beater. The striking bookplate carries the arms of a member of the Colleredo-Melz und Wallsee family, one of the most illustrious in the history of the Holy Roman Empire.

The history of café refreshments can be begun in January 1660 when on his return from Italy the maître d'hôtel Audiger found employment in the households of Colbert and the duc de Beauvilliers while waiting a privilege to sell "all kinds of liqueurs made in the Italian manner." The title of Audiger's book (the Bitting Collection has the first and second editions, 1692 and 1700) points to his two occupations. He is maître d'hôtel in the first half, *La Maison regleé et l'art de diriger la maison d'un grand seigneur,* where he is in the tradition of the old "whole house" book instructing on the conduct of the seigneurial home. He is *limonadier* (maker of café refreshments) in the second part of the title, *Avec la veritable méthode de faire toutes sortes d'essences d'eaux de liqueurs, fortes & rafraichissantes à la mode d'Italie,* and as *limonadier* he is a pioneer. Book Four of *La Maison regleé* describes the distillation of liqueurs from flowers, fruits, and grains and the preparation of creams, sherbets, chocolate, tea, and coffee, of which, he says, "I was one of the three who made the fashion." At his shop in the Palais Royal after 1680, Audiger furnished the court and the great lords with those things whose making his book describes.

The "fashion" of coffee of which Audiger talks was promoted by *De l'vsage dv caphé, dv thé, et dv chocolate,* an amalgam to whose making Ph.-Sylvestre Dufour and Jacob Spon contributed as yet precisely undetermined parts. The Bitting Collection has the 1671 Lyon first edition and its reappearances as *Traitez nouveaux et curieux* in 1685 in Lyon, Paris, and The Hague, and in Latin translation in Paris in 1691 and Geneva in 1699. The rival coffee book, *Le Bon Usage du thé du caffé et du chocolat* of Nicolas Blegny, charged by the King with testing all new medical remedies, is in the Bitting Collection in the first edition of 1689 with all of Hainzelman's curious plates. One of the plates in Jean de la Roque's *Voyage de l'Arabie heureuse* (Amsterdam: Steenhouwer et Vytwerf, 1716) may be the first generally correct depiction of "Mocha's berry" in its home in the land that the maps then called "Arabia felix." Before the outbreak of the French Revolution, the army doctor André Gentil's *Dissertation sur le caffé* (Paris, 1787) and the *Étrennes à tous les amateurs de café* (Paris: Hotel de Bouthillier, 1789) indicated that coffee had ceased to be a fashion and become a staple. The historian Michelet depicts coffee as the great animator of the intellectual life of Paris: the light Arab mocha, the timid beginnings under Louis XIV; the strong coffee of the island of Bourbon, Montesquieu and Voltaire; and finally, the exciting, light, nervous coffee of San Domingo, the *Encyclopédie.*

THE books that will be listed here are prime sources for the history of liqueurs, the characters of which include *populo* (anis-based, like today's *pastis*), cinnamon-based *rossolis, eau d'or, parfait amour,* and *ratafia,* greatest of the *potions cordiales* composed for the old Louis XIV, which we now call simply cordials. Comment on this history is provided by two members of the circle of Curnonsky, Comte Austin de Croze in *Ésprit de liqueurs* (Paris, 1928) and Maurice des Ombiaux in *Nobilaire des eaux-de-vie et liqueurs de France* (Liège: J. Mawet, 1927). Paul Claquesin's standard history of the limonadier-distiller corporation (*Histoire du communauté des distillateurs.* Paris: Cerf, 1910) is, the bookseller's catalogs say, *rare et recherché* for its twenty-nine plates.

By 1704 the corporation of limonadiers was doing so well that the king suppressed it so that he might again sell its privileges. Pierre Masson's *Parfait Limonadier, ou, la manière de preparer le thé, le caffé, et le chocolat & autres liquers (!) chaudes et froides* was published in the next year by C. Moette of Paris. The *Traité des liqueurs, esprits, ou essences* of the Belgian Du Verger appeared in Louvain in 1728 and is followed in our collections by Dejean's *Traité raisonné de la distillation* in the fourth edition of 1778. Polycarpe Poncelet thought Dejean's use of water excessive and prima facie proof of an intention to enrich corporation members. Poncelet's own 1755 *Nouvelle Chymie du goût et de l'odorat* (the Bitting copy of the 1800 edition) is notable for its confusion of the sense modalities. He proposes the existence of a gamut of flavors like that of sound, a gustatory gamut whose notes are acid: do, insipid: re, sweet: me, bitter: fa, bittersweet: sol, austere: la, and piquant: ti. J. K. Huysmans found in Poncelet the idea of an organ of liqueurs to provide music for the tongue and palate which he used in *À Rebours.*

Maradon, publisher of Grimod de la Reynière's *Almanach des gourmands,* also issued J. Machet's *Le Confiseur moderne* (1803, 1806). Machet talks of "tablets" of bouillon and of "portable" lemon, which he says would be "very precious for sailors and travelers." Bouillon-Lagrange's 1807 *Art de composer facilement et à peu de frais, les liqueurs de table* says Poncelet is not to be taken seriously. Bouillon-Lagrange himself must be taken seriously, for he appears in very good company in Adophe Fosset's *Encyclopédie domestique . . . extraits des ouvrages speciaux de M. Appert, Berthollet, Bouillon-Lagrange* (Paris: Raymond, 1822). Most interesting are the 1779 *Art du distillateur et marchand des liqueurs* and the 1804 *Art du limonadier* "extracted from the best writers . . . and principally from Dubuisson," who is also the unacknowledged author of the first-named work. We shall return to Dubuis-

Bibliothèque d'un Gourmand

ALMANACH
DES GOURMANDS,
OU
CALENDRIER NUTRITIF

SERVANT DE GUIDE DANS LES MOYENS DE
FAIRE EXCELLENTE CHÈRE;

Suivi de l'Itinéraire d'un Gourmand dans
divers quartiers de Paris, et de quelques
Variétés morales, nutritives, Anecdotes
gourmandes, etc.

PAR UN VIEUX AMATEUR.

SECONDE ÉDITION
revue et corrigée.

Tanquam leo rugiens, circuit
quærens quem devoret.
S. Petr. epist. 1, cap. VI, vers. 8.

A PARIS,

Chez MARADAN, Libraire, rue Pavée-
Saint-André-des-Arcs, n°. 16.

AN XI. — 1803.

Almanach des gourmands...par un vieux amateur
Paris: Chez Maradan, 1803).

Grimod de la Reynière's recent editor, J.C. Bonnet, thinks his basic theme to be the comparison of cookery and its preliminaries to an author's elaboration of a draft text. Bonnet points to the "mots=mets" equation displayed by this illustration of the library of the gourmet and to sentences like: "Vinegar enhances the flavor of the dish and epigrammatizes it into a kind of perfume." One can also think that Grimod de la Reynière saw himself as a Byronic figure (complete with deformity) writing for "the happy few" who like him understood life as an affirmation of personality.

son after taking the limonadier literature through Louis XVIII with Lenormand's *Art du distillateur des eaux-de-vie et des spirits* (Paris, 1817), whose plates show the distillation apparatus, and the 1825 Manuel Roret edition of the very popular *Manuel du limonadier,* "useful for all persons who find diversion in improving the pleasant sweetness of life." In the latter the author, "Cardelli" (Henri Duval), gives a process for instant coffee.

The *Almanach des gourmands* of 1808 laments that the Caveau and Zoppi were not what they were in the days of Dubuisson. The Caveau is known to the historians of gastronomy for the songs and poems of the three or four epicurean societies that have taken that name. Zoppi is known to historians of literature in the very broadest sense, for Zoppi was once Procope. Dubuisson of Zoppi's, the author of *L'Art du limonadier,* is the heir and continuer of that Francesco Procopio dei Coltelli who in 1686 furnished his establishment in what is now the rue de l'Ancienne-Comédie with elegant mirrors, chandeliers, and marble tables and hung the latest newspapers from the pipe of the stove that heated the café. Along with coffee he sold preserves, candied fruit, maraschino, crême de roses, fruit wines, and ices, the refreshments whose making Audiger had described. In 1689, the Comédie-Française opened across the street with a double bill of Racine and Molière, and the theater-goers, actors, authors, and their hangers-on made Procope the first literary café. Michelet says that the coffee drinkers at Procope during the Regency saw the French Revolution at the bottom of their cups. At any rate, on July 14, 1789, Camille Desmoulins mounted a table at the Café de la Régence to exhort the mob to storm the Bastille, and the café entered political history.

The geographic center of café life of Paris has changed, going from Montmartre to Montparnasse and, most recently, to Saint-Germain-des-Près. Diderot can represent the artists who imbibed ideas and personalities in the café in the eighteenth century; perhaps Verlaine, who went to the café "to drink, to talk, to dream," those in the nineteenth century. The French think the Jean-Paul Sartre of the Café Flore the café figure of our times; Americans remember the Hemingway of *A Moveable Feast.* When Hemingway lived at 113 rue Notre Dame des Champs, over the sawmill, he would go to Deux Magots and Chez Lipp to work. There, accompanied sometimes by Master Bumby, who would sip a glass of grenadine, he wrote *Three Novels & Ten Poems* and *in our time.* Paradoxically, Bohemia is a fiction but its capital has historically been Paris. The cafés of Paris have changed, but they have remained always the outpost of Bohemia, open to anyone with the price of a cognac or a cup of that coffee which Audiger "made the fashion."

Chapter Five

La Cuisine moderne

Je me suis emparé d'une heureuse matière;
Je chante l'Homme à Table, et dirai la manière
D'embellir un repas; je dirai le secret
D'augmenter les plaisirs d'un aimable banquet.
JOSEPH BERCHOUX

Be mine a new subject, both pleasant and gay,
I sing Man at Table, and here point out the way
To adorn a repast; the secret means I'll reveal
Of increasing the pleasures of a happy meal.

IN the Napoleonic period the French gastronomic writers popularized the high style of Versailles and eighteenth-century Paris to make all Frenchmen equal before the table. The import of this social shift downward is easiest explained by comparison with the English experience. The writers like Grimod de la Reynière, Berchoux, Brillat-Savarin, and Cussy who appear in *Classiques de la table,* the standard French nineteenth-century anthology of gastronomy, are all *ci-devants,* aristocratic survivors of the old regime. These men see themselves as hosts, or as drama critics reviewing the cook-actor's performance of a scenario prepared by the host-author, but never as cooks or housekeepers.

In a comparable English anthology, the writers of cookbooks for the middle-class housekeeper, like Mrs. Beeton, Mrs. Glasse, or Soyer, would have dominated. The difference is that in England, after the First Reform Bill, the middle class did not aspire to the culture of the aristocracy, insisting instead on its own values, and somehow getting them accepted by the aristocracy. The French gastronomic writers taught an aristocratic tradition to the socially ambitious bourgeoisie that had been put in power by the Revolution and was eager to assume the outward appearances of the old aristocracy. In addition to making fine cuisine an object of social aspiration at home, these writers gave French cuisine its special éclat abroad, so that every Western country today has two cuisines, its own and France's.

IT is said that in France everything ends in a song. Modern gastronomy may be said to have begun with a song, or more accurately with the four *"chants"* into which Joseph Berchoux divided his poem *La Gastronomie.* The word *gastronomy* is of Berchoux's coinage and like the word his poem was accepted everywhere. Three editions sold out in 1803, the first year; there were immediate translations into English, German, and Spanish. The Bitting Collection has the second edition of 1803 and an 1819 edition; Mrs. Pennell owned the Spanish translations of 1820 and 1830. Of the quadrivate of innovators of gastronomy with whom we shall be concerned—Brillat-Savarin, Grimod de la Reynière, Carême, and Berchoux—only the last has been left unstudied.[1] Some samples of Berchoux's alexandrines are provided here to show that he, as much as the others, was not born, as the French say, with his tongue in his pocket.

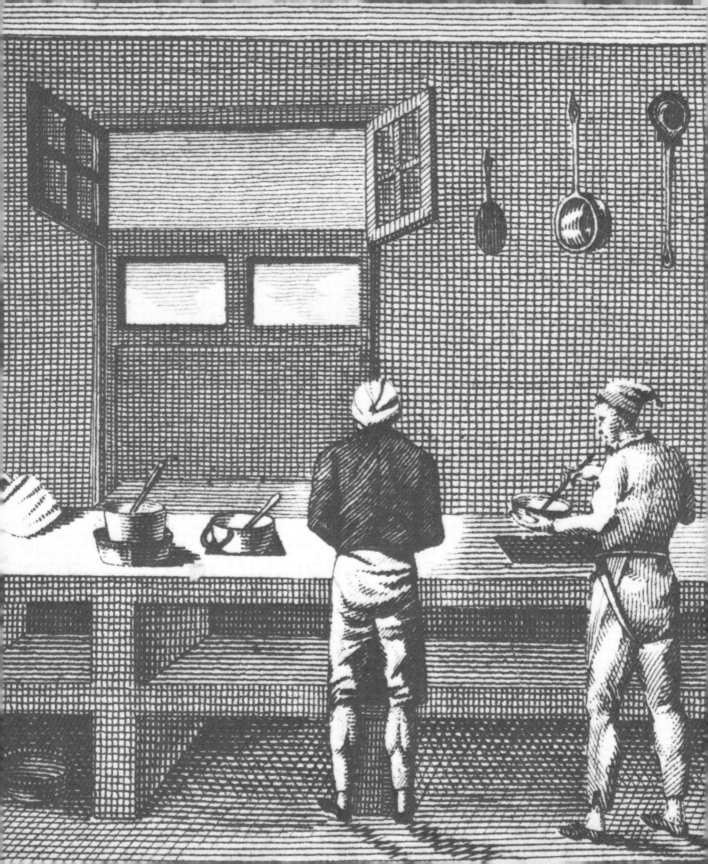

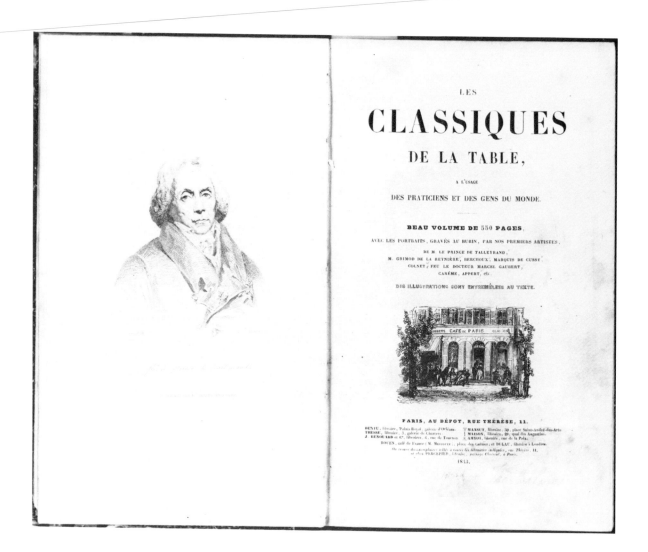

Alfred C. F. Fayot, *Les Classiques de la table* (Paris: Au Dépôt, Dentu, 1843).

Carême's advocacy is responsible for Fayot's introducing his anthology with the portrait of Talleyrand, the dandy who sold out in turn all the governments by which he had been bought. As France's representative abroad after the fall of Napoleon, Talleyrand informed his government that he needed casseroles more than diplomatic instructions. With Carême for cook and his young niece, the comtesse de Dino-Périgord, for hostess, Talleyrand gave dinners that quickly convinced the diplomats who had convened to punish France for Napoleon that Europe without France, indeed civilization without France, was inconceivable. Carême saw that "cuisine goes arm-in-arm with diplomacy" and presented his *Art de la cuisine au XIXe siècle* as a course in gastronomic diplomacy.

Berchoux recognized that a social upheaval like the French Revolution brings to the top many self-made men who stopped work too early as far as their manners were concerned. After the conventional references to Apicius and Vatel, he begins therefore with the host's central position in gastronomy to describe the art of selecting guests, maintaining them in harmony, anticipating their needs, and inspiring their intelligences. Brillat-Savarin will say that the host who does not give personal care to his dinners is not worthy of friendship. Berchoux has the distinction of having said it first and having said it in rhyme. Brillat-Savarin does not broach the manner in which wine spiritualizes the pleasures of the table. Berchoux catalogs the chromatic and gustatory gamut of the wines of France in bursts of song almost worthy of the subject. Conceding that wine robs men of their reason, he demands: how else can you lose so little and gain so much? "Has the reason you boast of with so much parade / By its precepts a change in your destiny made?"

Berchoux's most quoted lines are probably those warning against invitations welcoming you to a "potluck" or "family" dinner: "Souvenez-vous dans la cours de la vie / Un dîner sans façon est une perfidie." The English reader will find Berchoux's meaning in the Ephesian Antipholus' line in *The Comedy of Errors:* "A table full of welcomes makes not one dainty dish." When the servant argues "Good meat, sir, is common, that every churl affords," Autolycus refutes him decisively: "And welcome's more common, for that's nothing but words." Dr. Johnson remarked after one saddening experience that a family dinner is not a dinner to invite a man to: accept invitations only from those who will honor you culinarily. A personal favorite describes that poignant last moment when the coffee has chased away the vapor of the wine and the poet, now condemned to sobriety, hears the critics' final judgement, to which he himself must agree, "Un poème jamais ne valût un dîner." A poem is never worth a dinner, not even Berchoux's *La Gastronomie*.

First among the epigoni of Berchoux is Gouriet, whose *L'Antigastronomie* (Paris: Hubert, 1806) presents itself as a "manuscript found in a pâté, augmented with important remarks." Gouriet seemingly deplores not gastronomy alone but all eating, a jeu d'esprit difficult to carry through 215 pages. Montbrison's *Propos de table* (Montpellier, 1805) appeared in various small editions inscribed to the author's friends. There are six "Propos" in our two editions; one understands that the number and the farcical element increase with each later edition. Honoré Blanc's *L'Echo des Alpes* (Paris: Librairie de l'industrie, 1827) reprints his early verse

d'après nature

like "Les Rayolles," and adds verse like "L'Éloge du marasquin." Rayolles, something like the Italian ravioli, are a specialty of Provençal fetes so that Blanc might be considered an early advocate of regional cookery. His best claim to posterity's attention is a very early (1814) guide to Paris restaurants, not in these collections. Trambly's *L'Oenologie* (Chalons-sur-Saône, 1820) celebrates the wines of Burgundy and Champagne to demonstrate the superiority of Bacchus over Comus as a source of poetic inspiration. These poetasters are named here to indicate public taste; they wrote nothing without which the literature of gastronomy would have been irreparably damaged.

This statement is less true of some of their successors: Méry's *Le Café* (Paris: J. Ledoyen, 1837), Leon de Fos's *Gastronomiana* (Paris, 1870), and Franc-Nohain's *La Nouvelle Cuisinière bourgeoise. Plaisirs de la table et scènes du ménage* (Paris: Revue blanche, 1900). Mery's *Le Café* stands the comparison with anything in Berchoux, and his poem on the bouillabaise of his native Marseilles is a classic in the genre. It is not true at all of Raoul Ponchon, whose friends collected the verses he had scattered through a hundred journals to publish *Muse au cabaret* (Paris: H. Cyral, 1925). Curnonsky called Ponchon the greatest Bacchic poet; Guillaume Apollinaire thought him a great poet, without subject limitation. While all verse is untranslatable, light verse is absolutely untranslatable, so we quote only Ponchon's prose: "I know nothing about wines, I am not a sommelier. But when I have drunk wine it is I who become the bottle. The wine is in me, it ferments, the cork jumps . . . and I begin to sing."

Montbrison had dedicated his *Propos de table* equally to Berchoux, "the Boileau," and to Grimod de la Reynière, "the Pascal of the table." His family's fortune lost in the Revolution, this gastronomic Pascal worked first as a drama critic. In 1803, rightly judging the times, he published the first of the *Almanach des gourmands* and instituted a *jury dégustateur,* a tasting jury to grant seals of approval to the butchers, grocers, bakers, and cooks eager for mention in the next almanac. The frontispiece for the 1805 *Almanach* (like all the others composed by Grimod de la Reynière, designed by Durand, and engraved by Mariage) shows the eight judges solemnly eating while the applicants anxiously wait their verdict.

By 1807 the *Almanach des gourmands* had twenty-two thousand subscribers. There were two editions in 1803, but there were none in 1809 and 1811, so that on its completion in 1812 the now very rare *Almanach des gourmands* set totaled eight volumes. The stoppages were due to the litigation to be expected when a com-

This portrait of Joseph Berchoux and the ones of Grimod de la Reynière and Carême that follow are from *Les Classiques de la table.*

plaint about a shopkeeper began: "It is not because the widow Fontaine is a bad woman whose first husband died of frustration and whose second killed himself but because swindling and theft seem to be her natural elements that I call her . . . ." In 1808 Grimod de la Reynière also published the strikingly illustrated *Manuel des amphitryons*, which sometimes rather condescendingly instructs the new host in carving, menu-making, and *politesse gourmande*. The reviewers nicknamed the book Père-Lachaise after the cemetery for its brief, epitaph-like statements about the innovators of dishes and techniques in cookery.

Grimod de la Reynière expressed his significance in the development of the literature in a letter to the marquis de Cussy (March 5, 1825). His *Almanachs,* he observed, were not written "in the style of 'dish and serve hot' that is the *gloria mundi* of the cookbook writers. In them appears for the first time the kind of writing that is entitled *littérature gourmande*." The basic problem in communicating the appreciation of food is still that tastes and flavors with their variabilities do not allow the analysis into distinct elements that scientific methodology requires. Brillat-Savarin stated the dimensions of the problem:

> . . . given the fact that there exists an indefinite series of simple tastes which can change according to the number and variety of their combinations, we should need a whole new language to describe all these effects, and mountains of folio foolscap to define them, and unknown numerical characters for their classification.

Grimod de la Reynière untied the Gordian knot by cutting it, that is, by rejecting the whole concept of a Linnean-like taxonomy of flavors, offering instead of science, metaphor and simile—that is, literature. He demonstrated by example that the skilled writer's pen can nuance the differences of taste and flavor *à l'infini*. A contemporary, the anonymous author of *Le Cuisinier des cuisiniers* (Paris, 1825), discerning that Grimod de la Reynière represented a new departure in language, foresaw immortality for him "as long as we eat in France, [because] he ennobled the language while at the same time improving the taste, proving that the genius of our culinary science could be allied to all the gifts of the intelligence."

Grimod de la Reynière's *Almanach des gourmands* sets the pattern for gastronomical almanacs: the calendar of seasonal dishes, the walk around Paris to judge restaurants and provision merchants and to recall dinners and recipes, the light verse, special articles, saws, maxims, and learned instances of the code of *"politesse gourmande."* Horace Raisson and Léon Thiessé used the pseudonym A. B. Périgord (chosen perhaps because Périgord is Talleyrand's birthplace) for

Denon pinx.   Blanchard sc.

Mr. Grimod de la Reynière.

publication of three issues (1824–26) of the *Nouvel Almanach des gourmands*. They apostrophize Grimod de la Reynière as the restorer of the old cuisine, whose "voice has never ceased to maintain in our hearts the traditions of the dinners of yesterday." The frontispiece of the first *Nouvel Almanach*, like that in the Grimod de la Reynière *Almanach*, shows a room walled with books in which the gourmet sits at a table ready to indite the oracles of gastronomy. The map of the gastronomic specialties of France, borrowed from Cadet de Gassicourt's *Cours gastronomique*, is not colored in the Bitting almanac. The Library's copy of A. B. Périgord's *Trésor de la cuisinière et de la maîtresse de la maison* belongs to the "seventh edition," that is, to one of the six or seven appearing between 1875 and 1893 designated as the seventh edition.

The earliest of the Bitting almanacs is the *Almanach du comestible, contenant une suite de notices sur les repas des anciens et modernes,* which is the second supplement to the *Almanach du comestible nécessaire aux personnes de bon goût* that had appeared in 1778. The two supplements are impossible to date. According to Grand-Carteret, the bibliographer of French almanacs, our supplement appeared until 1791 with unchanged content under a cover carrying the caption "for the present year" and was released again in 1811 in the same way. The *Almanach des chasseurs et des gourmands* is an undated mid-nineteenth-century combination of gastronomy and the hunt. Audot, the Parisian publishing house most closely identified with cookery, addressed an audience of housewives and gourmets in *Almanach des ménagères et des gastronomes* in 1854. However, the great mid-century almanacs are the work of the gastronomic journalist Charles Monselet, friend of Dumas and the baron de Brisse, remembered by Anatole France as a "pot-au-feu with wings." The Bitting Collection holds the *Almanach des gourmands pour 1862,* the *Double almanach gourmand* (1866), the *Triple almanach gourmand* (1867), and their successors, the *Almanach gourmand* for 1868, 1869, and 1870, in addition to Monselet's *Gastronomie* (Paris: Charpentier, 1874). The contributors to Monselet's almanacs include the most important gastronomic writers of the time— Dumas, for example, writing articles on mustard and macaroni *au stuffato*. Monselet dedicated the *Double almanach gourmand* to Grimod de la Reynière, "he whose work has been most frequently consulted and stolen . . . and who under the Empire repaired the chain of gastronomic tradition broken by the Revolution." The latest of our almanacs, that published by F. M. Dumas in 1904, returns to Grimod de la Reynière's title: *Almanach des gourmands*.

In a biographic sketch for Michaud's *Biographie universelle,* Honoré Balzac wrote: "Since the sixteenth century, except for La Rochefaucauld and La Bruyère, no prose writer has known how to give a phrase so vigorous a profile." He was talking of Brillat-Savarin, author of the *Physiologie du goût*, excellently edited in this country by M. F. K. Fisher and in France by Roland Barthes, most recent of the *grands maîtres à penser* that the French set up over themselves from time to time. Brillat-Savarin published the first edition in 1825 at his own expense. On his death two months later, the estate sold the rights to the printer for the price of a good horse. Since then the book has been translated into many languages and gone into edition after edition in conformity with the biblical precept (as valid in publishing as in economics) that "to everyone who has will more be given."

The Bitting and Pennell collections hold the 1828 second Paris edition of the *Physiologie du goût* and the subsequent Paris editions of 1834, 1840, 1841, 1852, and 1926; the London editions of 1859 and 1889; the New York editions of 1870, 1884, and 1926; and the Philadelphia edition of 1854. The most beautiful copy in the Library of Congress is either the 1940 Bibliophiles du palais edition illustrated by Raoul Dufy or the 1961 version by Les Francs-bibliophiles with engravings by Mario Avati, both in our Rosenwald Collection. Perhaps most interesting for the history of literature is the 1838 edition that began the reprint series whose success enabled Charpentier to become the great publisher of nineteenth-century French romanticism. The fact is not without irony, since there is nothing in Brillat-Savarin of either romanticism or the nineteenth century. As Curnonsky recognized, Brillat-Savarin was an *honnête homme* of the seventeenth century. His work is not the revelation of a personal esthetics but a discourse on gastronomy in relation to history, geography, and social psychology in the aphoristically brief, surgically precise manner of the *Encyclopédie*. To attempt a summary would be an impertinence.

However, it cannot be said of Brillat-Savarin, as Matthew Arnold said of Shakespeare, "Others abide our question, Thou art free." Carême wrote that Brillat-Savarin recommended strong and vulgar things, was witty only in his writings, and "after dinner I have seen him fall asleep." In *Les Paradis artificiels* Baudelaire recoils in horror at Brillat-Savarin's surely very odd notion that the introduction of tea would lead Frenchmen away from wine. Baudelaire's indignation cannot be dismissed by reference to his own frequent lapses in taste. The kettle is none the less black for having been called so by the pot. Balzac worked on coffee and so was indifferent to wine, but he did wonder at Brillat-Savarin's failure to mention the satellite minor arts that enhance the pleasures of the table. It

A. BLAIZOT Libraire
22 rue Le Peletier PARIS

Albert Robida, *Les Aphorismes de Brillat Savarin* (Paris: A. Blaizot, 1905).

The artist Robida, contributor to *La Vie Parisienne* and *Caricature,* is remembered today for his science-fiction projections of the future. Perhaps Robida was struck by the fact that the only depiction of appetite in Brillat-Savarin should have been that of a woman, "une jolie gourmande sous armes." While the medieval moralists denied women a soul, most gastronomic writers would have denied them a palate. Grimod de la Reynière's use of sexual metaphor in describing new dishes reveals his view of woman-as-thing. Monselet and Baron de Brisse thought gastronomy unattainable not only for women but for one who

> . . . thinks less of good eating
>   than the whisper
> (when seated next him) of
>   some pretty lisper.
> Byron, *Don Juan.* (15.70)

should be remembered that in the *Traité de la vie élégante* Balzac's theme is the interdependence of the "accessories of life." Nelson Roqueplan saw nothing in the *Physiologie du goût* which could not have been written by many others and criticized specifically a theory of frying which calls the batter a kind of casing when it should be a second skin, light but adhering. Charles Monselet made a journalistic career of deriding Brillat-Savarin ("a drinker of seltzer water") for his over-intellectualization, as compared to the robustness of Grimod de la Reynière. It can be agreed that Brillat-Savarin is the greatest of gastronomic writers only if, like André Gide conceding Victor Hugo to be the greatest of French poets, one hastens to add: "Alas!"

Curnonsky called Lucien Tendret, author of *La Table au pays de Brillat-Savarin* (Belley: L. Bailly fils, 1892), "the second Brillat-Savarin." Tendret drew upon Brillat-Savarin family reminiscences for a lovingly written account (now *rarissime*) of the cuisine of Bugey, surely among the richest of the provinces of France. However, the easy presumption that Tendret's recipes, because of their association with his subject, are providential revelations has been questioned. A reviewer of Tendret in the authoritative journal *Grándgousier* (edited by Dr. Gottschalk of *Larousse gastronomique)* was horrified at the famous *pâté L'Oreillier de la belle Aurore* which is served cold, although containing veal sweetbreads and beef marrow.

Another accepted classic in the literary expression of transcendental gastronomy is Marcel Rouff's *La Vie et la passion de Dodin-Bouffant* (Paris, 1928). The protagonist here is the pot-au-feu served by Dodin-Bouffant to check and mate the pretentions to gastronomic preeminence of a visiting prince. There is a fine bravura piece in which the dish is eaten—not cooked. Rouff gives descriptions, not recipes, in conformance with Curnonsky's edict demanding the separation of cook and gastronomer. The gastronomer is the public and without him there would be no theater, but it suffices to appreciate Molière without writing a comedy oneself. The "pot-au-feu de Dodin-Bouffant" has become the Platonic archtype, the quiddity, of the superlative in food, although Brillat-Savarin had downgraded the pot-au-feu, as he had overpraised the turkey. Of the books that attend on Tendret and Rouff, the two that seem most likely to retain their interest are Pierre de Pressac's *Considérations sur la cuisine* (Paris: Gallimard, 1931) and the *Lettres à un gourmet* (Paris: Compagnie des graphiques, 1926) of "Fingosier," identified as "formerly cloistral prior of the Abbey of Sainte-Chergueule." "Pressac on the ideal cookbook" is quoted by Elizabeth David, "Fingosier on tripes à la mode de Caen" by the Academie des gastronomes' *Cuisine française. Recettes classiques.*

The last of the early innovators of gastronomy with whom these collections deal, Marie-Antonin Carême, was both cook and gastronomer, too strong a figure to be subsumed in only one category. When the imperial police questioned Grimod de la Reynière about his attitude toward Napoleon, he placated them by calling the Emperor a great man, adding, "Who knows how far he would have gone in the kitchen?" If Napoleon had gone into the kitchen, he would have been Carême. Carême's biography is that of the little lost child who founds an empire, Alexandre Dumas said, like those other little lost children, Theseus and Romulus. Carême's fate has been to live on in men's imaginations and to be spoken of as a nonpareil by after generations. Montagné and Nignon were probably the last great chefs to be directly influenced by Carême, but every cook knows the name for a perpetual search for perfection and an artistry never transcended.

Carême's body of doctrine is given in *Pâtissier royal parisien* (1841, 1854), *Pâtissier pittoresque* (1842), *Cuisinier parisien* (1828, 1842, 1858), *Art de la cuisine française au dix-neuvième siècle* (1828, 1858), and *Maitre d'hôtel français, traité de menus à servis à Paris, à Saint-Pétersbourg, à Londres, et à Vienne* (1822, 1842, 1854). His style is high neoclassic, cadentially tolling like Chateaubriand, causing one to wonder about the part played in the writing by M. F. Fayot, who later always signed himself "Secretary to the late Carême." The *Art de la cuisine française,* Carême's *summa,* was issued in five volumes, the last two of which were contributed by Plumery, trained in Talleyrand's household, but at the time cook to the Russian ambassador to France. The full title of *Maitre d'hôtel français* indicates that its menus were offered to George IV of England, Alexander of Russia, and Napoleon. Carême, the king of cooks, was fittingly the cook of kings.

An architect *manqué,* Carême himself would not have been happy in the simplicity of the present service practice, the *service à la Russe* introduced to Paris by Prince Kurakin in 1810. Yet his perceptions of his art medium were so selfless that he recommended, for bourgeois tables at least, that four dishes be served instead of eight and that they be served one after the other. The portraits of the great cooks of the preceding generation—Iliot, Robert, Lefèvre, Laguipière—in Carême's frontispieces are his acknowledgments of the great eighteenth-century tradition in which he worked, but which he materially simplified, for example, by rejecting the mixing of meat and fish and emphasizing the fumets, the light juices of meat and fish.[2] When Carême cooked for the Rothchilds, Lady Morgan noted

Steuben pinx.   Blanchard sc.

Antonin Carême.
de Paris.

Grand Buffet de la Cuisine moderne.

In *Le Pâtissier pittoresque* there are more than two hundred fifty line drawings of towering *pièces montées,* that is, windmills, military and naval equipment, lyres, harps, and Turkish mosques and Greek temples. Carême called pastry the most important branch of architecture. His own very real proficiency in architecture itself was shown by his *Recueil de projets* for St. Petersburg, which Tsar Aleksandr rewarded with diamonds. In his long hours of study Carême found and imitated for his table settings the landscape designs of Johann Kraft's *Maison de la campagne* and George Louis Le Rouge's *Jardinier anglo-chinoise.*

"every dish had its natural aroma; all the vegetables kept their color."[3] J. P. Aron theorizes that Carême sought to de-nature food in order to make it purely cultural, an artifact of human creativity.[4] Aron explains Lady Morgan's testimony, but does not succeed in explaining it away.

BERCHOUX, Grimod de la Reynière, Brillat-Savarin, and Carême are extensively represented in the standard anthology *Classiques de la table* published in 1843 by M. J. Fayot, "Secretary to the late Carême." The most important of the newcomers introduced are Colnet, of whose *Art de dîner en ville* we have no separate example, and the marquis de Cussy, who published nowhere else. Colnet continues the classical theme of the parasite and asks for a return of the hospitality offered hungry littérateurs by the salons of the eighteenth century. In addition, *Classiques de la table* has much ballast in the form of fugitive verse from poets like Panard, most interesting historically because of his founding of the first Caveau, and Béranger, certainly the greatest of all French popular poets. The title page vignette in the Bitting 1843 first edition is of the Café de Paris. The fourteen portraits in this edition of the gastronomic writers anthologized are pasted on the sheet as if to look like engravings. The 1848 edition repeats the 1843 text but has only five portraits. Justin Amero added a preface to his 1853 edition without increasing the number of portraits.

The rather disjointed *Art culinaire* of Louis de Cussy appearing in *Classiques de la table* is probably some notes preliminary to writing or Fayot's memories of Cussy's conversation. A marquis in the *Ancien régime,* Cussy had become a baron in the Empire by serving Napoleon as *préfet de palais.* He took over Grimod de la Reynière's place on the *jury dégustateur* and was thought the prince of gourmets in his time. His *Art culinaire* frequently falls into the seventeenth-century aphorism form. Despite the fact that his own name is associated with an onion soup made with cognac, he says, for example, "Soup is the preface to the meal and a good meal does not need a preface." Carême, who has five hundred soup recipes in his *Art de la cuisine française,* quarreled with him over this un-French heterodoxy. Cussy thought roasting the great art: "Happy those who are born rôtisseurs; I don't know any." Sometimes the aphorism form betrays Cussy. He says, for example, "Roasting is at once nothing and an immensity (à la fois rien et l'immensité)." This has the look of a very good aphorism and it is probably ungrateful of the reader to wonder what it means. Cussy is at his best in demolish-

Cadet de Gassicourt, *Cours gastronomique* (Paris: Capelle et Renand, 1809).

This is the first appearance in book form of the gastronomic map of France that would be reprinted frequently. Tourcaty, the designer and engraver, names the dish for which each place is famed and, on the rocks of the grotto of Epicurus, has written the names of members of the various epicurean societies known as the Caveau. The publisher of the *Cours gastronomique*, Capelle, had revived the Caveau by taking over the membership of the Vaudeville, the society which had published the *Dîners de vaudeville* in 1796. Capelle's Caveau, the third, met on the twentieth of each month at the Rocher de Cancale, which Balzac called "simply the best restaurant in the world." Edgar Allen Poe in "Some Passages in the Life of a Lion" represents the gastronomic lion by M. Fricassée of the Rocher de Cancale.

ing the legend of Vatel foisted upon posterity by that chatterer Madame de Seveigné. Vatel, the maître d'hôtel who committed suicide when an emergency arose was in effect deserting before the enemy. Cussy had had the advantage of living with Napoleon and so remarked simply that a good general always keeps something in reserve and that Vatel's fate would not have happened to Carême.

One is at first surprised not to find in the *Classiques de la table* the *Neophysiologie du goût* of the man baptized simply Maurice Cousin but representing himself as the comte de Courchamps, scion of an old Irish Jacobite family. The reason possibly is that in 1841 Courchamps had plagiarized a novel by the Polish count Adam Potocki, changing only the title and the author's name, and had been savaged in the newspapers for this latest partition of Poland. Roger de Beauvoir's *Soupers de mon temps* depicts his astonishment at their first meeting, when Courchamps received him in the feminine garb he donned to elude the enemies his paranoia saw everywhere. In the 1830s Courchamps's presence made the fortune of the restaurants he patronized, and other diners would ask him to select their meals for them. The Bitting Collection copy of Courchamps's *Neophysiologie du goût* is the second edition, titled *Dictionnaire général de la cuisine française* when published in 1853. In addition to the dictionary-style entries heavily larded with literary and historical references, there are selections from Grimod de la Reynière, a section on French menus since the twelfth century, and a pharmacology. The hauteur that made Courchamps feared in the cafés appears in his introduction of his work as the replacement of all the books about the kitchen "of whose charlatanism, inadequacy, and obscurantism the public has had too much experience."

WE should not pass over the period of the First Empire without "meditating the consequences," as Brillat-Savarin says, of a new social institution, the restaurant. The first restaurateurs were technically-trained men who had been dislocated by the Revolution and sought a new, remunerative way of selling their talents. They had been the cooks of the prerevolutionary aristocracy. The first restaurants therefore were re-creations in marble, mahogany, bronze, silver, and great mirrors reflecting lights and flowers of the old princely households, giving concrete examples of the aristocratic gastronomy that the writers could only describe. The chefs like Escoffier, Montagné, Gilbert, and Nignon who shaped haute cuisine came out of the restaurants, along with recipes like Noel Peters's *homard à l'americaine* and the *Tour d'argent's canard au sang*. Contemporaries had lamented that, of all the things destroyed by the Revolution, gastronomy would be the hardest to restore, since there was no aristocratic social edifice to support it. However, if the Revolution had demolished the old structure supporting gastronomy, it had used the remnants for a new social invention, so that gastronomy arose anew from the restaurants, like the phoenix from its ashes.

The great cookbook of the first restaurants is *L'Art du cuisinier* of Beauvilliers, once in the employ of the comte de Provence. With Beauvilliers at the Taverne de Londres begins the history of the gastro-sexual Parisian pilgrimages of foreign nobility. Later the aristocracy moves to the Café Anglais, then to the Maison Dorée, and finally to the restaurant with a French proper name put into the English genitive form. At Maxim's, when art nouveau reigned and the women all looked like Mucha's posters of Sarah Bernhardt, the man in the corner ordering from the twenty-four page menu might be Edward, Prince of Wales, happily sure that at Maxim's he would be "recognized but not noticed." The restaurateurs of Paris created *poulet Demidoff* for the Russian dukes, *selles de chevreuil à la Metternich* for the German barons, and *poularde à l'Albuféra* for the Spanish grandees. Beauvilliers' own English recipes—"rosbif," "the true 'bifteck' as it is done in England," "plumbuting," and "misies paes"—come in with the curious French post-Waterloo anglomania that also brought in the Baudelairean dandy.

Cadet de Gassicourt, Cadet de Vaux, Parmentier, Delessert, and Appert are members of the generation of Grimod de la Reynière who do not appeear in *Classiques de la table* but must be mentioned. Charles Louis Cadet de Gassicourt was one of the joyous band of poetic epicures of the Caveau, to whom he dedicated the anecdotal, literary, and philosophical work called *Cours gastronomique* (Paris: Capelle et Renand, 1809). Another member was Comte Louis-Philippe de Ségur, state councillor and grand-master of ceremonies for Napoleon, chief author of *Étiquette du palais impérial* (Paris: Imprimerie impériale, 1808), which revived Louis XIV's dining protocol at the court of Napoleon. The personae of Cadet de Gassicourt's *Cours gastronomique* are a parvenu and his son who seek instruction in gastronomy from their "phagotechnician" teacher. The reader is made to understand that gastronomy is part of the national culture and that newcomers to the upper levels of society require education in it. The instructor disdains the "details of daily practice"—he is a gastronomer and not a cook—but uses every dish as a text for instruction in history, philosophy,

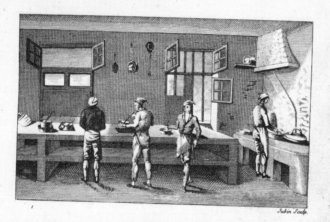

L'ART
DU CUISINIER,

PAR A. BEAUVILLIERS,

Ancien Officier de MONSIEUR, comte de Provence, attaché
aux Extraordinaires des Maisons royales, et actuellement
Restaurateur, rue de Richelieu, n° 26, à la grande Taverne
de Londres.

———

TOME PREMIER.

Jubin Sculp.

A PARIS,

CHEZ PILET, IMPRIMEUR-LIBRAIRE, RUE CHRISTINE, N° 5.

IL SE VEND AUSSI

CHEZ { COLNET, LIBRAIRE, QUAI DES PETITS-AUGUSTINS,
{ ET LENOIR, LIBRAIRE, RUE DE RICHELIEU, N° 35.

De Beauvilliers   1816.

Antoine Beauvilliers, *L'Art du cuisinier* (Paris: Pilet, 1816).

The 1814 date of publication should be corrected to 1816. *L'Art du cuisinier* can be thought an expansion of the menu Beauvilliers offered when, sword at side like an eighteenth-century maître d'hôtel, he welcomed Napoleon's conquerors ("nos amis les ennemis") who rushed to the Taverne de Londres to make up for the French food lost during the war. Beauvilliers never forgot a face and had the international restaurateur's talent for languages. Brillat-Savarin, who does not mention Carême, singled Beauvilliers out for praise. Carême, as was to be expected, thought him second-rate. In comparing the two, the English gastronomer Hayward used the distinction between classicist and romantic. Beauvilliers, he wrote, had exhausted the possibilities of the old world of art and Carême had invented a new one.

letters, and the arts as they relate to the table. On completion of the course, the students will be able to offer the dinner table conversation expected of every Frenchman.

Another of Cadet de Gassicourt's works in the Bitting Collection: *Le Thé, est-il plus nuisible qu'utile?* (Paris, 1800) is a reminder of the philanthropic activity of his cousin Cadet de Vaux, author of the very similar *Dissertation sur le café* (Paris, 1807) and of *L'Art de faire les vins* (Paris, 1803). These publications rise out of a concern for the quality of life for all Frenchmen that Cadet de Vaux showed elsewhere in founding the Free Bakery School to help Parmentier to popularize the potato, and in working with Delessert to organize soup kitchens in Napoleonic Paris. An American coming across Cadet de Vaux's history is pleased to discover that he and his cousin knew Benjamin Franklin, corresponded with him, and felt themselves inspired by him. When the bakery school was inaugurated (June 8, 1780), Franklin was in the audience, although he was indifferent to the potato. Always seeking converts to the Indian maize god (who Longfellow tells us is named Mondamin), Franklin gave Cadet de Vaux a copy of "Observations on Maize or Indian Corn," the last essay he wrote in Europe.

Antoine Parmentier's forty-year campaign against prejudice seems incredible today when *les frites* perfume the air of Paris (as if response to Sir John Falstaff's "Let the sky rain potatoes"), and Roland Barthes makes *"Bifteck et frites"* the subject of one of his *Mythologies*. The Bitting example of Parmentier on the potato is *Récherches sur les végétaux nourrissans . . . Avec des nouvelles observations sur la culture des pommes de terre* (Paris: Imprimerie royale, 1781). A pharmacist, like Cadet de Vaux, Parmentier devoted his career to the chemical evaluation of food, working passionately in many areas. He had learned, he said, that it is not enough to say what is good: it is necessary to say it in every way. Samples of his activity in these collections concern bread (*Parfait Boulanger*, 1788), wheat and flour (*Expériences et refléxions*, 1776), milk (*Précis d'expériences*, 18—?), and the use of grapes for sugar (*Instructions sur les sirops*, 1809).

Delessert is another of the selfless men of the period whose lines call to mind the passage in *Culture and Anarchy* in which Matthew Arnold says that "the impulses toward action, help, and beneficence . . . the noble aspiration to leave the world better or happier than we found it . . . come in as part of the grounds of culture, and the main and pre-eminent part." Delessert, a regent of the Banque de France as well as of the Bureau de bienfaisance, had founded the Société des soupes économiques, of which Cadet de Vaux was for a time president. Delessert's *Sur les fourneaux à la Rumford et les soupes économiques* (Paris: Labor, 1800) gives his experience in setting up soup kitchens using the newly invented Rumford stoves to make a pea, barley, and potato soup at a cost a seventh of that of the Paris hospital kitchens. The *Instruction sur les soupes économiques,* published without indication of authorship by the Imprimerie impériale, describes this welfare service in that horrible year 1812, when the survivors of Napoleon's Russian débacle could not get the hunger and cold out of their bodies. In that year also Delessert found the process by which to make beet sugar in quantities large enough to nullify the English blockade.

Beet sugar is one example of war as the mother of invention; another, contemporary with it, is commemorated by the presence in the Bitting gift of a bust of Nicholas Appert, which presides over the collection like a Roman household god. The Bittings purchased the first edition of Appert's great *Art de conserver,* the 1813 and 1831 editions retitled *Livre de tous les ménages,* the London translations of 1811 and 1812 called *The Art of Preserving All Kinds of Animal and Vegetable Substances,* and the Viennese editions of 1811 and 1812. Mrs. Bitting called her translation of the Appert first edition *The Book for all Households* (Chicago, 1920). Her glowing characterization of the man and his achievement is repeated here in part:

> His was the task of blazing a new path through the unknown and this he accomplished by short steps, always going forward and with confidence because that which he had achieved was well done. . . . In many ways Appert deserves to stand in the same relation to the food preserving industry as does Pasteur to the sciences of bacteriology and of medicine. . . . No single discovery has contributed more to modern food manufacturing nor to the general welfare of mankind.

In the Bitting Collection Charles Gellier's *Conservation de la viande et des matières organiques* . . . (Paris: H. Dunod et E. Pinat, 1913) represents the refrigeration concept that took the food industry one step further and Louis Pasteur's *Études sur le vinaigre* (Paris: Gautier-Villars, 1868) the process bearing his name on which Pasteur stumbled while seeking to preserve wine and milk.

THE 1828 Bourbon *Gastronome français, ou, l'art de bien vivre* (Paris: Charles Bechet) preceded the 1843 Orleanist *Classiques de la table* as an anthology of gastronomic literature but never attained its popularity. Along with Grimod de la Reynière and Cadet de Gassicourt the contributors are identified as members of the Caveau, then metamorphosed into the "Société épicurienne du Rocher de Cancale"; the contributions are largely reprints from Grimod de la Reynière's *Journal des gourmands et des belles* and from *Le Caveau moderne*. The editor is given as M. C.; the preliminary article is signed "the author of this article." Neither of these obscurities matters, unless the author of the preface is accepted to be the printer, who matters very much.

The modest printer's designation on the verso of the half title reads: "Imprimerie de H. Balzac/rue des Marais S. G., N 17." Balzac had begun in 1826 the mismanagement of a printing plant that would bring him into bankruptcy in early 1828. *Le Gastronome français* is one of the 167 publications of the Balzac press, apparently the model for that run by David Séchard in Balzac's *Illusions perdues*. In 1828 Balzac also printed the *Art de dîner en ville* of Marco de Saint-Hilaire, which the Bitting Collection has in an imperfect copy. It is the historian of the Balzac press, Georges Vicaire, who is also, curiously, the bibliographer of French culinary literature, who asserts that Balzac wrote the preliminary discourse for *Le Gastronome français*.[5] Immediately on leaving the rue des Marais Balzac joined Horace Raisson's stable of hacks. A Balzac biographer, André Billy, says that if not for the bankruptcy Balzac might have continued his insipid stories of love and adventure. The experience gave him his theme, for the Latin tag *pecunia non olet* to the contrary, Balzac's fictional world, where poor people are non-persons, surely stinks of money.

The most successful of Horace Raisson's potboilers were his light satires on conventions and manners presented in the form of the judicial code to amuse contemporaries still awed by the Code Napoleon. This form he applied to gastronomy in the *Code gourmand*, of which the Bitting Collection has the third and fourth editions of 1828 and 1829. Typical of the style and substance of the gastronomical codes is the injunction that if a child is seated next to you at table your duty is to get it drunk as soon as possible so that its mother will take it away. Raisson's law that dinner conversation must be entirely on what has been eaten, what is being eaten, and what will be eaten until the third course, after which one is obligated to be witty, is repeated throughout French gastronomic literature. Raisson's coauthor, Auguste ("Coco") Romieu, was famed even among boulevardiers for the propensity indicated by his having begun an anecdote, quite naturally: "One day, when I wasn't drunk. . . ." However, Romieu achieved a very respectable career in both literature and the bureaucracy, ending his days as superintendent of the royal libraries.

THE association of aristocracy and gastronomy continued through the middle decades of the century, although the aristocracy was a self-constituted one. The gastronomic writers of the period, almost without exception, were habitués of the boulevards, really of the only boulevard that mattered, the Boulevard des Italiens, in whose few hundred meters were concentrated the Opéra, the Théâtre des Italiens, Tortoni, Rich, Hardy, and the Café de Paris. They wrote for others like themselves, the *Paris qui s'am se,* the people whose business seems to be to do nothing. Nelson Roqueplan's *Parisine* (Paris: J. Hetzel, 1869?), for example, is reportage on Paris by a man who as journalist was editor of *Figaro* and as impresario manager of the Opéra, but whose great boasts were that he had introduced the silk strip sewn over the trouser seam in the 1830s and had put the Opéra orchestra into evening dress. *Parisine* has chapters on restaurants and cuisine. The section on foreign cuisines in the latter begins: "Outside France all eating is impossible."

Roger de Beauvoir is another boulevardier who seems never to have dined at home until gout imprisoned him there. Born with too much money and too many talents ever to work seriously, Beauvoir is reported to have stopped drinking champagne only to talk, and his talk was said to have the bubbly giddiness of what he had been drinking. Alexandre Dumas, who had used Beauvoir's *L'Écolier de Cluny* for his *La Tour de Nesle,* wrote his reminiscences of Beauvoir's verve to preface the posthumous *Soupers de mon temps* (Paris: A. Favre, 1868). Beauvoir's interest is the restaurant as background for eccentrics like Courchamps and boulevardiers like Romieu. Linked even more closely than Dumas and Beauvoir were Victor Hugo and Alfred Asseline, whose *Victor Hugo intime* is based on his childhood in the Hugo household. Asseline's *Le Coeur et l'estomac* (Paris: Michel Lèvy frères, 1853) deals in verse and prose more with the heart than the stomach, but with both from the boulevardier or quantitive point of view.

Eugène Briffault, duellist and boulevardier, who as drama critic for *Le Temps* had called Hugo's *Ruy Blas* a "paroxysm of delirium," belonged to the loose society around Balzac. When Briffault's *Paris à table* and *Paris à l'eau* appeared in 1846, Hetzel, the publisher, gave him Bertall for his illustrator and reissued Balzac's *Physiologie du mariage* as *Paris marié.* Briffault is amusing on Talleyrand and unique in the boulevardier literature for his appreciation of the wealthy bourgeois table served by the woman cook traditionally called "le cordon bleu." We record here in exchange the endorsement of one of the boulevard restaurants by the greatest female cook in French literature, Proust's Françoise: "There was a café,

Notre réalité est bien autrement merveilleuse que cette orgueilleuse fiction.

Quand Paris se met à table, la terre entière s'émeut : de toutes les parties de l'univers connu, les choses créées, les produits de tous les règnes, ceux que le globe voit croître à sa surface, ceux qu'il enserre dans son sein, ceux que la mer renferme et nourrit, ceux qui peuplent l'air : tous accourent, se pressent et se hâtent, afin d'obtenir la faveur d'un regard, d'une caresse ou d'un coup de dents. Pour la France, le dîner de Paris est la grande affaire du pays. La plaine, la colline, la montagne et la vallée, le bois, la forêt, le vignoble et les guérets, le potager et le verger, la

Eugène Briffault, *Paris à table* (Paris: J. Hetzel, 1846).

Briffault's illustrator was Charles Albert, vicomte d'Arnoux, comte de Limoges Saint-Saëns, known as Bertall. The verve and facility displayed here perhaps place Bertall in the rank immediately behind Gavarni, with whom Bertall illustrated *Le Diable à Paris*. Of the illustrations by Bertall for the 1845 and 1852 editions of Brillat-Savarin used here for end papers, one, "Les Boissons," reappears on the cover of Bertall's *La Vigne* (Paris: E. Plon, 1878.)

where it seems to me they had some notion of cooking. I'm not saying that the beef jelly was up to mine, but it was very nicely made and the soufflés had plenty of cream. . . . I mean a restaurant where they go in for good, simple home cooking." She was talking of the Café Anglais, whose apotheosis may have been on the evening of June 7, 1867, when it served Wilhelm I of Prussia, Bismarck, and the Tsar and Tsarevich of Russia.

The culinary ideals of the boulevardier writers were realized by Jules Gouffé, who is in direct succession in the line of Carême. Gouffé's father displayed in his pastry shop window some *pièces montées* made by his son. Carême, not a quick man with a compliment, came in off the street to meet the sixteen-year-old youth and kept him in his employ for the next seven years. After being *officier de bouche* at the court of Napoleon III, Gouffé was coaxed out of retirement by Dumas and the baron de Brisse to take over the kitchens of the Jockey Club. The reader must be aware of the aura of snobbery about that name to understand the first chapter in *À la Recherche du temps perdu,* when the narrator's grandparents entertain Swann, not knowing their guest to be "one of the most elegant members of the Jockey Club, a preferred friend of the Comte de Paris and the Prince of Wales, one of the most petted men of the high society of the faubourg Saint-Germain."

The preface to Gouffé's 1867 *Livre de cuisine* points to the existence in France of two cuisines, the first that of the family, to which the opening 333 pages are devoted, the second, "la grande cuisine," receiving the remaining 550 pages. In writing of the development and perfection of this grand cuisine of *fonds* and essences, Gouffé was assisted by his brothers, Alphonse of Buckingham Palace and Hippolyte, cook to Count Shuvalov in St. Petersburg. Like his master Carême, Gouffé detested the approximate in cooking, saying of himself that he never worked out a recipe without having at every moment the clock before his eyes and the scales at arm's reach. Like Carême again, however, Gouffé accepted unreservedly the mésalliance of architecture and gastronomy and the complicated displays of foods that were not intended to be eaten. The plates in Gouffé's *Livre de cuisine* showing this superabundance were designed "après nature" by E. Ronjat, a Prix de Rome winner. Gouffé is represented in the Bitting Collection by the *Livre des soupes et des potages* of 1876, an 1871 English translation of *Le Livre des conserves* called *Book of Preserves,* and the *Royal Cookery,* an 1869 translation of *Livre de cuisine.* Gouffé is Carême *redivivus,* but a Carême of the Second Empire, the reign of Napoleon the Little, when the decorative arts had fallen into excesses.

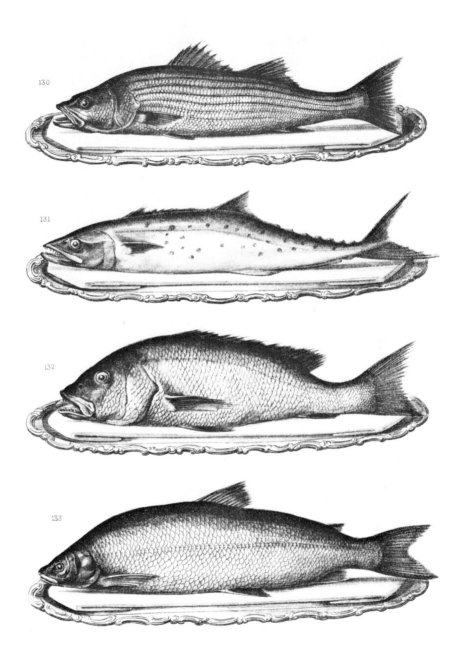

From Jules Gouffé,
Le Livre de cuisine
(Paris: Hachette, 1867).

Fig. 32. Position des mains pour faire la liaison.

Urbain Dubois, *Cuisine artistique* (Paris: Dentu, 1882).

Urbain Dubois writes: "I thought that these beautiful representations would interest equally the practitioner and the amateur, because I believe that they have not been shown in any culinary work in Europe or America in such realism. I owe these pictures to the courtesy of a friend and colleague, Charles Ranhofer, a distinguished artist, well known in New York for his devotion to the progress of the culinary art." Charles Ranhofer of Delmonico's was the author of the 1883 *Epicurean*, which gives Delmonico's bills of fare.

The other great book of the period, a book worthy to stand with those of Menon, Carême, and Escoffier, is *Cuisine classique,* written by Urbain Dubois and Émile Bernard and superbly illustrated by sixty-four plates *hors texte.* The place of this work in a fundamental change in the course of haute cuisine is indicated by its subtitle: "Practical studies on the French school of cuisine applied to service à la russe." While accepting the "Russian" or modern service in which portions are given in the kitchen, Dubois and Bernard strove to make each course visually more spectacular in the new system than in the old. To do this they kept on with the bad old practice of crowding the table with decorative inedibles. At the moment of writing, Dubois was cook to the Prussian king and other French cooks ruled the kitchens of the Emperors of Austria and Russia. Dubois himself had learned the art at Tortoni's, the Rocher de Cancale, and the Café Anglais. Among the bon-vivants and gastronomic writers who contributed articles to *Cuisine classique* was Théophile Gautier.

Dubois took over the copyright of *Cuisine classique* in 1868 (the Bitting copy is dated 1874) and thereafter devoted himself entirely to writing. Pierre Hamp describes in *Mes Métiers* Dubois's visit to get the recipe for soft macaroons, the specialty of the pastry shop in which Hamp then worked.[6] Hamp was impressed by Dubois's seriousness. The modern reader of Dubois is impressed by the crystal-clear style, polite in the sense of the French critical precept that clarity is the "politesse" of the writer. The Bitting Collection holds the *Cuisine de tous les pays* (1886 ed.), *Cuisine artistique* (1882 ed.), *Grand livre des pâtisseurs et des confiseurs* (1883 ed.), *Nouvelle cuisine bourgeoise* (1889 ed.), *Cuisine d'aujourd'hui* (1889 ed.), *École des cuisinières* (12th ed., 18–?) and *Pâtisserie d'aujourd'hui* (1894 ed.). The experts say that everything that really matters in Dubois is in the *Cuisine classique.* The *Cuisine de tous les pays* was inspired by the wish to prepare cooks for such contingencies as making clam chowder for the president of the United States.

In the *Cuisine de tous les pays* Dubois had said that Russia was a great new gastronomic power, while American practices made one recall involuntarily the excesses of antiquity. Russian gastronomy was francophone and an extension of boulevardier gastronomy. Théophile Gautier came back from a trip through Russia in 1867 to report that all Russian cooks were French. Kniaz Lobanov-Rostovskii, a great bibliophile, printed the menus of 320 dinners he had attended between 1841 and 1857 in the hundred-copy edition of *Tablettes gastronomiques de Saint-Pétersbourg* (St. Pétersbourg: Pratz, 1856–58). The hosts bear great Russian names, but the locale is the Yacht Club or the English Club, and the chefs and the menus are always French. The Lobanov-Rostovskii exlibris, sometimes accompanied by a notation of shelf location in the Hermitage library, appears in books of the Czars' Winter Palace library acquired by the Library of Congress in the 1930s. Alphonse Petit's *La Gastronomie en Russie* (Paris: Chez l'auteur, 1860) gives 257 recipes of the Russian kitchen as adapted by a French cook working for not quite the first rank of nobility; Ferdinand Grandi's *Les Nouveautés de la cuisine princière* (Paris: Audot, 1866) returns to the aristocracy (his employer was Prince Demidov) that played English games and ate French dinners.

The advance of French cultural imperialism across the Alps begun by La Varenne was furthered by Édouard Hélouis's *Les Royal-dîners* (Paris: Dentu, 1898). Cook for Charles Albert and Victor Emmanuel of Italy, Hélouis is one of the four men to whom Escoffier dedicated the *Guide culinaire*. The French conquest of transatlantic kitchens is witnessed by books like the rather oddly named *Domestic French Cookery* of the tireless Eliza Leslie (Philadelphia: Carey & Hart, 1836); *What to Eat and How to Cook It* by Pierre Blot, founder of the French cooking schools in America; and *La Cuisine française. French Cooking for Every Home* (Chicago: Baldwin, Ross, 1893) by François Tanty, who had been trained by Carême and had cooked for the Russian court. Tanty told his French colleagues that Americans ate like locomotives taking on water. Jules Breteuil's *Le Cuisinier européen* (Paris: Garnier, n.d.) is one of the few French cookbooks to take seriously foreign cuisines in general.

The baron de Brisse, one of the men who had brought Gouffé to the Jockey Club, was the first French gastronomic journalist (*gastrophile à plume*). He prepared a daily column for *La Liberté,* the first Parisian newspaper designed for mass circulation. His intention, according to his *Les 365 Menus de Baron de Brisse,* was to prepare simple and varied menus in accordance with the seasons. Brisse's menus are the prime sources exploited by J.–P. Aron in his groundbreaking survey of a typology of Parisian eating. Brisse followed his menus with one or two recipes. Early in his journalistic career he discovered that nothing increased the number of letters to the editor and the paper's circulation more than a really impossible recipe like *abricots au gratin de fromage* or *macreuse au chocolat.* In metaphor and simile, Brisse reads like Grimod; tomato sauce, for example, is "red mustard," and he is certainly among the first (with Monselet and Jules Janin) to have called the lobster the "cardinal of the sea." Of his two journals, *La Salle à manger* (1864–66) and *Le Baron Brisse* (1867), the first is in these collections. The Library's monographs include *Les 365 Menus de Baron de Brisse* (1868) and *Petite*

Cuisine de Baron de Brisse, Les 366 menus, and *Cuisine en carême,* all of 1872. The English-French version by Edith Matthew Clark (London: S. Low, 1882) gives 1,200 recipes in addition to the 366 menus. Alexandre Martin's menu-giving *Bréviare de gastronome* (Paris: Audot, 1828) is an early predecessor of the baron de Brisse; F. Barthélemy's *Menu quotidien* (Paris: Distel, n.d.) seems a worthy successor but never attained the baron's popularity.

The other member of the Jockey Club delegation to Gouffé, Alexandre Dumas *père,* "Alexandre the Great," sat down in 1869 to use pen, scissors, and paste to realize his wish to "crown my literary career of more than 550 volumes with a cookbook." In March 1870 he had ready a manuscript of about six hundred thousand words for Alphonse Lemerre, publisher of the Parnassian poets. Dumas's death and the Prussian war delayed publication, so the *Grande diction-naire de cuisine* did not appear until 1873. Lemerre dedicated the book to the hôtelier D.J. Vuillemot, who had read the proofs for him. When the book did not sell well, Lemerre issued it in 1881 in shortened form as *Petite dictionnaire de cuisine.* The editorial tasks he had entrusted to a clerk, Jacques Thibauld, who later used the pseudonym Anatole France. When André Maurois's wife asked the old Anatole France about this work, he answered "I would have been proud to have written the book. But . . . I was only a corrector of proofs and sometimes a *com-mentateur.*" Spoken by Anatole France the ambiguity of the word *commentateur* must be thought intentional. At any rate the first edition of the *Petite dictionnaire* is even more sought after today than the first edition of the larger work.

The preface has the author's characteristic verve, but the text seems labored and is spontaneous only when Dumas is talking of his own finds like fillet of kangaroo or lamb tails *glacées à la chicorée.* One searches Dumas in vain for the legendary recipe insisting on the left foot of the elephant because the animal's practice of sleeping while standing on its right rear foot makes that member hard and fibrous. The actual recipe, beginning in the true Dumas manner, "take one or several elephant's feet," requires only that the animal be young. A better example of the Dumas brio is his praise of the truffle. In Brillat-Savarin this tubercule is called "the diamond of the cuisine," a lapidary-cold phrase. Dumas does not check his gastronomic sensibilities: "You have asked the scientists what the truffle is and after thousands of years of discussion they answer, as they did on the first day, 'We don't know.' Ask the truffle itself and it answers: 'mangez-moi et adorez Dieu' (eat me and praise the Lord)."

If Dumas were not its author the book would long since have been dismissed

Émile Goudeau, *Paris qui consomme*
(Paris: Imprimé pour Henri Beraldi, 1893).

Émile Goudeau left a teaching assistant's position in Bordeaux to work in the finance office of a Paris ministry. In the effort to balance his own budget, Goudeau claimed exemption from the tax on house pets by calling his dog a working dog. When Goudeau proved his point by adding a sheep as a pet, Paris took him to its heart. In 1878 Goudeau founded the Hydropathes, a group of artists, writers, and musicians, selecting that name because it meant nothing and committed him to nothing. The Hydropathes lacked a permanent locale until in December 1881 Goudeau met Rudolph Salis. Salis built the *Chat noir* on Montmartre, the first *cabaret artistique,* where Goudeau invited Paris to share the wit of the artists and writers over whom he presided. In 1883, the year of the publication of *Paris qui consomme,* Goudeau also published his *Poèmes ironiques,* whose title sufficiently shows his style.

200

DICTIONNAIRE DE CUISINE

PAR

Alexandre Dumas

REVU ET COMPLÉTÉ

PAR

J. VUILLEMOT, ÉLÈVE DE CARÊME

Ancien Cuisinier, Propriétaire de l'*Hôtel de la Cloche*, à Compiègne, etc.

PARIS

ALPHONSE LEMERRE, ÉDITEUR

27-31, PASSAGE CHOISSEUL, 27-31

Alexandre Dumas, *Dictionnaire de cuisine* (Paris: Alphonse Lemerre, n.d.).

Dumas met Vuillemot when he went hunting near Compiègne, where Vuillemot owned the Hôtel de la Cloche. One of Dumas' recipes is *lapin Vuillemot,* for which, Dumas says, "you must absolutely have shot the rabbit yourself." Dumas was not born to the Paris boulevards. His *Memoirs* show him as a child running wild in the woods around the village where he was born like a bird or a fox. He would go to a farmer's house, offer a piece of game for use of the hearth fire, and cook his own meal. He made his first trip to Paris with a friend, each riding the one horse alternately, the man on foot shooting game along the way. What they didn't eat they exchanged for lodging. When asked from whom he had learned cooking, his proud reply was "I have studied under all the masters, and particularly under that great master called necessity."

This copy was given to Mrs. Pennell by W. E. Henley, a great name in periodical journalism *(New Review, Magazine of Art, National Observer),* who unhappily now seems remembered only for the poem "Invictus."

as a muddle aspiring to become a pastiche. Dumas himself would have agreed that his work anthologizes the eighteenth-century cookbooks, Grimod de la Reynière, Cussy, Courchamps, Beauvilliers, Urbain Dubois, and Carême (for the last Garnier Frères had given authorization). Sometimes Dumas bothered only to change a name: for example, in his reproduction of the paragraph on champagne from the *Physiologie du goût,* Corvisart became Roger de Beauvoir, Dumas's boulevardier friend. Dumas's most understanding editor rightly says: "Although criticism of Dumas's work is justified and overdue, it would be wrong to make it according to criteria by which he himself was not guided."[7] Of course, one should not criticize ungenerously an author like Dumas who announces three mousquetaires and gives four.

WITH Dumas we leave the Second Empire and enter the Third Republic and the period of the further embourgeoisment of haute cuisine. After Waterloo, French gastronomy had been appropriated by the middle classes; after Sedan and the fall of Napoleon III, the petty bourgeoise demanded its share of this national cultural heritage. The leader of the revolutionaries was Joseph Favre, who showed his class consciousness by membership in the First International and his pride in his profession by organizing trade unions and exhibitions and by founding *La Science culinaire,* the first journal to be run by a cook. There is a portrait of Favre by Courbet, who shared Favre's anarchist sympathies. Favre used *La Science culinaire* to publish excerpts of the *Dictionnaire universel de cuisine et de l'hygiène alimentaire,* of which the first of the four volumes appeared in 1883 and the last in 1890. The preface announces his intention to classify in dictionary form the etymology, history, culinary chemistry, and properties of simple and composite foods. A most interesting entry is Favre's own description:

> After the disaster of Sedan, the furnaces of princely cuisine were extinguished and the democratic wind that traversed France inspired in our learned colleague, J. Favre, the idea of vulgarizing French cuisine and putting it within the reach of the masses. He worked out a program of courses in practical public cuisine . . . which was later used and functions today with success in England and Switzerland. By means of his journal he formed a league of the French cooks who had been scattered throughout the world.

Favre's coprotagonist of cooking for the masses was August Colombié, who left aristocratic employment to form a Society for the Study of Cookery, to write tirelessly, and to teach at a cooking school where his lectures had an audience of six hundred cooks. In his *Traité pratique de cuisine* (Paris: Chez l'auteur, 1896), Colombié stressed the demands on domestic science made by modern industrial society. At a time when conservative cooks lamented the replacement of the old wood fires by the coal that burned too quickly, he advocated that modern miracle of speed, gas. It is understood that the gas company of Paris subsidized his work but that he was being paid to be of his own opinion. The Bitting copy of Colombié's cookbook for schoolgirls (*Éléments culinaires à l'usage des demoiselles.* Paris, 1893) carries the author's inscription to the bibliographer Georges Vicaire.

A special kind of leveling of the class distinctions in cuisine desired by Favre and Colombié was reported by Émile Goudeau, leader of the Hydropathes, one of the bands of poets that made Montmartre a nest of singing birds in the 1880s. Goudeau's *Paris qui consomme* (Paris: H. Béraldi, 1903) is very like Briffault's 1846 *Paris à table,* though Goudeau's text is less well served by Pierre Vidal's rather too pretty illustrations than Briffault's was by Bertall. Goudeau was struck by the simultaneous contraction of the menu in the boulevardier restaurants and its expansion in the others. In addition, the petty bourgeoisie were being offered the same dishes by these menus as the clientele of the Café de Paris or the Maison Dorée, although of course not in the same décor. A then new publishing phenomenon continuing as a leveling force in cuisine today was pointed out by Philéas Gilbert in the 1883 *Art culinaire.* Irked by the feminine invasion of Carême's "masculine and elegant art," Gilbert was particularly indignant that the readers of the new mass-circulation women's magazines should think themselves professionals because they followed the food columns. The effect of this vulgarization has been, Barthes complains in *Mythologies,* to make the glaze the most important part of the recipe, since the women's magazines care most about the picture.

If the period after Sedan was one of sowing, the harvest of the new ideas came at the turn of the century. The adjusting jolt to a new style was recorded by two classic cookbooks, Montagné and Salles's *Grande Cuisine illustrée* and Escoffier's *Guide culinaire.* These are classics in the sense that they stated to the satisfaction of the best contemporary professionals the principle toward which they themselves were working: sauces, garnitures, and condiments should accompany, enhance, and prolong the flavor of the dish, not disguise it. In 1900,

Prosper Montagné and Prosper Salles, both on the staff of the Hotel de Paris in Monte Carlo under Escoffier's friend and rival Jean Giroix, published *Grande cuisine illustrée*, 1,221 recipes of transcendental cuisine. Between the two world wars Montagné ran the gastronomic shrine called "Montagné traiteur," the favorite eating place of Paul Valéry and Léon-Paul Fargue. His free time he spent in reading Carême's notes in the Talleyrand manuscripts in the archives. The culmination of his very active publishing career is the *Larousse gastronomique* of 1938 with its 8,500 recipes.

In *Larousse gastronomique* Montagné called Auguste Escoffier more important in the history of cuisine than Carême, although giving the earlier figure far more space. Escoffier's apprenticeship is represented in the Bitting Collection by a second edition of his little book on the wax flowers he had learned to make in army barracks(*Les Fleurs en cire*. Paris: L'Art culinaire, 1910), and his maturity in his art by two English translations (1913, 1930) of the *Guide culinaire*, the rare *A Few Recipes of Mons. Escoffier, of the Carlton Hotel, London*. (London: Escoffier Limited, 1907), and *Livre des menus* (Paris: Flammarion, 1912). The dedication of the *Guide culinaire* to Urbain Dubois perhaps shows Escoffier's reluctance to break with professional tradition ostentatiously. By offering five thousand recipes in what he called only an aide-mémoire of practical cuisine and in assuming that the great stocks were always at hand, Escoffier designated this work as intended for the professional. Escoffier's *Ma cuisine,* with recipes like *poulet sauté bourgeois,* clearly is more appropriate for the housekeeper. Escoffier's bibliography should also include his contributions to *L'Art culinaire française,* which he founded with the journalist Maurice Dancourt, who used the pseudonym Chatillon-Plessis for his *Vie à table à la fin du 19ᵉ siècle* (Paris: Firmin-Didot, 1894). Escoffier appeared regularly in this professional journal even during the period when he and César Ritz were working to bring hotel keeping to new standards of excellence.

Perhaps Escoffier's experience at the Savoy and Carlton, as communicated in his columns in *L'Art culinaire,* did as much as his books to cut to essentials the structure of haute cuisine inherited from Carême. In table service Escoffier did away with the socles and trophies of sugar over plaster with which Carême had crowded the table. In the kitchen he minimized the use of the great sauces in favor of the fumets and reorganized the *brigade de cuisine* to benefit by the principle of the division of labor. In much of what he did Escoffier was making a virtue out of a necessity. Contemporary kitchens were too crowded and busy for the preparation of the grand creations and finicky delicacies of old. As Pierre Hamp, who

A. Escoffier.
D'après le portrait gravé à propos du jubilé culinaire de l'Auteur (1859–1909).

à Madame Sarah Bernhardt
son fervent admirateur
A. Escoffier
Londres Octobre 1910

LES FLEURS EN CIRE

August Escoffier, *Les Fleurs en cire*
(Paris: Bibliothèque de l'art culinaire, 1910).

Escoffier taught himself how to make wax flowers in the barracks at Nancy during his army service. The book also contains his ideas on menu making and a sampling of his poetry. Sarah Bernhardt was one of Escoffier's enthusiasms. He knew her roles by heart and attended all her opening nights. Escoffier said that "my success comes from the fact that my best dishes were created for ladies." Escoffier created Fraises Bernhardt for the "Divine Sarah" and for Dame Nellie Melba that masterpiece of simplicity, Pêches Melba. When Leonardo's Mona Lisa was loaned for exhibition in this country, the National Gallery of Art dinner signalizing the occasion delighted cookbook amateurs by serving Escoffier's Poires Mona Lisa.

worked in the Savoy kitchen during Escoffier's reign there, remembered, "What was wanted were appetizing dishes, quickly and daintily served, without ostentation or decoration. We worked in spasms, our hands moved as fast as was humanly possible, as rapidly as a fencer. Our tools were brought down with perfect precision, serving the joints of bone and shaving off the skins of vegetables without a particle of waste."[6]

THE books upon which this tour has been focused thus far are major suns that are far outnumbered in the collections by the scattered small stars. The great many, the authors of limited pretensions, in the aggregate reveal as much of the course of taste as the great men, the landmark figures like Escoffier or Montagné. In fact, anonymous constructions put together by the staff of a publishing house, Flammarion's "Mademoiselle Rose" books, for example, have been best-sellers. A review of the great many is so procrustean an undertaking that it will not here be possible to communicate briefly what one book does and how it differs from the others, but we can hope to give an idea of themes and currents. To avoid the confusion of Stephen Leacock's knight, who mounted his steed and "rode off in all directions," the great many will be introduced here in roughly chronological order and only in reasonably tolerable detail.

In the First Empire, the great book was that published in 1806 by Viard, once chef to the prince de Condé, as *Cuisinier impérial*. It became an almost comic example of a book chameleon, changing its title with every change of political régime. On the return of the Bourbons, it was renamed *Cuisinier royal*. When Louis Napoleon was president of the Second Republic, it was the *Cuisinier national;* when he ascended to the throne, it was the *Cuisinier impérial* again; and when he fell, *Cuisinier national* once more. These collections have the 1808, 1828, 1831, 1854, and 1873 editions. So many chefs reworked Viard over the years that the latest edition in the library's collections is double the size of the earliest. The culinary archaeologist digging down through the various levels deposited thinks Viard the equivalent of Schliemann's nine Troys.

Magiron's *Nouveau Cuisinier universel* (Paris: Ledentu, 1812) is as banal in presentation as Viard, but appeared in only one edition. Probably earlier than Viard is Leriquet's *Cuisine élémentaire et économique;* the Bitting copy is dated 1807 but calls itself the "third edition." Lériquet's frontispiece shows the stove and kitchen utensils he describes in a readable style and his recipe for "bifteck" precedes that in Beauvilliers. The enterprising widow Louise Friedel published her own *Art du confiseur* in 1801 and again in 1809 after renaming it *Confiseur impérial*. Her quasi-pedagogical *Petite Cuisinière habile* was published posthumously in 1822 and again in 1860. Neither Friedel nor Lériquet, it must be pointed out, was known to Vicaire. For the *Parfait Cuisinier* (Paris: Delacour et Levallois, 1809), Cousin d'Avallon used the pseudonyms A. T. Raimbault and Borel. The Bitting first edition is dated 1809 (not, as Vicaire states, 1810) and retains the frontispiece "Un Rôti sans Pareil," curious as one of the very few depictions of a woman eating. In the 1837 *Cuisinier modern* Cousin d'Avallon assumed only the name Borel, which was that of the cook of the Portuguese ambassador to Paris as well as of the chef of the Rocher de Cancale. The four plates that appear as frontispieces in this work originate in the same author's *Nouveau Dictionnaire,* which is not in the Library's collections.

In 1818 the publisher Louis Eustache Audot released *Cuisinière de la campagne et de la ville* without indication of authorship. He appeared as both publisher and author for the first time in the fortieth edition (1860). The collections hold the 1845, 1859, and 1876 editions, the two latter giving thirteen hundred recipes illustrated by three hundred attractive little figures in almost seven hundred pages. The Bitting *French Domestic Cookery Combining Elegance with Economy* (New York: Harper, 1855) is a reprint of an 1846 London translation of Audot. To explain his title, Audot describes himself as an admirer of both Grimod de la Reynière and the *Cuisinière bourgeoise* who devised in his country home the recipes he later tested in the city. Audot did announce his authorship of the *Bréviaire du gastronome* (1825), a menu guide which, in imitation of Grimod de la Reynière, is also "an interesting manual of table conversation." Pierre Quentin's *Art d'employer les fruits* (Paris: Audot, 1818), named in editions after the first *Art de conserver et d'employer les fruits,* is one of Quentin's two supplements to Audot. The other is the *Pâtissier de la campagne et de la ville,* whose long popularity is demonstrated by a 1930 edition.

An unsigned review in Horace Raisson's *Almanach des gourmands* for 1825 calls Archambault's *Cuisinier économe* the fruit of long experience, unfortunately somewhat marred by its vulgar insistence on economy. (Other reviews of Archambault pointed out an all too constant resemblance to Viard.) This review also comments that the certainty of commercial success for any kind of cookbook proves that "the gourmet population is enormous and that one always succeeds with the public by speaking to it of its true interests." The 1822 edition of the work of B. Albert, cook to Napoleon's uncle, Cardinal Fesch, is entitled *Manuel complète d'économie domestique* and the 1828 and 1833 editions, *Cuisinier parisien*. For a review of Albert we can use Charles Godfrey Leland's inscription of a copy of the 1828 edition to his niece Mrs. Pennell: "A very superior book—especially for all sweets, pastry, dessert, etc. . . . I incline to think that all things considered this is superior to any other French cook-book of its size."

The Bitting Collection has M. A. Chevreuil's *Cuisinier national et universel* in an 1836 edition and the Pennell Collection his *Maître d'hôtel* in an 1840 copy. A large folding plate at the end of the first work shows kitchen apparatus and table arrangements by courses. *La Grande Cuisine simplifiée* of Robert, chef for the British ambassador in Paris and then for the French ambassador in London, was one of Audot's 1845 publications. Robert's Tourne-Bride restaurant in the woods at Romainville is given a chapter in Paul de Kock's *La Laitière de Montfermeil*. Destaminil was chef of the Trois Frères Provençaux, the restaurant serving what Parisians thought was Provençal cooking. The recipes for the great specialties of the Trois Frères Provençaux singled out by Abraham Hayward in the *Art of Dining* like *potage à la puree de marrons* and *cotelettes à la Provençale* can be found in Destaminil's *Cuisinier français perfectionné* (Paris, 1844). Paul Chareau's *Science de bon vivre* (Paris: Bureau du Musée des familles, 184?) describes cuisine in its "intellectual, physical, and moral aspects," occasionally breaking into song, and goes on to a "thousand new recipes" and the always delicate topic of leftovers.

Antoine Gogué's *Secrets de la cuisine française* (Paris: Hachette, 1856), which takes the reader into the kitchen to demonstrate that cooking is fun, is attractive for its binding and forty-five illustrations by Rouyer. However, the book of the decade, one of those books that the professionals talk about with each other, is the *Cuisinier practicien* (Paris: E. Dentu, 1859) by Reculet, chef of the marquise de Courtarvelle. The journal *Art culinaire* called it an unquestionable masterpiece, "the best and most intelligent guide to the true science." Escoffier cited Reculet in the preface to *Guide culinaire*. Two other writers who appeared in this decade are classics in their specialties: Louis Bailleux on pastry (*Pâtissier moderne*. Paris, 1856) and Étienne on the *officier de bouche* (*Traité de l'office*. Paris, 1847). The animation of Bailleux's style has been attributed to the assistance of the actors of the Théâtre des variétés who patronized his pastry shop. In the Bitting Collection, Bailleux on pastry succeeds two Manuel Roret editions (1825 and 1850), Audot's 1838 publication *Pâtissier à tout feu*, and Belon's *Pâtissier national et universel* (Paris, 1836) and is in turn succeeded by a third Manuel Roret edition (1872), A. C. Bourdon's *Pâtis-*

serie pour tous (Paris: Rodière, 1874) and Bernard's *La Pâtisserie française* (Paris: Belon, 1887. Étienne, *officier de bouche* of the British Embassy in Paris, was the last great functionary to occupy that office. His book is a magisterial summing up of the *officier's* domain, and is followed only by Berthe's *Traité de l'office* (Paris: Garnier Frères, 1876).

The public of the 1860s which bought the non-boulevardier cookbooks seems to have been chiefly concerned with economy. The Ghent sausage specialist Cauderlier offered his *Économie culinaire* (Gand: De Busscher frères, 1869) to a public he thought disserved by books designed for the privileged of birth and fortune, citing Viard in example. Gabrielle de Gonet's *Nouvelle Cuisine simplifiée* (Paris: Hennequin, 1860) is for the lady of the house, as is F. Vidalein's *Cuisinière des familles* (Paris: Dentu, 1864), which condescends to "domestic cuisine taught by precepts within the reach of everyone's intelligence." The next decade is not represented in the Library's collections. The first book of the 1880s is the first to be devoted entirely to leftovers: *L'Art d'accomoder les restes* (Paris: Hachette, 1882) is dedicated "to those of small fortunes" by "a gastronomer emeritus." The books by women writing for women in this decade are Emmeline Raymond's *Nouveau Livre de cuisine* (Paris: Firmin-Didot, 1886) and the *Cent Recettes de Mlle. Françoise* (Paris: Pollendorff, 1887). The young wife or the lady of the house is promised everything on everything relating to the table, even on occasion how to go beyond cuisine bourgeoise to haute cuisine, in Emile Dumont's *La Bonne Cuisine française* (Paris: A. Degorce, 1889). Paput-Lebeau is as much gastronomer as cook in his *Gastrophilie ou art culinaire* (Paris: Audot, 1883), though most of his talk is directly related to his 60 menus and 275 recipes.

The young housekeeper books of the 1890s are Vincent Auguste's *Recettes d'Adèle* (Paris: A. Taride, 1893) and, equally brief and modest, Ch. Chemin's *Art de la cuisine* (Paris: Bernard, 1899). The Bordeaux chef F. Bouvière put together articles he had prepared for professional journals in his *Entretiens culinaires d'un père de famille* (Bordeaux: A. Bellier, 1890) at the request of the directors of some girls' schools. The collection contains Marinette's *Plats chics* of 1894 and *Petits Trucs de la ménagère* of 1895 but not the *Cuisine pratique* of 1899. Of the works of Alfred Suzanne, admired by his contemporaries as much for his *"poesie gourmande"* as for his mastery in the kitchen, there is only *Cent cinquante manières d'utiliser les restes* (Paris: L'Art culinaire, 1892). Fortunately, this edition also reprints some of Suzanne's culinary fantasies from *L'Art culinaire*. The other great chef *cum* littérateur of the time, Ozanne, is not in these collections. Gastave

Garlin's encyclopedic two-volume *Cuisinier moderne* (Paris: Garnier Frères, 1907) won him the appellation "Gouffé of the restaurants." Garlin browsed in the Seine bookstalls and his *Cuisine antique* (Paris: Garnier Frères, 1894) interests when he compares the recipes in the old books with his own practice. The great publishing event of the decade, excepting only Montagné and Salles, is Pierre Lacam's *Mémorial historique et géographique de la pâtisserie* (Paris, 1895), which sums up the contemporary state of the art of pastry as Éstienne's book had summed up that of confectionery. The even more discursive 1902 edition of Lacam gives three thousand recipes and seventeen portraits of the gastronomic great like Gouffé, Carême, and Grimod de la Reynière. It cannot be said that Lacam's is a well-edited book: the reader encounters at least three versions of the origins of the madeleines of Comercy.

The nineteenth century, which ended for France in 1914, ends for this tour with Escoffier's 1903 *Guide culinaire.* Without *Larousse gastronomique,* most of Montagné and Nignon, and all of Pellaprat and Babinski, we can only state, without demonstrating, that the literatures of the nineteenth and twentieth centuries, while similar, are not the same. Again ungoverned by any restrictive pattern, we indicate hurriedly some representative twentieth-century materials. Miquel Grandchamp's *La Cuisinière à la bonne franquette* (Aix-les-Bains, 1924) is in the best tradition of *cuisine bourgeoise;* Madame Saint-Ange's *Livre de cuisine* (Paris: Larousse, 1927) may be the best of the modern housekeeper books; Maurice and Germaine Constantin-Weyer's *Secrets d'une maîtresse de maison* (Paris: Rieder, 1932) are the secrets of a host and hostess most concerned with old wines in slim decanters. Paul Bouillard offers gastronomy on the cheap in his *Gourmandise à bon marché* (Paris: Michel, 1925) and *Cuisine au coin de feu* (Paris: Michel, 1928). In writing his *Dissertations gastronomiques* (Paris: Novel et Chavon, 1928) Ernest Verdier of the Café de Paris was not concerned with considerations of economy. Verdier and the chefs of Maxim's and Chez Marguery were the sources of the *107 Recettes* (Paris: H. Jonquières, 1928) of Paul Poiret, the couturier who took women out of corsets and clothed them in the colors of the Ballet Russe. A probably apocryphal story is that when asked "Why haute couture?" Poiret responded "Why champagne?"

Petits et grand plats (Paris: Au Sans pareil, 1929) is our only French edition of X.-M. Boulestin, the English restaurateur who is the Marcel of Colette's Claudine novels. The *Diet for Epicures* translation of Paul Reboux's *Nouveaux régimes* is our only example of the work of the enfant terrible who set out deliberately to pull the

To Mrs

Joseph Pennell.

With kind regards

of

Charles G. Leland.

Florence.

A book containing a
vast amount of coarse
cheap readily-made
recipes, suitable for
a third class hotel
of 'genteel' preten-
sions. E.g. the Mayon-
naise.

Left and opposite: Rosalie Blanquet, *La Cuisinière des ménages* (Paris: Librairie Adrien Demay, 1802).

In retirement in Italy, Charles Godfrey Leland searched the stalls for old cookbooks, which, after occasionally rebinding himself, he would send on to his niece, Elizabeth Robins Pennell. This critique of Blanquet continues on two more pages bound into the volume. The *Dictionary of American Biography* calls Leland "a burly, genial giant of a man, with a beard like Charlemagne's and a Gargantuan appetite for food, drink, and tobacco." Very popular in his lifetime for the gentle ethnic humor of "Hans Breitman's Barty," he is increasingly valued for his contributions to folklore, particularly his discovery of the Irish tinkers' language and his founding of the Gypsy Lore Society. Mrs. Pennell was an original member of the society as were Sir Richard Burton and the archduke of Austria. Leland is reported to have read through the membership list and commented: "What a rum lot—as the Devil said when he finished reading the Ten Commandments."

LE PATISSIER
DES MÉNAGES

Un volume in-12, avec gravures......... 3 fr.

LA
CUISINIÈRE
DES MÉNAGES

OU

MANUEL PRATIQUE

DE CUISINE ET D'ÉCONOMIE DOMESTIQUE

POUR LA VILLE ET LA CAMPAGNE

CONTENANT

L'ART DE DÉCOUPER, LE SERVICE DE TABLE

LES DEVOIRS D'UNE MAITRESSE DE MAISON, DES MENUS GRAS ET MAIGRES
POUR TOUTES LES SAISONS

UN TRAITÉ DE LA CAVE ET DES MALADIES DES VINS

ET UN GRAND NOMBRE DE RECETTES D'ÉCONOMIE DOMESTIQUE

PAR

Mme ROSALIE BLANQUET

Ouvrage illustré de 217 figures.

TRENTE-TROISIÈME ÉDITION

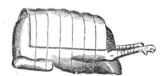

PARIS
LIBRAIRIE ADRIEN DEMAY

21, RUE DE CHATEAUDUN

routines of cuisine down over his elders' heads. Édouard de Pomiane, a distinguished member of the Institut Pasteur, exploited that new invention the radio to give the widest possible audience some notions of *"gastrotechnie,"* the scientific principles underlying gastronomy. His doctrine that cuisine was intended to please all the senses is presented convincingly in his *Radio cuisine* (Paris: Albin Michel, 1933) and *Code de la bonne chère* (Paris: Albin Michel, 1928). In *Radio cuisine* Pomiane states for us what has been the theme of this tour: "All the arts in the same period evolve in the same direction. The aesthetic rules adopted are all the same, whatever the area to which they are applied . . . . Today the dominating note in fashion is the simplicity of the line, whether in painting, couture, or gastronomy."

A very substantial work is Édouard Richardin's encyclopedic *Cuisine française du XIXᵉ au XXᵉ siècle,* which was used as a text in vocational schools. Our fifth edition (Paris: Éditions d'art et de littérature, 1914) is illustrated by Robida and offers 800 historical recipes, 550 modern, 220 from the great restaurants and master cooks, and 360 from writers and amateurs of cuisine. About the work of Édouard Nignon the authorities differ. Elizabeth David thinks it bombastic and overwritten, Robert J. Courtine, superior to Escoffier and Montagné. About the brilliance of his career there is no dispute. Nignon was chosen to serve President Wilson in 1918 and at his Café Larue welcomed Proust, Anatole France, and the marquis de Flers, who wrote the preface for his *Plaisirs de la table* (Paris, 1926). Calling routine in cuisine unpardonable, Nignon wrote broad sketches, letting the individual fill in the gaps to his own taste. Unfortunately, the collections lack the Nignon-edited *Almanach de Cocaigne* series (1919–29), which printed the music of Erik Satie along with contributions from Cocteau, Apollinaire, and Max Jacob and artists like Dufy and Segonzac. Maurice Joyant's *Cuisine de Monsieur Momo, célibataire* (Paris: Pellet, 1932) is surely the most beautiful book of the period for its twenty-four water colors and designs by Toulouse-Lautrec.

THE 1920s and 1930s saw a whole new category of culinary literature, the regional cookbook, appear in the publishers' catalogs. In their *Histoire de la société française* the Goncourts ascribe national awareness of the provincial cuisines to the assemblies of the French Revolution. It seems as probable that this awareness came only after the advent of the railroad and the automobile made tourism and truck gardening possible. The regional cuisines were

Maurice Joyant, *La Cuisine de Monsieur Momo, célibataire* (Paris: Pellet, 1930).

The frontispiece portrait for *La Cuisine de Monsieur Momo* is by Vouillard. The author, Maurice Joyant, was Theo Van Gogh's successor at the Boussod et Valadon Galerie and founder of the Toulouse-Lautrec museum in Albi. On the long sail around the Breton coast that is reported here, Joyant and Toulouse-Lautrec would stop to take on a load of lobster and fish. Cutting shallots and herbs, thickening sauces for *homard à l'americaine* and *bourrides bordelaises,* Toulouse-Lautrec was kept busy and, Joyant noted happily, away from his beloved American mixed drinks, the "kiss-me-quick" and the "corpse reviver." Curnonsky endorsed all Joyant's recipes, which include Toulouse-Lautrec's favorite, *ramereaux aux olives.* Toulouse-Lautrec's twenty-four designs of crustacea, fish, and fowl lack the touch of ugliness—art historians say that it was his own—that one seems always to find in his portraits of humans.

not exportable initially because of their individuality, individuality in the sense of being bound to the native soil for the products at their base and to the traditions of the province for their practices. Provincial cuisine has historically been a thing of tradition, almost of folklore, orally transmitted by the women in the family. Haute cuisine is professional, almost institutionalized; a cuisine of men, it had a written literature early. One of Curnonsky's master strokes in his campaign to link tourism and gastronomy was to emphasize regional cooking as *"la cuisine des femmes,"* thus invoking in a phrase the emotive aspects of the table associated with the wife/mother who personalizes each serving of the dishes she gives her family.

Some regional recipes are scattered throughout the old literature; the *andouilles* of Lyon, for example, can be found in the *Thrésor de santé* of 1607. However, the cuisine of so distinctive a region of France as the Provence began its literature only in 1830 in the *Cuisinier Durand*. The Library's copy is the rare signed first edition, which Durand published at his own expense. The eagerness of the public response is indicated in our collections by Durand's grandson's reedition of the work in 1877 and the Garnier Frères 1912 Spanish and Hispanic-American edition. Following Durand is the *Cuisinier meridional, d'après la méthode provençale et languedocienne* (Avignon: J. Chillot, 1835) intended for a less professional audience than Durand's. A classic like Durand is J. Reboul's *Cuisinière provençale* (Marseille: Ruat, 1913), as painstaking in detail and as clear in the presentation of techniques as the *Cuisinière bourgeoise*. In later editions Reboul gave the names of the recipes in Provençal, at the request of Mistral, the Nobel laureate poet. Alphonse Daudet similarly thought cuisine a weapon in promoting Provençal self-consciousness. He served Durand's *brandade de morue* recipe at the dinner-reunions when he and his compatriots came together "to eat the sun of Provence." Using the pen name "Pampille," his daughter-in-law wrote regional cookbooks in which Proust found the savory dishes with which he compared the vocabularies of Madame Guermantes. Other Provençal books in the Bitting Collection are Heyraud's *Cuisine à Nice* (1907) and Foucou's *Recettes de cuisine provençal* (1929).

A cuisine as distinctive as that of Provence is starred in a new literary genre, the detective story. When Simenon married Maigret off, he chose a girl from Alsace. To foreshadow the importance of food in that marriage the only words he has Louise speak in the first meeting are: "They have left the best cakes! Try these!" The regional cookbook for Alsace came out at about the same time as the *Cuisinier Durand* in Provence. *La Cuisinière du Haut Rhine* (Mulhausen: J.

Russler, 1829) is the French translation of a work which had four German editions as the *Oberrhenisches Kochbuch*. Vicaire and the Bittings following him could find no personal author. Charles Gerard's *L'Ancienne Alsace à table* (Paris: Berger-Levrault, 1877) ascribes the authorship to Madame Sperling, wife of a Mulhausen minister. Gerard's work is not a cookbook but a gastronomer's study of the cuisine that Montaigne thought excellent, particularly for fish, and Curnonsky called one of the richest and most original of France. In Georges Spetz's *L'Alsace gourmande* (Strasbourg: Revue alsacienne, 1914) a poem of more than one hundred pages on the glories of Alsatian cuisine is followed by one hundred and forty recipes in prose. The latest of the Alsatian cookbooks in the collections, Marguerite Hinkel-Rudrauff's *Livre de cuisine alsacienne* (Strasbourg: Heitz, 1933), has a twin German edition.

Perhaps more than any other single person Curnonsky fostered the appreciation of the provincial cuisines outside their geographical borders. This he did by coupling tourism and gastronomy to breed the "gastro-nomads," the tourists who like the Magi follow the stars of the *Guide Michelin*. After having worked in Willy's stable of hack writers, at a time when Colette was known only as Willy's wife, Curnonsky did publicity for Michelin, creating the rolypoly pneumatic Bibendum figure in 1907. Curnonsky and Marcel Rouff drove the highways of France in a pre-Lévi-Strauss effort to relate the historical and geographical structures of the provinces to the structure of their cuisine. Rouff died when twenty-eight of the little volumes of *La France gastronomique* (today *"introuvable"*) had been released. Working with Austin de Croze of the Office générale de la gastronomie, Curnonsky presented his tour of France again in the 1933 *Trésor gastronomique de la France*. Among those in the Library's collections reporting the cuisines of the provinces who wrote in the wake of Curnonsky and de Croze are Hughes Lapaire on Berri, Maurice Béguin on Poitou, Charles Blandin on Burgundy, Ferdinand Faideau on Aunis and Saintonge, and Jean Sequin on Normandy.

We shall conclude, as perhaps we should have begun, with the considerations on the literature of gastronomy advanced by Curnonsky, elected *prince des gastronomes* in the period with which this tour ends. Most perceptive is his characterization of gastronomy as a game whose rules the gastronomic writers have drawn up. Curnonsky here anticipates the concept later advanced by Johann Huizinga's *Homo ludens* on the affinity of play, order, and aesthetics. Gastronomy is a game, and "playing the game" rightly requires from the gastronomer the will to create orderly form and is therefore strongly aesthetic. Echoing Oscar Wilde on life imitating art, Curnonsky ascribes to the gastronomic writers the making visible of a culinary landscape that others have looked at without seeing. He was thinking of the writers like himself, the makers of the little literature of gastronomy with which this tour has been concerned. But in addition there has been a big, a gigantic French literature of gastronomy, for example, Balzac on the restaurants, Zola on Les Halles, Proust on the madeleines that sent him down the halls of memory. Today when the writers who live for and by the word convene to award France's literary prizes, first they sit down to dine. The Cartesian *cogito ergo sum* can be modified to explain French gastronomy: In France gastronomy is written and talked, therefore it exists.

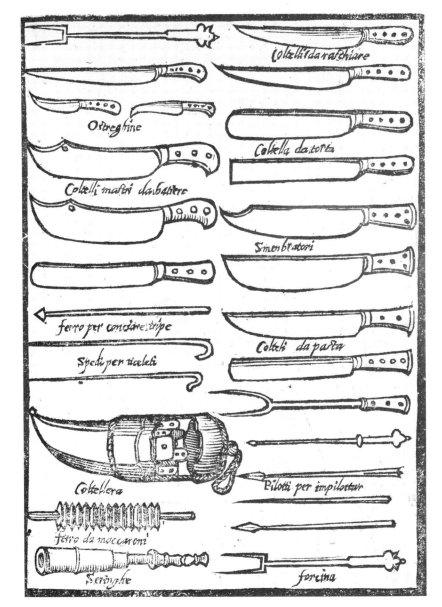

Bartolomeo Scappi, *Opera* . . .
(Venetia: M. Tramezzino, 1574?).

The first depiction of the *forcina*,
the fork used in bringing food to
the mouth as well as in carving, is
in the lower right-hand corner. In
Ben Jonson's "The Devil is an Ass,"
first performed in 1616, one of the
characters asks, "Forks, what be
they?" and is answered: "The laud-
able use of forks brought into custom here, as they are in Italy, to the
saving of napkins."

Notes

Chapter One
Praise Is Due Bartolomeo Platina

1. José Ruysschaert, "Sixte IV, Fondateur de la Bibliothèque Vaticane (15 Juin 1475)," *Archivium historiae pontificiae* 7 (1969): 511–23.

2. Alfred E. Housman, *The Name and Nature of Poetry* (New York: Macmillan; Cambridge: At the University Press, 1933), p. 26.

3. Joseph Vehling, *Platina and the Rebirth of Man* (Chicago: W. M. Hill, 1941).

4. Emilio Faccioli, *Arte della cucina; libri di recette, testi sopra lo scalco, il trinciante e i vini dal XIV al XIX secolo . . .*, vol. 1 (Milano: Edizioni Il Polifilo, 1966), pp. 119–204.

5. Ludwig Pastor, *The History of the Popes, From the Close of the Middle Ages . . .*, vol. 4, ed. F. L. Antrobus (St. Louis: B. Herder, 1898).

6. See Benjamin Farrington, "The Meaning of *Voluptas* in Lucretius," *Hermathena* 80 (November 1952): 26–31, and *Faith of Epicurus* (London: Weidenfeld & Nicolson, 1967).

7. T. S. Eliot, "Baudelaire in Our Time," in *Essays Ancient and Modern* (New York: Harcourt, Brace and Co., 1936), pp. 69–70.

8. Edith Wharton, *French Ways and Their Meaning* (New York, London: D. Appleton and Co., 1919), p. 133.

9. Vespasiano da Bisticci, *Le Vite* (Florence: Nelle Sede dell'Instituto nazionale di Studi sul Rinascimento, 1970).

10. Mary Ella Milham, "Toward a Stemma and 'Fortuna' of Apicius," *Italia medioevale e umanistica* 10 (1967):259–320.

The standard bibliographies in this area include Georges Vicaire's *Bibliographie gastronomique* (Paris: P. Rouquette et fils, 1890) and Richard Westbury's *Handlist of Italian Cookery Books* (Firenze: L. S. Olschki, 1963), in addition to the work by Mrs. Bitting cited in the text. Harry Schraemli's *Von Lucullus zu Escoffier* (Zürich: Interverlag AG, 1949) and Elly Cockx-Indestege's introduction to Gerardus Vorselman's *Eenen Nyeuwen Coock Boeck* (Wiesbaden: Guido Pressler, 1971) have also been consulted. Platina's *De honesta voluptate* appears in an English translation by E. B. Andrews as *De honesta voluptate; the First Dated Cookery Book . . .* (St. Louis[?]: Mallinckrodt Chemical Works, 1967). The quotation from Don Quixote is from Samuel Putnam's translation, *The Ingenious Gentleman Don Quixote de la Mancha* (New York: Modern Library, 1964); Montaigne is quoted from the *Essays of Michael Seigneur de Montaigne,* 7th London edition (London: Printed for S. and E. Ballard, 1739).

Chapter Two
The Renaissance Discovery of the "Inner Man"

1. Published in Paris by E. Paul, L. Huard et Guillemin, 1894.

2. René Sturel, "Rabelais et Hippocrate. (Notes bibliographiques)," *Revue des études rabelaisiennes* 6 (1908): 49–55; Roland Antonioli, *Rabelais et la médicine* (Genève: Libraire Droz, 1976). (Études rabelaisiennes, t. XIII).

3. *Phoenix Flame* 9 (1938): 10–12.

4. Oswei Temkin, *Galenism: Rise and Decline of a Medical Philosophy* (Ithaca and London: Cornell University Press, 1973), p. 40.

5. Samuel Taylor Coleridge, "Fragment of an Essay on Taste," *Biographia Literaria,* 2 vols. (Oxford: Oxford University Press, 1907) 2: 247–49.

6. Published in Hamburg by I.C. Bohn, 1716.

7. *The Colloquies of Erasmus,* trans. Craig R. Thompson (Chicago and London: University of Chicago Press, 1965).

8. Avenir Tchemerzine, *Bibliographie d'éditions originales et rares d'auteurs français . . . ,* 5 vols. (Paris: Hermann, 1975) 5: 587.

9. Published in Bergamo by Locatelli.

10. John E. Sandys, *A History of Classical Scholarship,* 3 vols. (Cambridge: Cambridge University Press, 1908) 2: 305.

11. P. Morton Shand, *A Book of Food* (London: Jonathan Cape, 1935), p. 236.

12. Published in Paris by E. de Boccard, 1922–23.

13. Leo Élaut, "Les Rêgles d'une gastronomie hygienique exposées par le médicin-humanist Georgius Pictorius," *Clio Medico* 3 (1968): 349–56.

Chapter Three
English Cookery Books

1. Dates in parentheses refer to editions in the Library's Bitting and Pennell Collections. To avoid capsizing under the weight of annotation, this chapter limits the description of individual titles to the year of the edition. For further bibliographic information the reader is referred to Lavonne B. Axford's *English Language Cookbooks, 1600–1973* (De-

troit: Gale Research, 1976) and A. W. Oxford's *Notes from a Collector's Catalogue with a Bibliography of English Cookery Books* (London: Bumpus, 1909.) There are two works entitled *Old Cookery Books,* the older by W. Carew Hazlitt (London: Eliot Stock, 1902) and the other by Eric Quayle (New York: E.P. Dutton, 1978). Recent facsimiles of the classic English cookbooks (e.g., Francatelli's, Glasse's, Acton's, Bradley's) give much incidental information; there is a biography of Soyer and three of Mrs. Beeton. These are the books that come immediately to mind. There are many others, indeed, too many others to list, although the journal *Petits propos culinaires* might be singled out.

Chapter Four
La France à Table

1. For the Toinet Collection, see his: "Les Écrivains moralistes au XVIIe siècle," *Revue d'histoire littéraire de la France* 23 (1916): 570–610; 24 (1917): 296–306, 656–75; 25 (1918): 310–20, 655–57; 33 (1926): 395–407.

2. X.-M. Boulestin, *A Second Helping* (London: William Heinemann, 1935), pp. 11–13; Arnold Bennett, "Omelettes, Soup, and Wines," in *Things that Have Interested Me,* second series (New York: Doran, 1923), pp. 245–47.

3. Alain Girard, "Le Triomphe de la 'Cuisinière bourgeoise,' Livres culinaires, cuisine et société aux XVIIe et XVIIIe siècles," *Revue d'histoire moderne et contemporaine,* 24 (Oct.-Dec. 1977): 497–511.

4. Bertrand Guégan, *La Fleur de la cuisine française* (Paris: Aux éditions de la Sirène, 1920), p. 57.

5. The present head of the La Varenne Cooking School in Paris writes: "*Le Cuisinier françois* belongs to [our] world . . . . Cuts of meat are easily identifiable and they are treated as now. . . . Both meat and fowl are simmered in subtly blended ragouts, and La Varenne recognizes the importance of reducing cooking juice to concentrate the flavor. La Varenne is the first French cook to add the classic thickening *roux* (of fat and flour) to bouillon to make velouté sauce. An astonishing number of modern dishes are mentioned. . . . He gives special attention to the preparation of vegetables, he uses a bouquet garni to flavor stocks and sauces, and introduces such techniques as using egg whites to clarify a gelée." Ann Willan, *Great Cooks and Their Recipes* (New York: McGraw-Hill, 1947), p. 48.

8. Edmond de Goncourt, "La Cuisine et les livres de cuisine au XVIIIe siècle," *Moniteur du bibliophile,* 3 (March 1, 1880): 1–7.

9. Georges Vicaire, *Bibliographie gastronomique* (Paris: Chez P. Rougette et fils, 1890).

Chapter Five
La Cuisine moderne

1. See Alexandre Grimod de la Reynière, *Écrits gastronomiques,* texte établi et presenté par Jean-Claude Bonnet (Paris: Union générale d'édition, 1978); Jean Anthelm Brillat-Savarin, *Physiologie* du gout/Brillat-Savarin, 1st éd., mise en order et annotaté avec une lecture de Roland Barthes (Paris: Hermann, 1975); *Physiology of Taste,* a new translation by M. F. K. Fisher, with profuse annotations by the translator (New York: Limited Editions Club, 1949). It is appropriate to point out that W. H. Auden said flatly of Mrs. Fisher, "I do not know of any one in the United States today who writes better prose" ("The Kitchen of Life," *Forewords and Afterwords,* 1973, p. 485).

2. Jean-Claude Bonnet, "Carême ou les derniers feux de la cuisine decorative," *Romantisme* 17/18 (1977): 24–43.

3. *Lady Morgan in France,* ed. E. Suddaby and P. J. Yarrow (Newcastle upon Tyne: Oriel, 1971), p. 237.

4. J. P. Aron, *Essai sur la sensibilité alimentaire à Paris au XIXe siècle* (Paris, 1967); —*Le Mangeur du XIXe siècle* (Paris, 1973); —"La Cuisine: un menu au XIXe siècle," *Faire de l'histoire* 3 (Paris, 1974), pp. 192–219.

5. Gabriel Hanotaux and George Vicaire, *La Jeunesse de Balzac* (Paris: A. Ferroud, 1931).

6. Pierre Hamp, *Mes Métiers* (Paris: Gallimard, 1943), pp. 45, 287–88.

7. Alexandre Dumas, *Dumas on Food,* trans. Alan and Jane Davidson, introduction by Alan Davidson (London: Michael Joseph, 1978).